A Guide to African International Organizations

Richard Fredland

HANS ZELL PUBLISHERS
London • Melbourne • Munich • New York • 1990

All rights reserved. No part of this publication may be reproduced or transmitted in any form or by any means (including photocopying and recording) without the written permission of the copyright holder except in accordance with the provisions of the Copyright Act 1956 (as amended) or under the terms of a licence issued by the Copyright Licensing Agency, 7 Ridgmount Street, London, England WC1E 7AE. The written permission of the copyright holder must also be obtained before any part of this publication is stored in a retrieval system of any nature. Applications for the copyright holder's written permission to reproduce, transmit or store in a retrieval system any part of this publication should be addressed to the publisher.

Warning: The doing of any unauthorised act in relation to a copyright work may result in both a civil claim for damages and criminal prosecution.

© 1990 Richard Fredland

Hans Zell Publishers
is an imprint of Bowker-Saur Ltd, a Reed International Books Company.
Borough Green, Sevenoaks, Kent, England TN15 8PH

British Library Cataloguing in Publication Data

Fredland, Richard
   A guide to African international organizations.
   1. Africa. International organizations
   I. Title
   068.6
ISBN 0-905450-90-6

Library of Congress Cataloging-in-Publication Data

Fredland, Richard A
   A guide to African international organizations / Richard Fredland.
   324p. cm.
   Includes bibliographical references.
   ISBN 0-905450-90-6
   1. International agencies--Africa--Directories. I. Title.
JX1995.F67 190   90-32206
060'. 1--dc20   CIP

Cover design by Robin Caira

Printed on acid-free paper.

Printed in Great Britain by
Bookcraft Ltd., Midsomer Norton, nr Bath

TABLE OF CONTENTS

	Foreword	
I.	Introduction	1
II.	Background to International Organization	3
III.	Main International Organizations in Africa	15
	1. OAU: Organization of African Unity	21
	2. EAC: East African Community	29
	3. OCAM: Organization Commune Africaine et Malgache	33
	4. ECOWAS: Economic Community of West African States	37
	5. SADCC: Southern African Development Coordination Conference	41
	6. UDEAC: Customs Union of Central African States	43
	7. PAC: Pacific-African-Caribbean States	45
	8. ADB: African Development Bank	47
IV.	Data: African International Organizations	49
V.	Biographical Data	159
VI.	Chronology	177
VII.	Appendices	
	1. A Note on Kenya and International Organizations	183
	2. Alphabetical Listing of Acronyms	185
	3. Founding Dates of African International Organizations	191
	4. Countries and Number of Memberships	199
	5. Individual Country Memberships	201
	6. Number of Memberships by Groups	267

VIII. Maps

1A. Customs Union of West African States	271
1B. Southern African Customs Union	273
2A. Central African Economic and Customs Union	275
2B. Entente Council	277
3A. African Postal Union	279
3B. Southern African Development Coordination Conference	281
4A. African Posts and Telecommunications Union	283
4B. African Postal and Telecommunications Union	285
5A. African and Malagasy Common Organization	287
5B. East African Community	289

IX. Tables (in text)

1. Variables Affecting International Organization	18
2. African Disputes Considered by the OAU	27
3. East African Community Institutions	32
4. Institutions Associated with OCAM	34

X. Bibliography 291

XI. Index 307

FOREWORD

This volume serves two purposes. First, it is a compilation of about 400 *intergovernmental* organizations which have existed and do still exist in Africa. Second, it offers a commentary about the institution of African international organizations and evaluates several of the major extant or recent organizations. This is essentially a reference work which will further one's tracing the political activities of African states particularly through the dynamics of the independence period.

Every publication suffers from a time lag in reporting evolving reality, and nowhere is this more true than in a field as ephemeral as international organizations among newly-independent states. While acknowledging full responsibility for all that appears, no pretense is made that there are not errors of omission, commission, ignorance, and sorts not predictable. This is akin to a printed image extracted from a film or video; we have captured an impression of reality at one moment in time. The problem is that there are myriad films running simultaneously, and the image captured will not necessarily be of all at the same moment. Another caveat: The tables were prepared by computer; this required certain conventions which are "unconventional" such as the strange date notations in the list of founding dates. It also facilitated the replication of errors many times. These have hopefully been caught and remedied.

Thanks are due to Nancy Carfree of the Association of International Organization (Bruxelles) for generous assistance in the early research. Richard Samko converted data into computer readable form, Lee Anne Sakellarides and Emma Hall patiently proofread, Mae Annexton provided editorial suggestions, and Don Smith expertly provided final manuscript preparation.

INTRODUCTION

This volume provides an overview of the institutions of that portion of the international political system which is Africa. The three decades of African independence have been filled with the creation and demise of numerous international organizations. If one were to look for a biological metaphor to describe the process it would have to be something like the rabbit or fruit fly in that the number has been substantial but the longevity has been, in general, limited. However, there have been created some other metaphorical specimens, perhaps cats or even lions--organizations which have demonstrated greater longevity and survivability, e.g. the Organization of African Unity or ECOWAS. Some of the minor specimens with a narrow technical focus, e.g. the component agencies of STRC, have also demonstrated a substantial lifespan. As with the study of global international organization, one must keep in mind that the concept of the political international organization has only been a major feature of the international landscape since the creation of the League of Nations in 1919, so we are examining an essentially new feature in international politics. Sovereign states in Africa are even a newer phenomena, arriving first in the 1960's in significant numbers, as can be seen from the table of dates of founding elsewhere in this volume. While some African international organizations antedate the independence era, most are creatures of the political decisions made by sovereign states.

Since the ability of international organizations to thrive and prosper is at least in large part a function of the political will of the member states to forego a portion of their sovereignty, the most potent force on the international scene for a couple of centuries, it is not surprising that the transition to a new age dominated by international organizations has not come about smoothly or even with much evidence of being welcomed. It is, in fact, ironic that the League of Nations was the institution that rendered the concept of international organization universal while at the same time the Treaty of Versailles also articulated the even more appealing idea of "one nation, one state" which foreshadowed the era of independence which has been characterized by the fissiparation of political power rather than its aggregation. It has become apparent in observing the more mature states that the surrender of sovereignty is something that is done with great reluctance; it can hardly be expected to occur readily among the new states of Africa.

Still, this volume records almost 500 international organizations which have appeared on the African continent in this century. A substantial portion of them survive to this day. None has been so successful as have several in Europe. That is understandable in that maturity, wealth, and the remembrance of devastation served to foster the political will that moved Europe into its age of international organization. Africa is politically some time away from that affluence or maturity; hopefully it will ever remain free of the two holocausts experienced in Europe in the first half of this century. International organization is more effective against human-induced catastrophe than natural ones, of which Africa has had a surfeit. This volume provides both a broad overview of the processes at work in the evolution of international organizations as well as details about specific organizations on the African continent.

BACKGROUND OF INTERNATIONAL ORGANIZATIONS

The concept of an international organization can be seen on the one hand as a logical progression in the evolution of political entities from the basic family or tribal grouping of pre- and early historic times to the feudal arrangements of early Europe and on to the more or less homogeneous territorial nation-states of Europe which emerged following the Peace of Westphalia in 1648.[1] That is, in terms appropriate to economics, political organization has been seeking an economy of scale over recorded human history. It is clear, for example, that some minimum size is needed for the specialization which accompanies the modern, technological state. Iceland, with a quarter million population, appears to have achieved this in its unique environment; at least it is recognized as having sustained "state" status by those states which "matter." Other microstates, for instance, the old European ones of Liechtenstein, Monaco, and San Marino, have opted to join with larger neighbors (arguably a form of regionalism) for certain important state functions, e.g. fiscal and security matters. The newer microstates, particularly island states of the Pacific and Caribbean, have generally not proceeded beyond the thrill of independence to reach the point of coming to grips with the realities that must be addressed in dealing with long-term survival in a dynamic and sometimes-hostile international environment. As technology becomes increasingly sophisticated (e.g. launching communications satellites, generating nuclear power, or construction of railways), increasingly larger entities are needed to develop and deploy the skills to produce and operate those technologies as well as to make economic use of them. There is no magic size; the minimum is a function of many variables. Iceland does well, at least in part, because of isolation, a long tradition of doing what it does, and regular external injections of U.S. military assistance. Much larger Tanzania, in many ways better endowed naturally, however, does less well for complex reasons.

A second perspective on international organization is that as being something antithetical to the state, in effect an external entity which may subsume or destroy the state.[2] This latter view is held by many chauvinists and protectionists who find the economic, political and cultural mongrelization which they claim follows political regionalism an unacceptable outcome. Implicit in the concept of regionalism in relation to a body politic is the necessity of one "group" having to surrender its autonomy to another "group." The drive for self-governance which was given both impetus and sanction with the founding of the League of Nations and the Treaty of Versailles has proven to be one of the most powerful political forces of modern times. We see in this idea the potential solution to pervasive and persistent problems being sought beyond the boundaries of a single political entity, even though "our political thinking has been so long rooted in the notion that every authority must be linked to a given territory."[3] The concept of surrendered sovereignty suggests, incidentally, an interesting analogy regarding the similarity between the melting

---

1. See Mark F. Imber, "The Intellectual Bases of Functionalism," paper prepared for International Studies Association, Atlanta, 1984, for a discussion of the concept from one perspective.
2. At least two African countries, Ghana and Zaire, have had constitutional provisions for the voluntary surrender of sovereignty to a pan-African entity, Ghana in the era of Kwame Nkrumah and Zaire in its most recent constitution under President Mobutu.
3. David Mitrany, "The Prospect of Integration: Federal or Functional?" in Joseph S. Nye, Jr., *International Regionalism* (Boston: Little Brown & Co., 1968), p. 59.

pot origins of American culture and the potential political culture which could eventuate under a regional arrangement over a long period.

The view that regionalism is part of a logical epistemology of states is implied by many scholars who have followed the evolution of international organizations, particularly since World War II when the number has proliferated geometrically. The roots of pan-Africanism can be found in several sources. First there are the ideals of the French Revolution emphasizing the rights of man, particularly relevant to post-colonial Africa. Marxism added the concept of organizing the masses in the face of bourgeois domination. Woodrow Wilson's "fourteen points" furthered the conception of self-determination. Finally, Kwame Nkrumah articulated the pan-African ideal of Marcus Garvey and others in contemporary terms appealing to Africa's newly-acquired sense of international participation. Africa came to regionalism not as a means primarily of economic development or economic efficiency but as a means of organizing in the face of continuing control by the former colonial powers. Regionalism provided the opportunity for the "creation of facilities literally beyond the physical capacity of any one state to provide."[4]

A major theorist in the field, in addition to Mitrany, has been Schmitter, whose concept of functionalism has been demonstrated by the European (Economic) Community.[5] It has, in its three decades, grown from a few organizations of limited competence to a transcontinental mechanism for collaboration on many fronts and including twelve members promising economic unity in 1992. Some theorists hold that co-operation in non-controversial areas such as technical matters, e.g. customs forms, visa requirements, greenhouse temperatures, adoption of daylight savings time, or telephone dialing codes, will lead inevitably to more significant areas of cooperation through what he terms "spillover."[6] While other regional groups have developed, e.g. ASEAN, CARICOM, or LAFTA[7], none has been so successful in achieving integration as the European example, and it has benefitted from this effort substantially.[8]

Reasons for the success of European regional co-operation are not difficult to come by. The following factors would have to be included in an explanation of the success of the EC: (1) cultural homogeneity and common history, (2) economic diversity and even complementarity (industrial north, agricultural south), (3) geographical contiguity, (4) economic dynamism, (5) affluence (expected costs could easily be borne), (6) high level of

---

4. Imber, op. cit., p. 6.
5. See, for example, Phillippe C. Schmitter, "A Revised Theory of Regional Integration," in *Regional Intregration; Theory and Research*, Leon N. Lindberg and Stuart A. Scheingold, eds. (Cambridge: Harvard University Press, 1971). The term "economic" is parenthetical because the original, more limited concept of economic collaboration was broadened as time passed to include more areas than only things economic (see, for example, *Journal of Common Market Studies*, XIII:4, 1975).
6. See, for example, Ernest B. Haas, "International Integration," *International Organization*, vol. 15, 1961.
7. ASEAN: Association of Southeast Asian Nations; CARICOM: Caribbean Common Market; LAFTA: Latin American Free Trade Area.
8. See, for example, Leon Lindberg, *Europe's Would-be Polity; Patterns of Change in the European Community*. (Englewood Cliffs, NJ: Prentice-Hall, 1970).

political commitment on the part of post-World War II leaders in the original six members who saw no alternative to close cooperation in post-war Europe, (7) a close and visible threat in the Soviet Union and its empire, (8) substantial external pressure (from the United States), and (9) a desperate search for a mechanism to prevent another European war such as those which "twice in their lifetimes" (as the UN Charter Preamble puts it) had consumed their populations.[9] Few of these factors characterize Africa, certainly to the extent that they can be applied to Europe. It might be added that the European Free Trade Area (EFTA) has been largely superseded by the European Community because it lacked many of the characteristics noted above.[10]

Not surprisingly, the development of African international organizations has been decidedly different from that of Europe. In Europe we see the world's oldest and most successful nation-states from the point of view of cultural and economic homogeneity, advanced technology, interwoven infrastructure, and political integrity. This is particularly as a result of political and economic redevelopment following the Second World War. African international organizations have not approached the success of the European Community for several reasons. The most important are the pervasive poverty of Africa along with the relative youth of the modern state system in Africa and the concomitant practice of "testing the new wings" for an indeterminate period before being willing to discuss seriously infringements upon their new-found autonomy. Not unlike the maturing process in humans, the state, almost anthropomorphically, experiences an essentially psychological need to establish its own identity. This was particularly evident as a consequence of the anti-colonial revolution of the 1960's and 1970's and as a means of establishing itself is a bipolar international system.[11] The need to prevent another war which was so impelling to Europeans is not so great in Africa where military capability is substantially limited.

There have been previous interregional polities as Azikiwe reminds us: "In other terms, in spite of racial, linguistic, and cultural differences, conscious efforts have been made during all known periods of African history to form a political union with a regional or continental base."[12] These historical attempts at union, e.g. the kingdoms of Mali, Ghana, or Songhai, occurred in a different context, however. There was an amorphous external environment and threat was uncertain, unpredictable, and unknown, and these polities did not consist of discrete units. Now, the global environment is much better understood, the potential of a threat is much greater, and the international role to be played by African states is far more significant, if much more tenuous.

---

9. The United States role in this evolution came in requiring that its economic assistance be received not by individual states, but by international entities. See Secretary of State George C. Marshall's Harvard University remarks, 5 June 1947, excerpted in Daniel M. Smith, ed. *American Diplomatic History*, vol. II. (Boston: D.C. Heath and Co., 1964).
10. See Emile Benoit, *Europe at Sixes and Sevens*. (New York: Columbia University Press, 1961) especially pp. 82-85.
11.This is discussed in Donald Rothschild, *Politics of Integration* (Nairobi: East African Publishing House, 1968) part I; and Richard A. Fredland, *Africa Faces the World*, (Washington,D.C.:Carrollton Press, 1980) pp. 135-141.
12. Nnamdi Azikwe, *The Future of Pan-Africanism*, (London: Nigeria High Commission, 1961) p. 11.

Most importantly, the domestic heterogeniety of many African states has required substantial energy to establish the authority of the government within its own domain; any effort at transnational co-operation, particularly if there was any real or apparent cost, was politically counterproductive to the extent of being unacceptable. The start-up costs of integration efforts are visible at several levels; benefits are often diffuse, subtle, and perceived as well as received for the most part by the elite. In any case they are delayed. In that same vein, the process of industrialization and modernization which was the core of any African government's domestic economic policy, resulted in developments which were contraindicative of international co-operation, e.g. protection of infant industries, the need to identify external enemies in order to consolidate or maintain internal control, or infrastructure development which accentuated internal networks to the exclusion of regional ones.

Imber argues that "[T]he politics of the lowest common denominator is not incompatible with the search for universal values [of] welfarism and developmentalism."[13] He argues that these two goals are unarguable for any state and should be adequate to induce international cooperation.

At a more mundane level, Hazlewood, both a consultant to and critic of the East African Community, suggests that there has been less push for regional integration in Africa than in Latin America because of the large domestic market potential through import substitution in Africa.[14] This results from the lack of industrial development during the colonial period and has meant that for developing domestic industry in most states there has been an ample market at home without the need to press for a troublesome political decision to expand the market. To the extent that industrial development was directed externally, there was also little incentive for regional arrangements because multinational business inherently represents non-political regionalism. When one realizes the substantial interconnectedness of business and political elites in many African states,[15] one can easily see how pressures for autarky would be the case: business leaders would want protected markets, i.e. within the boundaries of their own states and within a political system susceptible to political control within their grasp. It is simpler administratively to diversify one's business within the system over which one has influence than to run the uncertainties of participating in a larger market whose administrative machinery is beyond the control of a single national elite.

Infrastructure development in Africa could be compared with, for example, a highway map of an American state. American highways can be seen connecting major population (i.e. economic) centers without regard to the state in which they are located. This is particularly evident when viewing the system of interstate highways. A look at a similar map of an African state would show all major infrastructure, i.e. transport and

---

13. Imber, op. cit., p. 14.
14. Arthur Hazlewood (ed.), *African Integration and Disintegration*, (London: Oxford University Press, 1967) p.12.
15. See, for example, Gavin Williams, "Nigeria: The Neo-Colonial Political Economy," in Dennis L. Cohen and John Daniel, *Political Economy of Africa*, (London: Longman, 1981) pp. 45-66.

communications systems, oriented on the major city within the state, often to the virtual exclusion of transnational connections. One such example frequently cited, even into the 1980's is that telephone calls from Accra, Ghana, to Lomé, Togo, about 250 miles distant, were routed through London and Paris, an expensive indication that infrastructure had been developed in order to connect metropole and colony, but not neighboring colonies. The remnants of this situation can still be seen in such matters as varying railway gauges in different former colonies, educational systems employing British books and techniques on the one hand and French on the other; or agricultural development in which French desires for groundnuts led to their being planted across wide areas without regard to how little that did for intraregional trade or even what it did to production of subsistence food crops. Colonial policy as a whole was anything but conducive to integration.

One specific element of collaboration in developing areas illustrates the difficulty of regional co-operation, that of the complementarity of economies. In general, African economies are primary-producing in agricultural and mineral products. One of the more industrialized African states, the Cote d'Ivoire, Kenya, or Zaire, for example, may derive no more than 15% of its gross domestic product from manufacturing. The perceived need for tools of development involves secondary and tertiary economic activities, the technologies and skills for which must be imported from developed countries, particularly at the early stages of economic development.

While African states are all relatively poor by European standards, there is substantial variation among the states, albeit at a low level, thus impeding any cooperation. As an example of the problem, there is no possibility for trade, to put it oversimply, between Kenya and Uganda in tea. Rather, they will both be competing in the international marketplace for the same buyers to the extent that competition exists in the face of international cartel-like arrangements in many primary product markets. This activity is antithetical to economic collaboration. Cobalt from Zaire and diamonds from Angola, other things being equal, would provide very little basis for trade since both are commodities demanded by a technologically sophisticated society and are of little inherent value in a developing one. The basic industrial activity at the outset of industrialization is in textiles and basic commodities of everyday life plus infrastructure development. Economic relationships inherited from the colonial situation operate contrary to this.

Any effective system of regionalism will eventuate in a regulated customs union, at least in the first instance, the usual device for creating an enlarged market which will lead supposedly to economies of scale. Many of the regional groupings in Africa announced this as an early objective. Common markets provide the expanded incentive which serves to justify adequate initial investment to get a new industry underway, whether it be in import substitution or introducing a new product. Regulation is needed to assure an acceptable balance of placement of new industry at a minimum. A successive level of planning would see to optimal geographical location, integrating related industries, i.e. vertical development, and planning horizontally integrated projects for which outside funding could be sought. This last consideration is not inconsequential: During the privatization drives of the Reagan and Thatcher regimes in the U.S. and the U.K., aid for development of private initiatives was much more easily come by than funds for public enterprises; aid from Scandinavian states for social development is possible, from Israel for security, and so on. But the availability of external funds relates to needs of donor, not recipient, states.

The usual first concrete step in economic co-operation is a customs union. Once a customs arrangement is made, in order to regulate the benefits, as Hazlewood points out,[16] an even greater surrender of sovereignty to the regional authority is necessary, and this, in turn, imposes additional perceived costs and threats upon the more advantaged states in the organization. This may lead to its residents' seeing their participation in the arrangement being, in effect, a transfer of wealth from the richer state in the organization to the poorer members, or more likely, the populace of the relatively richer state's seeing its resources being drained toward the poorer, and the poorer state seeing the richer state continuing to get richer in spite of the arrangement. In actuality, at least in the case of the EAC, the redistribution efforts simply tapped the future income of the states in a way that gave the poorer members a slightly larger share than they would otherwise have received and the rich member, Kenya, slightly less. It was not actually a transfer of wealth from the rich to the poor; it provided enhanced opportunity for income to the poorer states. Such a technical analysis was easily lost on Kenyan public opinion. Of course, no one knew what the benefits would have been to any specific participant of a collaborative arrangement in its absence, but imaginings about lost potential can provide fodder for political opposition by those who wish to make use of it.[17]

An additional problem more prevalent in Africa than elsewhere is its fourteen landlocked states, more than half of such states in the world. With them, regional cooperation presents special problems with customs collection from imports to be transported through a landlocked state's coastal neighbor. This problem aggravated the imbalance in the EAC between Uganda and Kenya, and a similar problem affected Chad and the Central African Republic within UDEAC.[18] Then there is the lessened incentive for incoming industry to expose itself to two sets of potentially unstable polities; why go, for example, to Uganda if one can settle in Kenya at similar cost, have access to the entire community, and only have to deal with one set of customs agents, tax collectors, political elite, and the like? We have seen the economic stranglehold South Africa exercises over its neighbors, e.g. Botswana, Lesotho, and Swaziland as well as more remote states by controlling transportation access to the outer world. This problem of access can be solved with good will, but this is an additional burden along the path to a difficult political goal. And the supply of international good will has never been, nor is it likely ever to be, adequate to the opportunities, absent some major external forces.

From the perspective of a developing economy, one of the problems created with collaborative activities is the siting of new industry. If a new (infant) industry is to be developed to process domestic raw materials for local consumption, for example, the ideal situation is to have an optimally large market which permits an economy of scale to be achieved. This usually requires more than the 10 million or so impoverished people in the average African state. It follows then that the industry (or university, or service institution-- the principle is the same) should be located in one state and serve several adjacent states.

---

16. Hazlewood, op. cit., p. 14.
17. Hazlewood, op. cit., p. 16.
18. See Lynn K. Mytelka, "Common Market with some Uncommon Problems: UDEAC Chooses Cooperation despite Unequally Share Poverty and Some Sever Clashes of Interest," *Africa Report*, XV, 1970.

As an example, if plywood is to be manufactured from the abundant timber supplies in Cote d'Ivoire, the neighboring states will at best be able to market some lumber to the Cote d'Ivoire, but purchases of plywood would be from Cote d'Ivoire. Thus the lion's share of economic activity will remain within that one country. The apparent costs are consequently visible at the outset: Construction of a plywood mill is precluded in others states; purchases of plywood must be made from the Cote d'Ivoire; geographical proximity favors suppliers in that location, and so on. The benefits of presumably lower-cost plywood available to everyone who has access to the mill and trickle-down effects to suppliers and other entrepreneurs in all the economies involved are neither so great at the outset nor so visible in the long run as the visible costs foregoing the construction of a plywood mill in another state of the region at the outset. The longer this autarchic tendency continues, the more difficult it is to consider regional development.[19] Even though there may be a successful plywood mill in one state and a less successful one in an adjacent state, the costs of closing the second in favor of the first are great, and consequently not likely to be voluntarily incurred. The corollary of siting one industry in one state is the siting of another industry in a second state, thus tending to equalize benefits over time. This theoretical principle is obscured by timing, i.e. one industry will come first; by relative differences in profitability and potential market; and numerous other variables. The effect is that substantial political will must be expended to make such an integral provision of economic regionalism function.

This is the obverse of this process that has been underway in the United States in recent years: Theoretically, the collective economic wellbeing of the United States is better served by the free importation of, for example, automobiles. This has provided lower-cost automobiles to the consuming public, but it also led to job losses in the automobile industry. The benefits are far less clear to the consumers than to the producers, and those upon whom the costs are imposed see them much more vividly than the recipients of the benefits. So, politically it is easier to protect the relatively few jobs at the expense of the much larger number of consumers who would stand to save by the purchase of less expensive imported autos. (This, of course, has ignored the questions of reciprocal trade benefits, taste, and quality which are assumed in such analysis.) The point illustrated is that the common good is more diffuse and obscure than the good of particularistic groups.

Another factor which underlies the limitations on collaboration is political uncertainty. With few exceptions, the states of Africa have experienced "irregular" changes of government, some with distressing frequency, some painfully violently. Under such circumstances, it is unlikely that political leaders will have interest in devoting time or energy to furthering international collaboration. And it is unthinkable that many leaders under many circumstances will go before their people with a proposal to incur costs in order to achieve a vague and uncertain long-range benefit. Regional agreements require careful negotiations and stable conditions for development and not the prospect of a change of regime which might obviate established modes of co-operation. Three exceptions to this reticence can be suggested, and the reader can be left to draw conclusions regarding motives. First, President Nkrumah in Ghana saw to inclusion in the Ghanaian constitution of 1960 a provision for the surrender of Ghanaian sovereignty to a united states of Africa.[20]

---

19. Hazlewood, op. cit., p. 13.
20. Amos J. Peaslee, *Constitutions of Nations*, vol. I, (The Hague: Martinus Nijhoff, 1965) p. 214 (Art. 1(2).

He was in an unassailable position of dominance and could have led the Ghanaian people and government wherever he chose. As a vocal and aggressive proponent of African integration, he was able to exhibit this concretely by participating in the founding of the OAU as well. As time went on other matters took precedence, culminating in his ultimate overthrow and exile in disgrace. Ghana has not since had the resources or inclination to explore regional collaboration at a similar level of intensity.

A more successful "integrator" was President Julius Nyerere of Tanzania, who, incidentally, voluntarily surrendered his Presidency in 1985, a rare phenomenon in Africa, and an indication that maintenance of total power was not his only political value. One of the most articulate and thoughtful of African leaders, he saw to the postponement of Tanganyikan[21] independence in 1961 so that Kenya and Uganda could move in step with his country into independence and a co-operative regional venture, the East African Community. His efforts in this direction, supported by Presidents Kenyatta and Obote of neighboring Kenya and Uganda, respectively, resulted in extensive and elaborate mechanisms of cooperation, building, one must add, upon existing infrastructure from British colonial days, but also producing the most extensive regional institutions Africa has seen to date.[22] Before the full effects of unhappiness with perceived uneven costs and benefits among the states could be felt or an irresistible institutional momentum could be developed, Idi Amin appeared, and in the wake of the havoc created within Uganda, the East African Community collapsed. A tribute to the functional legacy of such an organization is that some of the technical institutions created under the aegis of the EAC remain.

The third example of an integrator is President Mobutu of Zaire. His constitution (and "his" is the proper adjective, for he promulgated the document) contains a provision similar to that of the first Ghanaian document. This constitution is part of Mobutu's efforts to transform the Zairean polity and simultaneously assert his leadership internationally in Africa. In the case of Nkrumah it was an authentic representation of Nkrumah's intent (especially if he were to be selected to lead the organization which might have been created) and consistent with his proclaimed pan-Africanism.[23] In the case of Mobutu, sincerity is more difficult to discern. Certainly, the "ad hocracy" of contemporary Zaire, as one commentator put it[24], precludes the careful planning and development necessary to effective and long-lasting integrative efforts. Mobutu envisions himself as a legitimate contemporary pan-African leader, since he is one of the doyens of African heads of state.

Of the three leading integrators, the evidence is still being accumulated on Mobutu. With regard to Nyerere, he clearly achieved the greater success because of his complete commitment to the concept. Nkrumah was unable to establish an institutional legacy;

---

21. It was Tanganyika, continuing the name of the pre-World War I German colony, till after independence. In 1964 a merger with Zanzibar resulted in Tanzania.
22. See Christian Potholm and Richard Fredland (eds.), *Integration and Disintegration in East Africa*, (Lanham, MD: University Press of America, 1981).
23. Kwame Nkrumah, *Africa Must Unite*, (New York: F.A.Praeger, 1964).
24. Michael G. Schatzberg, *The Dialectics of Opperession in Zaire*, (Bloomington: Indiana University Press, 1984).

however his rhetoric and energy gave impetus to supranational thinking and organization which might have been delayed years without his impetus, particularly the OAU.

The major international organizations which evolved and survived for some time as viable examples of international organization in post-colonial Africa are few: The Organization of African Unity (OAU), The African Development Bank (ADB), Common African and Malagasy Organization (most often referred to in the US by its Anglicized acronym, OCAM), the East African Community (EAC), the Central African Economic and Customs Union (UDEAC), the Southern African Development Coordination Conference (SADCC), and the Economic Community of West African States (ECOWAS). A non-institutional collaborative scheme is the arrangement between the member states of the European Community and their former colonies, the 50-plus Pacific-African-Caribbean (PAC) states, regularly referred to by the site of its last several treaty revisions, Lomé. Of these, the EAC and OCAM are dead and, SADCC exists by virtue of the common external enemy, South Africa. Of the five remaining, all have substantial external institutional and financial impetus. The ADB is closely related to the United Nation's Economic Commission for Africa (ECA) and receives funds from industrial states, thus justifying its existence. Here the cost is borne by non-African states and the benefits are received by the Africans. ECOWAS, OCAM, and UDEAC all involve Francophone states which are intimately tied to France through central bank arrangements as well as mutual defense treaties and other links. It is to the distinct benefit of France to sustain these organizations, so the necessary energy does not have to be contributed by the members alone. The Lomé agreement is another example of a one-sided arrangement with the visible costs being borne by Europe with the ostensible benefits accruing to Africa, among others.

From the observations in the preceding paragraph one could be led to conclude that, empirically, the African states have demonstrated a lack of commitment, i.e. willingness to bear the costs of regional organization. The question suggests itself, then: Why have the European states moved so far along this path and the Africans not, even though their need for every possible assistance in economic development is clear. At least four reasons seem to predominate in explaining the differential: immaturity, lack of complementarity of economies, ethnic stress and front-heavy economic and political costs in creation of co-operative arrangements. The last two reasons will not go away. The last can be attenuated by selective collaboration, e.g. jointly seeking external assistance to construct an international highway, and at this late date the World Bank is apparently adjusting its lending procedures to facilitate regional co-operation.[25] The first situation will, definitionally, ameliorate with time, though if 200 years has not sufficed in the United States with its recurrent protectionism and even occasional chauvinism, the span of time required is moot for contemporary analysis of Africa. Ethnic problems could be affected by redrawing boundries--an unlikely path--or through political socialization, a process which requires substantial time. There are other crucial variables which differentiate the United States from Africa, so this comparison is of limited utility, at best. Non-complementarity of economies could improve with time thorough joint planning, e.g. build a furniture factory in timber-producing country A, a plywood mill in timber-producing country B. If, on the other hand, all countries seek to develop the same infant industries to replace imports, future costs of integration will be increased, not lessened.

---

25. *The Economist*, 28 September 1986, pp. 19ff.

The University of East Africa which was a potentially outstanding example of an economy of scale achieved by the co-operation of three neighboring states foundered, essentially not on economic considerations (though one cannot know what would have happened had the three participating states had access to rapidly increasing resources). The participating states, though agreeing to be tightly tied together, decided they wanted autonomous universities and did not want to depend upon a neighbor to provide, for example, medical training or a law school, so the university foundered for political, not pragmatic, reasons.

Taking recourse to the benefits of functionalism provides the best model for considering cooperation in Africa. One "functional" organization which has gone unmentioned thus far is a creation of the ECA and OAU, the Scientific, Technical, and Research Committee. This body has spawned numerous technically-oriented groups dealing with topics which are essentially non-political, e.g. solar energy or soils. While acknowledging that conceivably any topic can be made political, least provocative are those issues which are most technical and, hence, generally obscure to the layman and politician alike. If one can demonstrate that the soil and climate of one location is superior for the production of a particular crop, it is a reactively small leap to encouraging that crop's production at that site to the exclusion of other areas. This can, of course, lead to complementarity of economic--in this case agricultural--development in two states. This assumes that agricultural scientists and development workers are not so chauvinistic as to have autarky as their predominant goal rather than the maximization of agricultural production.

The common thread in all serious regionalism is provision for a customs union. A customs union does not operate automatically; only when there is when there is careful control and a modicum of political will can it succeed; otherwise, inherent inequalities between any pairing or group of states will result in the relatively most advanced states continuing to gain in their advantage.[26] Short-term costs and dislocations tend to over shadow larger purposes.

As collaboration proceeds, there eventuates Schmitter's "spillover" effect, the accumulation of consequences from technical collaboration, but this is prior to integration, both conceptually and temporally. For example, an international highway suggests the possibility among the states being connected for uniform specifications in highway construction and maintenance, common driving practices, a common driving license, standardized truck size and weight, easier inter-state travel and trade, and so on. To pursue the questions of truck size: If there is free travel among states, there will naturally evolve a truck size which is acceptable to all the participating states, and so long as the standards are reasonably similar, there will be achieved a unity of one technical factor without a single common policy having been adopted. This would lead logically to a common truck size being sold by vendors in all participating states which, in turn, would suggest, for example, common warehousing of spare parts, and so on. Functionalism. Some issues are more political than the technical decision to construct the highway but could still be dealt with at the administrative level rather than the political level if leadership were willing. Perhaps

---

26. See Potholm and Fredland, especially chaps. 3-6.

this could be a virtue of the non-participatory political systems prevalent in Africa. In few cases would such a decision have to pass before a politically visible body such as a parliament, but could be taken by a cabinet member or in consultation with an executive. In the typical non-participatory African state, such a decision could be essentially invisible politically.

This process is already rapidly underway and provides the area in which most future integration appears most likely to occur. There are several reasons for this. First, the process is being encouraged by combined research and planning under the sponsorship of such organizations as the ECA, OAU, STRC, and others. State-specific planning is often not economic or reasonable. Second, the artificiality of African boundaries means that indigenous peoples will move back and forth without regard to those boundaries, taking with them common economic and technical practices. Third, the necessity of achieving economies of scale in economic development increases as technological complexity increases, meaning that the "average" African state cannot afford to seek economic development alone, regardless of political pressures. Fourth, the presence of external factors will continue to pressure African states to collaborate in enhancing their collective strength in confronting these external actors. This is particularly true in the short run regarding South Africa, but is also a factor regarding the dominant former colonial powers, most especially France.

Leys points out that economic growth is a function not simply of money but also of political power. If a state is to develop, there must be a unified elite as in Kenya or Cote d'Ivoire, something missing in Uganda and most other African states as well.[27] The same is true if movement into regional economic activities is to take place. The absence of political will makes almost any movement in the direction of regionalism impossible. One conclusion that can be drawn from the absence of regional integration efforts in Africa is that the political will requisite for such drastic political action has been lacking.

After a quarter-century of African independence and the process of autonomous development, the retrospective report on international co-operation is negative. "Since the mid-1970's, African regional integrative systems have been in decline."[28] Not much has happened despite the existence of some 450 or so international organizations during the course of this century. The prospects, however, appear to be brighter and to the extent that non-political factors are emphasized, one may see significant strides in this direction in future decades. One must realize that over the millions of years of human history, or even the 6000 years of recorded history, international organization as we are examining it has only existed for only about one percent of that period (the League of Nations being the benchmark of modern international organization). One cannot expect the institution to be mature, widely-accepted, and unerring or to have reached its full range of potential variation. When one concentrates upon the African context and sees political entities 25 years old compared to European states which have existed in essentially the same form, at

---

27. Colin Leys, "African Economic Development in Theory and Practice," in *Daedalus*, 101:3, 1982, p. 113.
28. Lynn K. Mytelka, "Competition, conflict and decline in the Union Douanière et Economique de l'Afrique Centrale (UDEAC)" in Domenico Mazzeo, ed., *African Regional Organizations* (Cambridge: Cambridge University Press, 1984) p. 131.

least socially and culturally, for centuries, it is easier to be patient with the fitful state of international organization development in contemporary Africa. One final, ironic note: Even though regional organizations have proliferated in Africa, the charter of the Organization of African Unity, unlike the United Nations Charter, contains no provision addressing the topic.

THE MAIN AFRICAN INTERNATIONAL ORGANIZATIONS:

OAU, EAC, OCAM, ECOWAS, SADCC, UDEAC, PAC, ADB

Numerous books and more numerous articles have been written about each of the major African international organizations dealt with in this section of the book (see bibliography). Given the comprehensive nature of this volume, however, it is appropriate to single out several of the more significant organizations to display the range of activities which concern international organizations in Africa. The particular organizations included in this chapter generally meet the criteria of being relatively long-lived in the African context (a generation or so), having a substantial number of members (the average is roughly seventeen), appearing to be fairly stable over much of their lifetimes, and displaying a relatively wide range of competence.[1] Two of the organizations included clearly do not meet these criteria: the EAC and the ADB. They are included nonetheless because, in the first instance, we are able to conduct a post mortem on an organization that was substantial and dynamic at one time but came to an end about fifteen years into its existence. Lessons can be learned from looking at its history. The second example, the ADB, on the other hand, is single-purpose, i.e., of limited competence, but broad-based. It is included because of its significance and because it has been a precursor to several regional development banks.

The broad view of these several organizations provides conceptual models through which most of the other organizations included in this volume can be viewed. There are a few models which the majority of the contemporary organizations follow. A remarkably small number of the organizations actually serve as conduits for funds, indicative of both the poverty of Africa as well as their determination to organize in spite of their poverty. This poverty also demonstrates that much regional collaboration can be undertaken essentially cost-free, e.g. there is no greater cost in developing highway plans in conjunction with neighboring states than in doing it alone.

The first model in a typology of African international organizations is the development bank. This is an organization which aggregates funds from member states but, more importantly, from developed states and disperses them among its members for development purposes. A second model is the customs union or the augmented customs union, e.g., the Union of Central African States. Over time there has evolved a standard type of organization with similar treaties, structure, goals, and actions. These were the low-cost, potential-benefit organizations. The ease by which a state could expand its possible market for home-produced goods through creating a customs union by the stroke of a pen has been an attractive mode of operating. For reasons discussed elsewhere, benefits are more easily anticipated than reaped. Recent international economic dislocations, particularly petroleum price rises and the subsequent dramatic rise in international debt, usurped control of much economic assistance thinking, leaving the development bank

---

1. Competence in terms of international organization refers to the organization's range of activities. For example, an organization of limited competence would be the Benin-Niger (Railway) Authority. An organization of broader competence would be committed to a customs union or even political goals, e.g. ECOWAS, OAU, or EAC.

approach marginalized and consequently not fulfilling the possibility of becoming a primary conduit for dispersal of North-South aid. The World Bank (the United Nations agency) has successfully steered a moderate course for forty years. As African institutions mature they can either follow its lead or surrender their individualistic objectives to the larger view of the global institution. This latter possibility presents an interesting opportunity for regional institutions to move the last step up the aggregation ladder and concentrate aid for development projects and infrastructure creation through a single institution. The application of the principle of superregionalism might be as well attempted in this arena as any.

The most frequently seen model is the third type, technical co-operation, or in Nye's term, a functional organization. These organizations focus narrowly on an activity that is essentially not political, or that is susceptible of international administration or technocratic collaboration. Two diverse examples are the Equatorial Office of Posts and Telecommunications and the Inter-African Bureau of African Health. This subject is dealt with elsewhere, but a short comment is appropriate in the context of listing models. Of the approximately 450 organizations included in the data base for this volume, probably half are found in this category. That number alone indicates the relative ease with which such organizations emerge as well as the vast opportunities both as a result of the age of technology as well as the extensive needs for technological development in Africa. Many of them have been instigated by United Nations agencies (particularly ECA) to facilitate their work in Africa. The essentially apolitical nature of technical collaboration makes these organizations attractive and the absence of widely-perceived costs further enhances their appeal. Since many instances of co-operation can be as modest in terms of institutionalization as identifying a place for sharing information or presenting queries, these organizations proliferate.[2]

Somewhat different from the functional model is the fourth category: the single-purpose organization. Here the objective may be selected from a wide range of possibilities, but the common feature is that it is clearly and narrowly defined, often even in the name of the organization. Examples include the Liptako-Gourma Integrated Development Authority and the East African Examinations Council. As the first example indicates, organizations of this type can overlap with the model explained above. It is conceivable that such organizations could achieve their stated objectives and cease to have a further purpose, though most of the organizations identified as being defunct reached their ends for political, not administrative reasons. African international organizations follow the same administrative culture of other bureaucracies and do not frequently volunteer to go out of business.

Self-help organizations, the fifth type, result from a commonly-perceived external threat. They also do not fit into the other four categories. Under such circumstances it is relatively easy for states of widely-differing views to be brought together for what they perceive to be the common good. Two diverse examples are the Southern African Development Co-ordinating Commission and the Desert Locust Control Organization for

---

2. *The Directory of International Organizations* includes some 25,000 organizations, most of them of this type, e.g. beekeepers, shopping center managers, mapmakers, etc. Many, of course, are not intergovernmental.

MAIN INTERNATIONAL ORGANIZATIONS

Eastern Africa. A standard device in the hands of political leaders throughout time has been the use of an external threat in order to rally the populace to the defense of the system. A look at the repeated resolutions of the OAU assemblies dealing with South Africa illustrates how easily a large and varied group such as the OAU membership can come to agreement when responding to a perceived external enemy, particularly when there is little or no apparent cost. SADCC is a more specific phenomenon in that vein which has been strongly supported by Western states in an effort to develop infrastructure in Southern Africa that would be independent of South Africa. (It can be seen as a diffusion mechanism, i.e. redirecting the energies of the front line states toward regional development rather than concentrating upon anti-South African hostility.) Locust control is an activity for which the potential cost to be avoided is very clear as well as being widely understood and feared. SADCC works to provide infrastructure alternatives which are very costly and for which the benefits are not readily apparent.[3]

Finally, there are a few comprehensive organizations which cover a broad range of functions and theoretically hold the potential for assuming a sovereign role under some conceivable circumstances. The OAU, the recently-collapsed OCAM, and the long-defunct EAC are examples of this type. These organizations, anthropomorphically, could be said to wish for political unity among their members. The EAC moved quite far along this path until the collective political will of its three member-Presidents was drained out by Idi Amin's accession to, and abuse of, power. The OAU's fifty-plus members are extraordinarily diverse and seized of far too many immediate and desperate problems to be expected to consider a "United States of Africa" under the aegis of the OAU in the foreseeable future, but the framework has been created. It would undoubtedly need substantial remodeling over future decades, but the genetic material, borrowing a metaphor from another field, is there which could become the basis for such an effort. The recent demise of OCAM and the earlier death of the EAC suggest that success is dangerous in general all-purpose African international organizations. Or it could be that a broadly-competent international organization presents too great a threat to individual political systems.

Cautions about the use of models abound; this comment is, therefore, brief. With the 400-plus organizations covered in this survey some device is needed to bring order to thinking about them, and loosely-defined models serve that purpose. The risk comes when one assumes that these six models encompass the entirety of concerns of African international organizations. That would be misleading. For example, especially with organizations from the colonial period there are other types of concerns. French West Africa and French Equatorial Africa were administrative mechanisms which bore little similarity in terms of objectives to those attributed to the six contemporary models. Likewise, the Franc Zone and the French Community. These models are useful, but they must be used with restraint and not preclude conceptualizing other functions for international organizations.

---

3. Supposing the success of SADCC in replacing the dependency of South Africa's neighbors on her rail system: There will be a substantial cost, presumably borne by donor states, but the benefits are solely abstract. A carload of paint delivered over the rails from Durban through South Africa will cost roughly the same and cover the same number of square feet of plaster as the same paint offloaded at Maputo and delivered over Mozambican rails.

No attempt is made here to compare the regional organization in any empirical way. As Dahlberg points out, different variables have different significance to different organizations.[4] While some of the common market organizations, e.g. Eastern Africa, ECOWAS, EAC, etc., proclaim similar goals, one can see by reviewing the six models described above that there is actually wide variety of purpose. In looking at African international organizations, the number of variables to be kept in mind goes beyond what is reasonably possible to encompass with empirical measurement. The following table contains a list of variables by which international organization might be judged. Beyond broadening the frame of reference for the topic it also provides a basis for not making general comparisons. The relevance of any one variable or cluster of variables has meaning only in conjunction with an appreciation of the stated objectives of the organization being evaluated.

Other variables could undoubtedly be identified; this list illustrates the complexity of considering and comparing regional organizations. The literature is devoid of such comparisons, undoubtedly for this reason. This writer attempted such an evaluation of measurable benefits of OCAM in relation to the rest of Africa employing World Bank data[5], but the findings were inconclusive. As organizations mature and data specific to the decisions taken becomes available, more detailed comparisons will become possible.

TABLE 1

VARIABLES AFFECTING INTERNATIONAL ORGANIZATION
(with particular attention to Africa)

1) What has been the time of establishment relative to independence of member states, i.e. how mature have the states become in terms of willingness to surrender latitude of decision-making?

2) What are the external environmental effects which create the climate in which the organization must operate regardless of its competence, intentions, or membership, e.g. the Cold War?

3) How homogeneous are the members in terms of development, colonial background, international political orientation?

4) What is the level of the political leaders' will to make the organization succeed, collectively and within the individual states, e.g. Senghor's commitment to regionalism versus Amin's disinterest?

---

4. Kenneth A. Dahlberg, "Regional Integration: The Neo-Functional versus a Configurational Approach," *International Organization,* XXIV:1, p. 123.
5. See R.A. Fredland, "OCAM: One Scene in the Drama of West African Development," in Domenico Mazzeo, *African Regional Organization* (Cambridge: Cambridge University Press, 1984), pp. 121-122.

5) What are the absolute and relative levels of economic development of participants? (Relatively richer states can be expected to bear costs for the benefit of poorer states.)

6) What are the fiscal and monetary constraints? For example, states in the Franc Zone will have less freedom with regard to fiscal and monetary policies than will, say, Nigeria, which, given its economic entanglements resulting from oil investments and the resulting debt burden, will have less freedom than Morocco, perhaps.

7) What is the quality of the preparation for the treaty and the organization, including the specificity with which it articulates goals, establishes procedures, and provides for dealing with problems which might arise in interpretation, implementation, or enforcement?

8) How sophisticated are the institutions which have been created to implement the organization's objectives?

9) What is the quality of the organizational leadership, political as well as administrative, i.e. capabilities, experiences, commitment, staff support, security from petty political reprisals for taking unpopular stances or decisions?

10) The foreign debt situation of member states is a current issue as are the international consequences stemming therefrom, e.g. IMF agreements.

11) Physical circumstances affect a state's political capabilities, e.g. natural disasters, regional conflicts not associated with the organization, effect of international economic activities or exports, or lack of a coastline.

12) What is the history of collaboration or conflict among members?

13) What is the effect of the organization's antecedents, e.g. UAM's becoming OCAM?

14) Is there external support for the organization adequate to needs and expectations?

15) Are the expressed goals of the organization authentic, i.e. is a customs union genuinely desired by its members and is it feasible, or is it created to spite a neighboring group or satisfy a faltering leader?

16) How persistent are the political and administrative leadership in pursuit of the expressed goals?

17) Is corruption present in the administration of the organization?

18) The purpose of the organization can be evaluated relative to functional or political goals of its members, recalling that on balance functional goals are more easily accomplished than are political goals.

19) Are members geographically contiguous?

20) Will the organization need to create constituent institutions, e.g. OAU's STRC, to achieve its goals?

21) Is there an adequate commitment of resources by members both to maintain the administrative structure and to undertake projects to fulfill objectives?

22) Is the site of the secretariat supportive, e.g. Dakar or Nairobi where numerous other organizations are located versus Kinshasa which is politically remote?

23) Physical circumstances of the headquarters such as the level of civil order in the city and state, access to communications facilities, the administrative infrastructure, accessibility and attractiveness of the location for experts as needed, adequate facilities for accomplishing tasks, and employable support staff all affect the ability of an organization to fulfill its charge.

24) The size of the organization, particularly with regard to specificity of objectives is important: The larger the organization, the more difficult to achieve goals and the more likely the organization is to be inefficiently diverse. Too small an organization can render decision-making difficult as extraneous concerns intrude unduly as well as minimize available resources.

25) Overlapping membership affects the "culture of co-operation." E.g., if several states such as former French West Africa, participate in several organizations with the same or similar memberships, collaboration may be more easily accomplished than with states which participate infrequently. An alternative possibility is "meeting fatigue" characterized by lack of creativity or enthusiasm.

26) Goals will not be met if skilled staff is not available. Both relative as well as absolute availability is important. Put differently, will the member states make available staff for secondment to the organization?

27) What is the popular support level? While there are few participatory regimes in Africa, there must be popular willingness to bear the costs which are endemic in virtually any organization.

28) Will members incorporate the goals of the organization into their domestic decision-making? Both the lack of autonomy as well as the paucity of resources suggest that effective organizations must have the support of constituent governments to become effective.

OAU: ORGANIZATION OF AFRICAN UNITY

The OAU is the preeminent African international organization. Founded in 1963, all African states, except South Africa and Namibia, of course, belong. Established at a conference there it is headquartered in Addis Ababa along with the UN's Economic Commission for Africa. It serves both political as well as functional purposes. The concept of pan-Africanism was given institutional meaning in conference of independent African states held in Accra (1958) and Addis Ababa (1960) as well as in UAM. The OAU is modelled on the United Nations. Its membership is universal for the continent with the necessary exception of South Africa and Namibia.[1]

The stated objectives of the OAU, faithful to the dreams of its primary instigators, Nkrumah and Touré, are:

to promote the unity and solidarity of the African states;
to coordinate and intensify their cooperation and effort to achieve a better life for the peoples of Africa;
to defend their sovereignty, their territorial integrity and independence;
to eradicate all forms of colonialism from Africa; and
to promote international cooperation, having due regard to the Charter of the United Nations and the Universal Declaration of Human Rights.[2]

The proposed unity has never been defined, and, consequently, has not been disputed, nor achieved. Concrete outcomes of the activities of the OAU are difficult to ascertain. They can be examined in three areas: political, conflict resolution, and technical cooperation. In sum, the OAU has been successful in about that order, from least to most.

The primary organs of the OAU are the Assembly of the Heads of State (which meets annually in the capital city of the year's OAU President), the Council of Ministers (generally foreign ministers), (which meets semi-annually), the General Secretariat in Addis Ababa, and the Arbitration Commission. There are specialized commissions similar to those of the United Nations in addition to the Liberation Committee. The OAU Assembly is akin to a combination of the opening session of the United Nations General Assembly with the appearance of national leaders, combined with the body's function of policy making. The Ministers' conferences are preparatory for the Assembly. The Liberation Committee was created in 1963 to encourage independence for remaining colonies, particularly in southern Africa; its work is essentially completed, largely as a result of forces beyond its control. The work of the Arbitration Commission is discussed below.

The bloc's homogeneity is second only to that of the former Eastern bloc. The African bloc existed before the OAU was created and would doubtless have continued had the OAU never appeared., but the bloc's actions have redounded to the benefit of the OAU by creating a sense that Africa is organized and unified. The role played by the OAU is, in terms of political analysis, interest agglomeration and articulation and less decision-making.

---

1. If Namibian political developments continues on course, one can logically expect it to join the OAU upon independence.
2. "Charter of the Organization of African Unity," Article II.

It does provide an information channeling role for state with a common set of interests, but without the resources to gather data independently and develop positions on its own. There is evolving slowly a cadre of African international civil servants (see the biographical section) with a level of institutional loyalty to something larger than their own states, an essential precursor to more complex integrative efforts. More vaguely still, the OAU, by simply existing, provides a focal point for the sense that there is indeed one Africa, despite many indicators to the contrary.

In the recent literature on Africa, probably only the turmoil in South Africa has evoked more scholarly writing and certainly more journalism than the OAU. Its attraction is that it encompasses all of Africa and consequently it ostensibly speaks for the entire continent. Just as votes at the United Nations, though largely ineffective in the world of *realpolitik*, do still reflect the expressed opinion of the international community, so it can be said that the OAU in effect represents Africa. And again, like the United Nations, its impact and visibility are far our of proportion to the material resources it is able to command or influence.

In terms of specific policies which can be attributed to the OAU as accomplishments int he political arena, there are few, and most of them will be considered under the topic of "conflict resolution." One humanitarian topic which has elicited OAU concern has been refugees. In 1967 the OAU established the Coordinating Commission on Assistance to Refugees as well as the Commission of Fifteen on Refugees. This led to the 1969 Convention on Refugee Problems. At its 22nd summit in Addis Ababa, 1986, the OAU established a council of "wise men" assigned the task of reconciling the parties to inter-state disputes in Africa. "The idea of such a conciliation commission has been on the agenda of OAU summits for many years, but this is said to be its most concrete embodiment to date."[3] The dispute settlement technique which has worked best in the recent past has been the use of disinterested heads of state to serve as mediators.[4] This 1986 proposal institutionalizes the idea. Time can only reveal its effectiveness.

The OAU has seized upon no fewer that forty-four disputes in its twenty-four years of existence. Meyers examined sixteen conflicts during the first ten years of the organization's existence; Shaw and Ojo covered the six years, 1975-1980. These data are summarized in Table 2 at the end of this section.

Meyers concluded that as a result of OAU efforts the Congo civil war, Africa's major internationalized armed conflict to date (1964-65), even though it had disengaged itself after an unsuccessful attempt at mediation, "its reputation was tarnished by its ineffectiveness." Shaw and Ojo are no less critical: "In sum the OAU has failed woefully to harmonize and regulate African affairs."[5] Polhemus provided an evaluation of the

---

3. *West Africa*, 18 August 1986, p. 1722.
4. It is tempting to point to President Mobutu of Zaire as a current example as this is being written: he is claiming responsibility for bringing about a resolution to the protracted civil war in Angola, but it is clear that, as a client of the United States, he could not have done that without substantial US participation. Similarly, the Angolan government, as a Soviet client state, doubtless needed prodding from Moscow.
5. Op. cit., p. 177.

Arbitration Commission in a 1977 article entitled, "The Birth and Irrelevance of the Commission of Mediation, Conciliation, and Arbitration of the Organization of African Unity!"

Despite OAU efforts to resolve the continent's major secession, Biafra from Nigeria, only military considerations finally caused the collapse of the revolt; the same result has been seen in several other disputes which the OAU considered. In 1971 the OAU was actively involved in the Arab-Israeli conflict. The ten-person commission established to see to the implementation of UN Resolution 242 was unable to reach agreement, having split along moderate-radical lines. On balance the best the OAU was able to do in its first decade was to assuage concerns of leaders in relatively minor disputes. Perhaps its most successful effort was in providing a military force to assist in maintaining order in Tanzania after an army revolt. The OAU, unhappy with President Nyerere's recourse to British troops to help maintain control of the country, provided a small military force consisting of Ethiopian and Nigerian troops to bridge the gap until a new Tanzanian army was trained.

From the perspective of international organization, the technical co-operation which the OAU has induced (and which would have undoubtedly expanded in its absence under the auspices of the ECA or other such organizations) laid the groundwork for more intricate integration over future decades in a more concrete fashion than most of the rest of the organization's work. The STRC has spawned numerous collaborative activities which have led to international cooperation in areas from remote sensing to highway construction to coping with endemic diseases. It is in these areas that an international institution establishes itself, just as the United Nations has spawned technical organizations whose essentiality no one questions, e.g. the World Meteorological Organization, the International Civil Aviation Organization, or even the World Bank or International Labor Organization, though the latter two are more political and consequently more controversial.

When one is reminded of the numerous impediments to continental cooperation which are endemic and appear prior to more ephemeral political impediments which are raised it is not surprising that the OAU has been less than successful. A listing of the major endemic problems casts a sobering pall over the "rosy prospects" view. First, there is poverty. When allocating resources, it is difficult for the decision-maker in a state with a per capita gross national product of $300 per year to justify siphoning any meaningful amount to contribute to OAU-sponsored activities, much less for institutional maintenance. Second, there are enormous gaps in Africa which are expensive to bridge: Arab-sub-Saharan; Francophone-Anglophone; pro-West and anti-West; homogeneous versus ethnically-split states; prosperous-impoverished; socialist-capitalist (or East-West, or whatever the prevailing terminology might be); conservative-adventuresome (leadership style, not global politics); well-endowed versus poorly-endowed; littoral or landlocked; stable or anarchic; large or small; densely- versus sparsely-populated; Eurocentric, Sinophilic, or Arabcentric; educated or uneducated; and on and on. While Africans would have it otherwise, the differences among the states are fully as great in their impact upon the potential for intraregional cooperation as are the differences between African states and other areas of the world to which they look for comradeship, assistance, and models. Third, there is little history of concrete interstate cooperation. During the two decades of independence and participation in the international arena, the African states have been operating for the mostpart in a mode of interstate competition and not infrequently conflict rather than cooperation. To be sure, there has been superficial unity in condemnation of South Africa (while several states trade quietly but willingly with the Pretoria government); there has been sound condemnation of having been forced into Cold War politics (while looking more or less eagerly to the benefits of playing off the United States and the Soviet Union for the highest bidder in granting their favor), and there has been a high level of rhetorical coherence as the United Nations was persuaded to adopt the proposal for a New /International Economic order. But when looking at the level of administration, detailed planning, project development and execution, assignment of costs, collecting of benefits, and aggregation of internal support for the projects, cooperation has been virtually non-existent.

The groundwork for regional or continental co-operation is firmly laid in historical events, and no matter the fate of the OAU or any other sub-continental arrangement, the fact of co-operation exists and cannot be totally erased. Only in the face of maniacal behavior such as that of a Bokassa in the Central African Republic (sentenced to death in a 1987 trial) or an Amin in Uganda (in exile) would any state want to totally sever itself from the benefits of technical co-operation as it has emerged. At the quarter century mark in the African independence era, it is too early to attempt to draw definitive conclusions about the impact of the OAU. The fact that it has survived in the face of its difficulties cannot be dismissed as less than a mean accomplishment. Its future in some form or other should be promising. (The adoption of an OAU anthem at the 1986 summit may be an auspicious sign!)

Similar to the United Nations, the OAU has spun off numerous nonpolitical structures in pursuit of its objectives. The primary ones include the following (others are included in the Appendix):

>African Civil Aviation Commission (Dakar)
>Inter-African Bureau of Languages (Kampala)
>Supreme Council for Sport in Africa (Yaoundé)
>Organization of African Trade Union Unity (Accra)
>Pan-African Postal Union (Arusha)
>Pan-African News Agency (Dakar and regional offices)
>Pan-African Telecommunications Union (Kinshasa)
>Scientific, Technical, and Research Committee (Lagos)
>   (STRC has spawned numerous technical sub-committees)
>Union of African Railways (Kinshasa)

To sum up an evaluation of the OAU one could use a report of the 1986 summit meeting which appeared in *Africa Now*[6]:

>African leaders present at the recent OAU summit in Addis Ababa did not only show unanimity on all major issues discussed (a far cry from the old days of perpetual bickering) but also illustrated that the organization was no longer the talking shop of Africa. They radiated the impression of determined

---

6. September, 1986.

men with a better grasp of the forces poised against Africa's independence, unity and economic progress.

An estimation of the resources available to the international organizations can be gained by looking at the miniscule operating budget of the United Nations (about double that of Indiana University at the time of this writing). In 1989 it was US$1.3 billion. The budget of the OAU, while more difficult to discern, is much less than that; for 1987-88 it was approved for US$23.2 million, a drop of US$2 million from the preceding year's budget, a time when only two of the fifty members paid their dues in full. Members are expected to contribute in proportion to their United Nations assessments with the proviso that no state will be expected to pay more than 20 percent of its UN apportionment.[7] Secretary General Telli reported in October, 1965, that less than half of the proposed budget of US$4.4 million had been paid in. For 1984-85 the budget had grown to US$25.3 million, dependent upon actual contributions.

In none of its realms of intended activity have the OAU's accomplishments been outstanding. The reasons have been primarily economic and political. The poverty, natural disaster, superpower play, mismanagement, and political competition among states have rendered cooperation difficult, at best. The absence of the requisites for effective regional cooperation has meant that many of the lessons which have evolved, especially in Europe, were not applied in Africa.

Two limitations deserve particular attention. Economic collaboration requires complementary economies, and this was lacking in Africa. When neighboring states produce similar products, there is little opportunity for a common market. When there is political competition or mistrust between neighboring states, even minimal cooperation is difficult. These limitations have characterized Africa with the consequence that an organization such as the OAU has struggled to create an identity and purpose.

The founding of the OAU in 1963 resulted from the perceived presence of an "outside" threat to African independence. While not necessarily shared equally by all African states, it was both discernible and credible. In addition to the residue of colonialism which often manifested itself as neo-imperialism, there was the imposition of cold war choices by the superpowers which forced unwilling third world states into political choices regarding East and West which were largely irrelevant to their aspirations, circumstances or progress. This sense of threat served a useful purpose, but it was not adequate to sustain a organization with the political needs and potentials of the OAU.

As the most apparent external "devil," colonialism, was vanquished the luxury of intra-African feuding grew. As the number of members grew from the original thirty-one to the present fifty-two, diverse political and economic systems appeared stretching the organization's ability to encompass them all. The contemporary external "devil," international debt, has not been effectively addressed by the OAU.

Regional political and internal economic reasons resulted in frequent underpayments of dues. And local hostilities resulting from, for example, cross-border raids

---

7. This can be inferred to be OAU member approval of the UN budget allocation process.

or ethnic rivalries multiplied the problems for the OAU without concomitant solutions. For example, in 1985 there was a crisis when Morocco quit th organization over its agreement to seat the Algerian-supported Saharan Arab Democratic Republic representatives as the legitimate government of Moroccan-claimed Western Sahara.

Structurally the OAU consists of five components:

The Assembly of Heads of State and Government is the annual gathering which determines basic policy. Not unlike the UN, its resolutions have no coercion attached, so enforcement is sporadic, at best.

The Council of Ministers (Foreign Ministers) is the executive organ of the OAU. It meets biennially or upon the call of an aggrieved member.

The General Secretariat, housed in Addis Ababa, is self-explanatory. Lack of "muscle" compounded by lack of funds renders its largely impotent. It has numbered around 300-500 staff over most of its existence. Regional offices are maintained in most African capitals.

Specialized commissions finally came, after a period of jealousy, to cooperate with UN agencies in developing technical information for use by member states. The overarching one is STRC. Others created by the OAU include AFCAC, OATUU, PANA, PAPU, PATU, the Supreme Council for Sports in Africa, the Union of African Railways, and the International Scientific Council for Trypanosomiasis Research and Control.[8]

The Liberation Committee has largely fulfilled its mission of decolonization, with the exception of South Africa. How much credit it should be accorded is arguable.

The Commission of Mediation, Conciliation and Arbitration, established in 1964, was intended to solve some of the political problems resulting from disputes between members. It has been largely ineffective. It has provided a regional forum for dealing with disputes short of taking them to the UN.

Dispute resolution is clearly one of the greatest opportunities for a regional international organization as encouraged by Article 52 of the UN Charter. There has been no shortage of disputes within Africa to which conflict resolution could be applied. Mathews identifies twenty-eight conflicts which were taken up by the OAU 1963-1981. About one-third were settled primarily as a result of OAU efforts.[9] Not unlike the UN, without a competent military force, without the legitimacy which derives from past successes, and without a substantial level of political will among the disputants to make the organization and its dispute-resolving effort succeed, there is little on which to premise optimism.

---

8. There are seventeen such organizations listed by Amate receiving annual subventions from US$15,000 to US$110,000. C.O.C. Amate. *Inside the OAU*. (New York: St. Martin's Press, 1986) p. 580.
9. K. Mathews. "The Organization of African Unity," in Domenico Mazzeo (ed.), *African Regional Organizations* (Cambridge: Cambridge University Press, 1984) pp.66-72.

The final section of one of the definitive works on the OAU is entitled "The Undoing of Illusions." Throughout history regional-international solutions to the problems which beset mankind have been attempted. The Lagos Plan of Action, adopted in 1980, which projects an African common market by the year 2000, will likely be another illusion. The illusions of solutions have failed more often than they have succeeded. The future for the organization will probably focus on refugees, international debt, infrastructure development, and food production. These are largely unarguable issues, except for refugees, within the African political setting and can meet the acceptable criteria for consideration: (1) They do not pit one African state against another. (2) A convenient external "devil" can be identified, particularly regarding debt. (3) The input of external resources can be useful in attacking these problems, and that can be maximized by a unified appeal. Whatever the final answer to the question of a pan-African political organization, it has not been revealed.

TABLE 2

AFRICAN DISPUTES CONSIDERED BY THE OAU, 1963-1980[10]

DISPUTANTS	ISSUE	OUTCOME (AS OF DATE OF WRITING)
Algeria-Morocco	territory	settled
Ethiopia-Kenya-Somalia	territory	ongoing
Ghana-Burkina Fasso	territory	settled
Equatorial Guinea-Gabon	territory	quiescent
Ghana-neighbors	subversion	settled
Rwanda-Burundi	subversion	quiescent
Guinea-Senegal	subversion	ongoing
Tanzania-Uganda	subversion	ongoing
Ghana-Guinea (1)	kidnapping	settled
Ghana-Guinea (2)	kidnapping	ongoing
Guinea-Cote d'Ivoire	kidnapping	ongoing
Tanganyika (internal)	peacekeeping	settled
Congo (Zaire)	civil war	settled
Nigeria (internal)	secession	settled
Sudan (internal)	secession	settled
Burundi (internal)	unrest	ongoing
Algeria-Morocco	territory	ongoing
Algeria-Mauritania	territory	settled
Angola	civil war	settled (?)
Angola-South Africa	incursions	settled (?)
Angola-Zaire	intervention	settled

10. See B. David Meyers, "Interregional Conflict Management by the Organization of African Unity," *International Organization*, XXVIII:3, and Timothy Shaw and Sola Ojo, *Africa and the International Political System*, Washington: University Press of America, 1982, especially Chapter 7.

TABLE 2 (cont.)

AFRICAN DISPUTES CONSIDERED BY THE OAU, 1963-1980

DISPUTANTS	ISSUE	OUTCOME (AS OF DATE OF WRITING)
Benin	intervention	settled
Botswana-Rhodesia	incursions	settled
Chad (1)	civil war	suspended
Chad (2)	civil war	ongoing
Chad-Libya	intervention	suspended
Comoros (internal)	invasion	settled
Ethiopia-Eritrea	secession	ongoing
Ethiopia-Somalia	territory	quiescent
Ethiopia-Sudan	subversion	settled
Ghana-Togo	border dispute	settled
Kenya-Somalia	territory	quiescent
Libya-Egypt	border dispute	quiescent
Libya-Tunisia	subversion	settled
Mauritania-Burkina Fasso	border dispute	settled
Mozambique-Rhodesia	incursions	settled
Mozambique-South Africa	incursions	settled
Nigeria-Chad	border dispute	ongoing
Uganda-Tanzania (1)	subversion	quiescent
Uganda-Tanzania (2)	territory	settled
Uganda-Kenya	border tension	settled
Zambia-Rhodesia	incursions	settled
Zaire (Shaba 1)	subversion	settled
Zaire (Shaba 2)	incursion	settled

EAC: EAST AFRICAN COMMUNITY

One can more easily deal with a completed past activity in terms of evaluation than attempting to assess an institution with only a nebulous present, a tentative future, or a limited past. Consequently, by way of evaluation, it can be said of the EAC that it did have substantial impact and has left behind a residue of intraregional co-operation that has continued despite the demise of the organization several years ago. In recent years there has been talk as well as tentative steps toward reincarnating an East African organization spanning East Africa from Ethiopia to Mozambique. Realization of this goal will certainly depend upon settlements of problems at the northern and southern extremes of this potential organization, in Ethiopia and Mozambique.

Again, the areas of technical cooperation--which did not present unacceptable perceived levels of cost to the region's inhabitants--have continued, e.g. the East African Marine Fisheries Institute. Those elements which were seen as costly to pride or pocketbook have been terminated, e.g. the University of East Africa which met its end, in 1970 for reasons of national pride. Another institution which foundered was East African Airways which was one of the more visible points of contention among the members. In general, the citizens of East Africa appeared to have been thoroughly imbued with their "East Africanness" and readily accepted the essentiality of the institutions of the Community. Once stability returns to Uganda, as it appears to be doing slowly and painfully after the decade of Idi Amin's carnage, and assuming that unexpected disorder does not infect the other two member states, one should expect the reconstitution of co-operative arrangements. In 1986 talks took place among the three Presidents--all new to their positions since the breakup of the EAC--toward that end. For example, regular traffic resumed between Kenya and Tanzania in 1983; Uganda was subsequently included.[1] This foreshadows further steps which may likely result in either the reconstitution of a tripartite community or involve a larger region such as that encompassed by the Preferential Trade Area.

A retrospective look at the EAC shows it to have been a dynamic institution with a long tradition, having its roots in British colonial politics of the early 20th century. As early as 1902 the East African Court of Appeal was created. A university and an income tax were added in 1952. With the East African Common Services Organization in 1961, the heart of the financial arrangements for the community-to-be was put in place. The distributable pool was the key component.

A careful examination of its problems is instructive to those who would avoid the pitfalls in the development of successive regional organizations in Africa, as well as other developing areas. Particularly important was the perceived inequitable distribution of benefits, perhaps an outcome that can only be overcome by producing so many and such diverse benefits that no one member of the group would feel intolerably disadvantaged to the point of crying "foul." Among the problems which led to the demise of the EAC must be included the following: (1) The divergence between Kenya and Tanzania over social and economic paths. (2) The predominance of outside investment in Kenya relative to the other two members. (3) The pre-Community dominance of Kenya as a result of white settlers (in

---

1. *Africa Now*, September, 1986, pp.13-14.

the "white highands"). (4) Disorder in Uganda. (5) The inherent problem in the "rule of three:" If a three-way decision is not unanimous, the only alternative arrangement is a two-to-one split. This can lead to a sense of being conspired against by the one state in the minority. These problems need to be added to the general problems which confront any regional organization.

The lessons Hazlewood suggests are to be drawn from an examination of the EAC are presented in the form of questions:

1. Must all members benefit equally, or should development gaps narrow?

2. Is there a limit to the difference in levels of development and size?

3. Can members be induced to take the long-term view regarding benefits?

4. If all gain, can it be assured that all perceive the gain?

5. Can common incentives for investment be agreed upon to encourage an acceptable distribution of new investment?

6. Can the scheme be insulated from a scarcity of foreign exchange?

7. How much co-operative planning is needed?

8. Are members prepared to accept constraints of common planning?

9. How does one cope with investor preferences?

10. Does complex co-operation resulting in some benefits for all participants more likely assure all members' perceiving these benefits, or is a less comprehensive scheme preferable?

11. Are "functionally specific" arrangements best?

12. Is broadly similar ideology necessary among members?

13. Must continued political harmony exist?

14. How far must sovereignty be surrendered?

15. Can the regional scheme be protected from wavering commitment by one or more leaders of participating states?

16. Will the absence of political rewards reduce the level of political will?

17. What are internal and external influences which will support and will benefit from integration?[2]

With these questions in mind, an overview of the EAC provides a guide to thinking about regional international organizations of Africa.

The EAC was an extension of the East African Customs Union Organization created by the British in 1917 to serve the colony of Kenya, the protectorates of Uganda and Zanzibar, and to which would be added the Tanganyika mandate following World War I. In 1961 the East African Common Services Organization was created, a textbook example of functional co-operation in non-political activities. This was easily accomplished, of course, because there was a single responsible metropole, the British. Early on, however, jealousies arose in Uganda and Tanganyika over [accurate] perceptions of disproportionate benefits to Kenya.[3]

Independence for the three areas in 1961 and 1963 led to the formation of the EAC, supported particularly by President Nyerere of Tanzania. The key to equitable distribution was the "Distributable Pool" which consisted of customs and excise duties collected in all three states. Half of the total was used to support administration of the Community and the other half was distributed equally among the three members. This arrangement provided a clear example of one way of dealing with inherent inequities within a regional organization: Kenya, as the wealthiest member of the trio, would almost certainly accumulate the largest share of customs, particularly since virtually all Ugandan imports passed through Kenyan ports. By distributing the customs income equally, a small portion of Kenyan income was foregone for the benefit of its poorer colleagues. Since these were indirect taxes and they constituted a minor portion of Kenya's income, this made for a politically tolerable means of both supporting the institution and redistributing wealth at the same time, albeit slowly.

East African institutions proliferated (see Table 3 below). Some were important infrastructure components, e.g. railways and airline. Others were low-level examples of functionalism, e.g. the Institute of Malaria and Vector-Borne Diseases. Unfortunately, with the demise of the community, virtually all were terminated, though professional activities do continue. With the arrival of the barbaric and incompetent Idi Amin, problems for the community multiplied, and the momentum which had developed was inadequate to sustain the political will of the Community. At the end, open hostilities between Uganda and Tanzania had broken out with the latter finally providing troops to assist in Amin's overthrow.

In the years immediately following the collapse of the Amin regime, while disorder reigned in that exhausted state, talk emerged regarding the successor organization. Small steps have been taken, and if East African regionalism is an idea whose time has certainly come, temporary political setbacks will not keep it from coming to fruition.

---

2. Adapted from Hazlewood, "Economic Instrumentalities of Statecraft and the End of the EAC," in Potholm and Fredland, pp. 141-143.

3. Springer, in Potholm and Fredland, pp. 14ff.

TABLE 3

EAST AFRICAN COMMUNITY INSTITUTIONS[4]

AFRO	Agriculture and Forestry Research Organization
CAB	Civil Aviation Board
CED	Customs and Excise Department
CMT	Common Market Tribunal
CSC	Community Service Commission
DCA	Directorate of Civil Aviation
EAA	East African Airways
EADB	East African Development Bank
EAHC	East African Harbours Corporation
EALB	East African Literature Bureau
EAPT	East African Post and Telecommunications
EAR	East African Railways
EARW	East African Railways Workshops
FFRO	Freshwater Fisheries Research Organization
IMR	Institute for Medical Research
IMS	Inland Marine Services
IMVBD	Institute of Malaria and Vector-Borne Diseases
IRO	Industrial Research Organization
ITD	Income Tax Department
LRC	Leprosy Research Center
MD	Meteorological Department
MFRO	Marine Fisheries Research Organization
TPRI	Tropical Pesticides Research Institute
TRC	Tuberculosis Research Center
TRO	Trypanosomiasis Research Organization
VRI	Virus Research Institute
VRO	Veterinary Research Organization

---

4. Taken from Potholm and Fredland, p. x.

OCAM: ORGANIZATION COMMUNE AFRICAINE et MALGACHE

OCAM was the successor organization to several West African regional groupings in the early independence era: Mali Federation, Ghana-Guinea Union, UDE, UAM, OAMCE, UMOA, and UAMCE. (All are included in the data section of this volume.)[1] The original signatories of the treaty were : Burkina Fasso, Cameroun, Central African Republic, Chad Congo, Cote d'Ivoire, Dahomey, Gabon, Malagasy Republic, Mali, Niger, Rwanda, Senegal, Togo, and Zaire. They represented the core of Francophone Africa, a group seen repeatedly combining and recombining in regional groupings, now most visible in ECOWAS.

Regionalism was a natural consequence of the geographical and administrative contiguity of the former French colonies in the area (with the exception, of course, of Madagascar and Djibouti). There was administrative continuity resulting from the French Equatorial and French West African entities and the *Loi Cadre*, the French Communauté created upon independence, and the subsequent Franc Zone. Its roots also go back to the Mali Federation of 1958 with later incarnations in UDE, UAM, OAMCE, UMOA, and UAMCE. The founding of Air Afrique was a concrete linking of these francophone states.

OCAM's objectives were expressed in Articles 2 and 3 of its Charter, which was ratified at Tananarive 27 June 1966:

Article 2: The OCAM is based on the solidarity of its members. In the spirit of the OAU, its purpose is to strengthen cooperation and solidarity between the African and Malagasy states in order to accelerate their economic, social, technical, and cultural development.

Article 3: For this purpose the Organisation shall seek to harmonize the action of the Member States in the economic, social, technical, and cultural fields, to coordinate their development programs, and to facilitate foreign policy consultations between them, with due respect for the sovereignty and fundamental rights of each member state.[2]

On the one hand there is a proclamation of substantial intent: solidarity in development. On the other hand, this is mitigated by the respect for rights of member states. As with most other regional groupings, OCAM was more visible in words than in action. One observer described its appeal: "Gossamer though it sometimes seems, OCAM offers a way of attaining some of the goods of independence without sacrificing the benefits of continued specialized dependence on the former metropole."[3] In the mid-1970's its

---

1. See R. A. Fredland, "OCAM and West African Development," in Domenico Mazzeo, *African International Organizations* (Cambridge: Cambridge University Press, 1984), pp. 104-106.
2. The text of the charter is contained in American Society of International Law, *International Legal Materials,* 1967, pp. 53-56.
3. Philip M. Allen, "Madagascar and OCAM: The Insular Approach to Regionalism," *Africa Report*, January, 1966, p. 15.

budget was close to CFA500 million. Its sugar agreement was one of its major accomplishments. By the time of its demise in 1985, there was little remaining.

In the area of conflict resolution, OCAM, along with other organizations, was involved in the civil war in the then-Congo, now Zaire, on the side of the conservative elements. It was also involved in the Nigeria-Biafra secession; neither time with success. Internally it confronted conflict in 1969 when the government of Zaire saw to the assassination of Pierre Mulele, an exile just returned from fellow member-state, Congo, without effect.

The removal of the first administrator of UAM for overzealousness presaged the demise of OCAM. Further, much of the impetus for OCAM was antipathy to the pan-Africanist pretensions of President Kwame Nkrumah of Ghana. Anxious to resist his expansionist politics, the Francophone states proclaimed a greater intention toward unity than was actually the case. The fact that half OCAM's membership had dropped away by the time of its ultimate demise suggests a failed organization; on the other hand, the fact that eighteen states belonged at one time or another suggests the potential which is now partially fulfilled by ECOWAS in the region.

OCAM has produced several subsidiary organizations and activities, particularly the sugar marketing agreement and Air Afrique. See the table following for a complete listing.

TABLE 4

INSTITUTIONS ASSOCIATED WITH OCAM[4]

African and Malagasy Bureau of Legislative Studies
African and Malagasy Coffee Organization
African and Malagasy Institute of Applied Economics and Statistics
African and Malagasy Institute of Architecture
African and Malagasy Institute of Bilingualism
African and Malagasy Office of Industrial Property
African and Malagasy Sugar Agreement
African and Malagasy Union of Development Banks
African and Malagasy Union of Posts and Telecommunications
African, Malagasy and Mauritania Cultural Institute
African Institution on Information
Air Afrique
Architectural Institute
Center for Training of Cadres
Conference on Statisticians
Council on Administration of Information
Governmental Experts of OCAM on the Problems of Film Production
Institute of Sciences and Veterinary Medicine
Inter-State School of Engineers of Rural Equipment

---

4. Fredland, op. cit., p. 117.

Jurist Experts
Merchant Fleet
Organization for Meat Marketing
Organization for the Development of Tourism in Africa

Further, conventions on diplomatic representation, movement of persons, shipping, insurance, and other issues were adopted. It was the mechanism of OCAM through which General DeGaulle pursued his chauvinistic concept of francophonie. In 1967 a student movement was created with the purpose of spreading consciousness about the organization among that segment of society.

There is no standard measure for the success of an international organization, but reference to Table 1 (p. 18) provides some guidance. Writing earlier, I attempted a measure of OCAM's impact upon the living circumstances of its citizens compared to the rest of Africa. Taking standard World Bank and United States Agency for International Development data, I compared life quality levels for the OCAM states on the one hand and the rest of Africa on the other (minus South Africa). On eighteen measures of change, e.g. literacy, OCAM fared better that the rest of Africa on eight measures; less well on ten. The only reasonable conclusion was that OCAM states had experienced dramatic change in only two areas: OCAM members experienced an average 14 percent increase in their trade with developing areas during 1960-1978 while the comparable figure for the rest of Africa averaged 4.3 percent. Presuming this increase was a result of trade which transpired predominantly with other OCAM members, there was a sign of measurable benefit. The other area of significant difference was in secondary education enrollments for which OCAM accomplished a 640 percent increase in 1960-1977 compared to an increase of 250 percent for the rest of Africa. These are meagre benefits and of little visibility to the average citizen. Nor was there evidence of OCAM's being the direct cause of this outcome. "On balance, there is little to distinguish OCAM states from the rest of Africa on the basis of empirical data."[5]

Members of OCAM came and went, and by the late 1970's only half remained of a high total of the original eighteen. Intraregional political disputes have taken the forefront to the exclusion of functional efforts at cooperation. There was, therefore, little apparent benefit, resulting in the demise of the organisation in 1985 with the explanation that all its goals had been achieved! In many ways similar to the crisis that has been building within the United Nations for several years, OCAM reached the point at which centripetal forces outweighed centrifugal ones, and the only feasible reconciliation was to discontinue efforts to maintain the organization. The numerous francophone organizations which were created provide avenues for cooperative ventures if the political will remains.

---

5. *Ibid*, p. 124.

ECOWAS: ECONOMIC COMMUNITY OF WEST AFRICAN STATES
(CDEAO in French)

ECOWAS can best be described as a plus-sum activity[1]. It has survived for over a decade and threatens no one. It has been perceived by its membership as a positive force. Widely disparate states such as Sierra Leone, Nigeria, and Mauritania belong to the regional economic grouping founded in 1975. ECOWAS includes all the Anglophone states of West Africa as well as all the surrounding Francophone and Lusophone states to make a geographically integral grouping. It is, incidentally, the largest regional group in the world in terms of number of members, sixteen.[2] "ECOWAS [was] created to foster economic integration and development.... Given the old barriers of language and geography....,the ECOWAS treaty must be regarded as the beginning of a brave new experiment..."[3]

Among the major provisions of the 1975 treaty establishing ECOWAS are provision for free movement of individuals among the members (still to be implemented), a customs union to be fully implemented in fifteen years, establishment of a common external tariff, a coordinated transportation and communication infrastructure, equalized development banks, common monetary policies, a unified development fund, and a fifteen-year transition period. The treaty proclaims the objectives of raising its people's standard of living, increasing and maintaining economic stability, and fostering closer relations. (Art. 2) All of this was to transpire in three stages. Its institutions include an Inter-Ministerial Council, the Authority of Heads of State and Government (which meets annually), four Commissions, and an Executive Secretariat.

A recent annual meeting paid attention to two regional disputes, though no formal mechanism exists for dispute settlement. One of the major impediments to success for the organization is hostility between Sierra Leone and Liberia, Ghana and Nigeria, Senegal and Mali, Cote d'Ivoire and Nigeria, among others.[4] In 1980 hundreds of thousands of aliens were expelled from one ECOWAS state to return to their homes in other ECOWAS states, a reflection of both economic and social strains. As with most regional groupings, there are ideological differences among the sixteen members, which are periodically changing with changing regimes.[5] This exacerbates cooperation. Poverty also impedes achievement of goals; in 1986 only Nigeria and Cote d'Ivoire had paid their obligations in full.

---

1. In game theory an activity in which participants see their actions as mutually beneficial is described as "plus sum." If not seen as mutually beneficial, the actions would be either "zero-sum," i.e. cancelling one another out, or "negative sum."
2. Cited by J.E. Okolo, "West African Regional Integration: ECOWAS," paper prepared for International Studies Association, 1984, p.45.
3. Address by Nigerian Chief of Staff, Brigadier Shehu Musa Yar'adua, to West African Economic Association, 13 April 1978, in Vremudia P. Diejomaoh and Milton A. Iyoha, *Industrialization in the Economic Community of West African States*. Lagos: Heinimann Educational Books, 1980.
4. Okolo, op. cit., p.19.
5. See Okolo, op. cit., pp. 10-20.

In 1980 the United States paid special attention to encouraging investment in the region through a trade mission as well as a forum held in Washington. Europe's connection with the region is through the Yaoundé and Lomé conventions. It is argued by some[6] that "the interests of the EEC are basically incompatible with the major objectives of the ECOWAS strategy of self-reliance."[7] This is because Europe sees itself as an exporter of manufactured goods and the ACP states as providers of raw materials. Relationships are further complicated by close ties between European multinational corporations and the economic elites in the ECOWAS states.[8] During the decade from 1968 to 1978 the percentage of imports obtained from ECOWAS states dropped for seven of the sixteen member states and exports to ECOWAS members declined for nine states, suggesting that not only was the organization not achieving its objectives, it was losing ground.[9]

There are favorable characteristics which move the ECOWAS states toward their objectives. Not the least is the simple fact of survival from 1972 in an environment which is not conducive to regionalism. Okolo points out, however, that ECOWAS does not meet the standards for success articulated by Haas and Schmitter[10]. ECOWAS established a Fund for Cooperation, Compensation and Development which is the mechanism for taking into account differential levels of development among its members. This provides a mechanism for, in effect, distributing the benefits in greater proportion to the poorer members and in lesser proportion to richer members.

A measure of the difficulty of the task facing ECOWAS, or any similar organization, is set out by the Executive Secretary of ECA. He points out that if Africa is to reach the level of two percent of global value added in manufacturing by the year 2000, all of Africa would have to maintain an annual growth rate of 11.3 percent. This was achieved by Cote d'Ivoire [in the 1970's], but is highly unlikely regionally.[11] One measure of the barriers to development in the region is the percentage of the workforce engaged in manufacturing: In the mid-1970's it ranged from about three percent in Liberia to fourteen percent in Cote d'Ivoire to seventeen percent in Nigeria to twenty-one percent in Burkina Fasso.[12] By 1980 comparable figures were eight percent in Cote d'Ivoire and twelve percent in Nigeria.[13]

---

6. For example, see S.K.B. Asante, "ECOWAS, the EEC and the Lomé Convention" in Domenico Mazzeo, *African Regional Organizations*, Cambridge: Cambridge University Press, 1984.
7. *Ibid*, p. 188.
8. *Ibid*, p. 191.
9. Okolo, op. cit., p.7.
10. Ernst B. Haas and Phillipe C. Schmitter, "Economic and Differential Patterns in Political Integration: Projections About Union in Latin America," in *International Political Communities: An Anthology*, Garden City: Doubleday, 1966. Their specified conditions which affect integration are: size-power homogeneity, rate of transactions among them, extent of pluralistic socio-political structure, and complementarity of elite values.
11. Adebayo Adedeji in Diejomaoh and Iyoha, p.21.
12. Ibid., p. 51.
13. World Bank data reported in *Africa Insight*, 17:4, 1987, p.73.

Despite the inherent fact of better-off and less-well-off participating states[14], no provision is made for a compensatory mechanism comparable to the "distributable pool" of the East African Community.[15] There is provision for "compensation due to loss of revenue" as a result of customs, but it is to be dealt with *ad hoc*, not as a matter of general principle.[16]

While the economic future for virtually all of Africa is clouded by factors both human and natural, ECOWAS appears to be able to survive, even with hope: There is proposed for 1992 a common currency (not coincidentally aligned with the similar proposal for that date in Europe).

"The central objective of ECOWAS as an institution is substantially to alter [the] pattern of (under)development."[17] While it has been in existence for a relatively short time, there is little evidence that ECOWAS has been able to overcome institutional, environmental, and economic impediments which have, in effect, condemned West Africa to an unpromising future in terms of economic development.

---

14. In the better-off category: Nigeria, Ivory Coast, Senegal, Sierra Leone; in the less-well-off category: Benin, Guinea, Mali, Niger.
15. See Arthur Hazlewood, *Economic Integration: The East African Experience*, New York: St. Martin's Press, p. 39 ff. for a discussion of this.
16. The text of the treaty is contained in Diejomaoh and Iyoha, op. cit., pp. 465-484.
17. Asante, op. cit., p. 187.

SADCC: THE SOUTHERN AFRICAN DEVELOPMENT COORDINATION CONFERENCE

With the convenient and provocative external enemy of South Africa as impetus, the nine states of the region just to her north formed SADCC in 1979. SADCC wes defined in the Lusaka Declaration adopted at Lusaka in that year. SADCC took effect 1 April 1980; a headquarters was established in Gaberone. It was an expansion of, and concrete manifestation of, the concept embodied by the Front Line States of Angola, Botswana, Mozambique, Tanzania, Zambia, and Zimbabwe. SADCC encompasses a population of 60 million. For some years previously the Front Line States had assumed the role of articulating Africa's displeasure with the remaining minority regimes in South Africa and Namibia. Rather than allow discussions of the Southern African "problem" to be monopolized by the major Western powers and the South African government, a process which had resulted in no satisfactory solution in African eyes, SADCC was an initiative taken in behalf of majoritarian interests. SADCC was an institution which would enable sympathetic states in the West to assist in developing infrastructure components which would strengthen SADCC members in finding alternatives to dependence upon South Africa, particularly regarding overland transportation and imports. The founding agreement provides for a regionally integrated economy as well. It has resulted in corollary institutions such as an organization of SADCC universities.

The SADCC program of action focuses on ten sectors, each the responsibility of a single member state: energy (Botswana), agriculture and natural resources (Malawi), food security (Zimbabwe), livestock (Botswana), soil and water conservation (Lesotho), industry and trade (Tanzania), mining (Zambia), manpower development (Swaziland), tourism (Lesotho), and transport and communications (Mozambique). The primary infrastructure activity is the rehabilitation of the 200-mile Beira corridor consisting of rail, highway, and pipeline links between the Mozambican port of Beira and the interior. By 1987 four hundred of five hundred proposed individual projects had been approved by members at a projected cost of US$5.4 billion. An example was the announced intention to construct Maize silos with 430,000 tons of capacity in Malawi.[1] Over a third of this amount had been pledged by Western donors by early 1987. Only with substantial aid can SADCC achieve its goals.[2]

However, the reality was that there were few concrete changes in their economic situations, and the states of the region were continuing economic hostages of the continent's most dynamic economy. For example, goods from South Africa accounted for from ten percent of Angola's imports to over eighty-five percent for Malawi and Swaziland, affording the opportunity for substantial economic destabilization in SADCC states. Still, seven SADCC states maintain direct air links to South Africa.[3] SADCC was the result of an attempt to focus economic activity away from South Africa by developing alternative infrastructure. In cooperation with donor states, which pledged US$650 million at a donor

---

1. *Daily Times* (Blantyre), 16 April 1985.
2. J. Barron Boyd, Jr.,"The Southern African Development Coordination Conference: A Subsystemic Analysis," paper prepared for International Studies Association, 1984, p. 7.
3. J. Gus Liebenow, "SADCC: Challenging the South African Connection," *UFSI Reports*, No. 13, 1983, p.7.

conference in 1980 in Maputo, projects were identified and some changes in regional economic patterns did occur. There have been periodic pledging conferences since.[4]

There are substantial problems which beset SADCC. For example, South African-supported RENAMO guerillas have wrought havoc with the already-lamentable Mozambican economy. The changing policies of the United States and the Soviet Union in the region have also had impact. Other problems, actual or potential are enumerated by Boyd: The members are heterogeneous, "varying in type of regime, level of development, economic orientation, ideological bent, degree of dependence upon South Africa, and geograph[y]."[5] Another problem is the economic dependence upon foreign workers; the vast majority in South Africa are from SADCC states. It is estimated by SADCC consultants that US$25 billion has been lost and that losses continue at the rate of US$5 billion annually.[6] As this is being written, the process of independence is underway in Namibia and an agreement has been signed to end the fourteen-year-long civil war in Angola. If these processes are consumated, SADCC's opportunities and promise will be bolstered.

Because there are two essentially divergent variables which gave rise to SADCC, its impact will be difficult to evaluate. On the one hand, there is the anti-South African sentiment which has both political as well as economic aspects. The SADCC states want to see South Africa liberated, but they also want to minimize their dependence upon her. The SADCC states are not without resources, e.g. ten percent of South Africa's electricity is provided by the Caborra Bassa Dam in Mozambique. Apart from South Africa, the SADCC states propose strengthening their elements of regional cooperation with the hope of enhancing their economic development. Certainly by focussing some donor resources on this latter goal, they have moved along their intended path.

---

4. See David S. Cownie, "Regional Cooperation for Development: A Review and Critique of the Southern African Development Coordination Conference," paper prepared at National Institute of Development, Research and Documentation, University of Botswana, n.d.
5. Boyd, op. cit.
6. *The Christian Science Monitor*, 15 July 1986.

UDEAC: CUSTOMS UNION OF CENTRAL ARICAN STATES

The Customs Union of Central African States is essentially just that: A customs union, created in 1964 as a result of an agreement between the members of UDE (consisting of former French Equatorial Africa (Central African Republic, Chad, Congo, Gabon) plus Cameroun. It succeeded the UDE of 1959 as "a necessary bridge between the colonial federation and a more extensive customs and economic union."[1] Created in 1964, UDEAC typifies the customs unions which have proliferated in post-independence Africa.

The key operative policy of UDEAC is the "single tax," a device intended to compensate for unequal levels of development. Its purposes are to stimulate industrialization by replacing import duties on materials needed for manufacture with the lower tax and also to build up a fund from which compensation can be paid to member states for lost revenues.[2]

The unevenness of development led to unhappiness on the part of Chad and the Central African Republic, despite compensation for a Solidarity Fund intended to redress the imbalance. These states finally withdrew and joined Zaire in the UEAC, a similar organization. The unimpressive data for UDEAC intraregional trade presented by Mytelka[3] suggests a similarity to the data referred to earlier regarding OCAM[4]. The short run impact of regional customs unions is not visible in the data--which of course has its own lag time, and that is compounded by a perceptual lag as well. As is argued regularly with regard to regional integration efforts, perceived costs at the front end are so great that no likely perceived benefits will be adequate to tide over either the populace or the leadership during the crucial first decade or so. If that period could be survived benefits could be expected, both actually as well as perceptually.

The primary subsidiary of UDEAC is the BDEAC, a development bank. Funded at CFA16 billion, it dispersed CFA5 5 billion during 1978-1981[5]. It is owned in equal shares by the member states and the central bank (BEAC) with lesser shares owned by Germany, France, Kuwait, and the ADB.

In evaluating the UDEAC Mytelka concludes that the treaty's effects have been less than salutary:

> [T]he single tax system and investment code have strengthened the market dominance of the foreign-owned companies, have guaranteed their profitability, have eliminated incentives to efficient production, have

---

1. Lynn Mytelka, "Competition, Conflict and Decline in the Union Douanière et Economique de l'Afrique Centrale (UDEAC)," in Domenico Mazzeo, *African Regional Organizations,* Cambridge: Cambridge University Press, 1984, p. 132.
2. *Ibid.*, pp. 133-134.
3. *Ibid.*, p. 137.
4. See Richard A. Fredland, "OCAM: One Scece in the Drama of West African Development" in Domenico Mazzeo, *African Regional Organizations,* Cambridge: Cambridge University Press, 1984, pp. 121-122.
5. Mytelka, op. cit., p. 140.

promoted capital and import-intensive production and have encouraged duplication of plants and products throughout the region.[6]

---

6. *Ibid.*, p. 146.

EUROPEAN COMMUNITY RELATIONS: PACIFIC-AFRICAN-CARIBBEAN STATES

As a consequence of negotiations between the members of the European Community and their former colonies, primarily within the British Commonwealth and the French *Communauté*, a treaty was concluded at Yaoundé in July, 1963 establishing "special arrangements" between these two groups. The arrangment is a "convention," not an "association," reflecting the sensitivity to neo-colonialist connections.[1] Original members were the six states of the Community plus French West Africa, French Equatorial Africa, Madagascar, French Cameroon and Togoland, Belgian Congo, Ruanda-Urundi, and Italian Somaliland, all African dependencies, numbering at the outset eighteen states. The agreement was renewed in 1969 in Yaoundé, at Lomé in 1975, 1979, 1984, and 1988. Presently the membership numbers sixty-six, including all the states of sub-Saharan Africa execpt Namibia and South Africa.

Yaoundé I (20 July 1963) established the Associated African States and Madagascar creating the "associated" status applied first to African states, later to other former colonies. Institutions created include a Council of Ministers which elects a Secretary General, a Parliamentary Conference, and a Court of Arbitration. These all continued under subsequent agreements. In 1980 the Secretariat staff numbered 90.[2]

The European Fund for Overseas Development, a creation of the Treaty of Rome, was the primary development assistance effort transferring funds from the developed states of Europe to Africa. In 1963 it was valued at EUA580 million. The primary characteristics of the arrangements, however, related to trading preferences. The European states agreed in Lomé to provide, in effect, a common market for African primary exports ranging from bananas to tomatoes to timber. Lomé I introduced STABEX, a complex system for stabilizing agricultural and mineral prices of the basic exports of the PAC states[3]. Over the ten years of Lomé and Lomé II 1,037 million ECU's wre transferred to PAC states.[4] A similar system, SYSMIN, which applies only to minerals, was introduced in Lomé II. In subsequent treaties this aspect of the relationship was more fully developed. The Africans, for their part, agreed to provide more favorable conditions of trade for manufactured exports from the EC. (This gave rise to one observation that the arrangement provided "peanuts for VW's.")

Yaoundé II, signed in May, 1969 and which came into force in January, 1971, made specific provisions to achieve the ends of Yaoundé I which had not been fulfilled, most particularly with regard to regional development. It was found that overall trade with Europe in the period 1958-1971 had increased at a lower rate than the rate for the rest of Africa, but that EC sales to the African member states had increased faster than sales to

---

1. *The Economist*, 8 February 1975.
2. The Secretariat publishes a bimonthly journal, *The Courier*.
3. The principal products (in terms of value) covered by STABEX include: coffee, cocoa, and groundnuts. Other products are cotton, copra and cocoanut, iron ore, oilcake, raw sisal, wood, and some lesser produce.
4. "Ten Years of Lomé," report by the Directoprate General for Development, Commission of the European Communities, 1986, p. 25.

other developing states. In other words, the Africans were purchasing more VW's while selling relatively fewer peanuts to Europe than before the arrangement.

With the accession of the United Kingdom to the EC, a new arrangement was needed to accommodate Commonwealth relationships. Lomé I (28 February 1975) expanded the common market provisions and also led to the Sugar Agreement which guaranteed European purchases of African sugar production at fixed levels and at European prices. Special emphasis was laid upon industrialization, training staff to manage and maintain projects provided under the terms of the agreement; funds for disaster aid were also laid aside.

The results of EC-APC have not been impressive: During the 1973-78 term the APC states provided only about 6 per cent of non-EC imports into the Community. Actually, in 1973 the figure was 7.4 per cent, and in 1978 it was 6.7 per cent. Put otherwise, the PAC states were providing 20 percent of third world imports to the EC in 1975; now it is 12-14 percent.[5] Major contributory factors to the absence of change were drastically lower world prices for copper and cotton, two of the major foreign exchange earners for several African PAC states.

Continued agitation on the part of the states of the South against perceived economic exploitation by the states of the North will undoubtedly be reflected by continued "adjustments" in EC-ACP economic relations. Whether these will result in "special" favors for the former colonies remains to be seen. Lomé IV, to be implemented in 1990, suggests that the system has become permanent: Lomé IV will not have a fixed duration.

---

5. Interview with Edwin Carrington, Secretary General of PAC, *West Africa*, October 24-30, 1988, p. 1988.

ADB: AFRICAN DEVELOPMENT BANK

The African Development Bank is the regional counterpart of both universal and subregional institutions, e.g. the World Bank (IBRD) and the West African Development Bank. Its purpose is not substantially different from similar institutions: elicit external funds and disburse them to member states with attention to regional considerations and agreed-upon development criteria. Specifically its charter calls for: financing investment projects, assisting in selecting projects, mobilizing non-African resources, promoting investment in Africa, and cooperating with other institutions to fulfill these objectives. It began with twenty-two member states, adding six additional ones by the end of the first year. The Bank was slow to start, having been established in August, 1963, and not becoming operational till July, 1966, largely as a result of inadequate funding. Its initial capital was US$300 million, half of it paid in. By 1970 it had committed only US$.04 per capita per annum in loans.

In 1982 the ADB decided to accept non-African members in order to expand its capital base, and within a year twenty non-African states had joined. Their contributions doubled the share capital to US$6.333 billion and enabled the Bank to raise US$1.6 billion in foreign capital markets. Originally, capital was split evenly between paid-in and callable funds; now only 25 per cent is paid in. Non-African states hold one-third of the seats on the Board of Directors exercising 36.57 per cent of the voting power as well as holding one-third of the capital commitments.

Management is by the President who is elected by the Board of Governors (one per member state) upon the recommendation of the Board of Directors (numbering 18). This is similar in structure to the World Bank. Not surprisingly, leadership has been a problem, balancing administrative expertise with political needs.

The Bank's five-year plan, adopted for the 1982-1986 quinquennium, emphasized food production with a minimum of one-third of its commitments to be made in that sector. As of the end of 1985 US$6.8 billion in loans had been approved. They were distributed sectorally as follows: agriculture 36.7%, transportation 26.7%, public utilities 19.16%, education 11.78%, and industry 5.66%. A proposal has been considered to authorize capital at the level of US$18.4 while lowering the paid up requirement to 12.5 percent from the present 25 percent.

In 1973 the Bank established the African Development Fund as a "soft money window." Interest-free loans were available with a .75% per annum service fee, a ten-year grace period, and fifty-year repayment period. Similarly, the Nigeria Trust Fund, which the Bank also administers, offers 4 percent loans with a five-year grace period and twenty-five year repayment period. By the end of 1985 the NTF had committed US$127 million in twenty-nine loans.

Institutions associated with the Bank are: Africa Reinsurance Corporation, Shelter Afrique, Association of African Development Finance Institutions, and Société Internationale Financière pour les Investissements et le Developpement en Afrique (all of which are detailed in the organizations section).

AFRICAN INTERNATIONAL ORGANIZATIONS

(ALPHABETICAL ORDER)

ORGANIZATION: Abidjan-Niger Railway Regime
ACRONYM: RAN FOUNDED: 1960
HEADQUARTERS: Abidjan
MEMBERS: Ivory Coast Upper Volta

RAN is intended to further economic development through railway expansion. The railway operated by RAN was built under French colonial administration and turned over to RAN in 1959. RAN employs a Director who is overseen by a twelve-member committee.

ORGANIZATION: Advisory Board of Inter-African Bureau for Animal Health
HEADQUARTERS: Lagos, PM Bag 2359

Created by STRC.

ORGANIZATION: African Accounting Council
ACRONYM: AAC FOUNDED: 1979.10
HEADQUARTERS: Kinshasa
MEMBERS:

Algeria	Angola	Benin	Burundi
Central African Rep	Congo	Equatorial Guinea	Gabon
Gambia	Guinea	Guinea-Bissau	Ivory Coast
Lesotho	Liberia	Libya	Madagascar
Malawi	Mali	Mauritius	Morocco
Niger	Nigeria	Sao Tome Principe	Senegal
Sudan	Tanzania	Togo	Tunisia
Upper Volta	Zaire		

Open to all OAU members, its purpose is to establish standard accounting procedures within the member states.

ORGANIZATION: African Agricultural Credit Commission
ACRONYM: AACC   FOUNDED: 1966.09
MEMBERS:

Algeria	Congo	Ivory Coast	Libya
Morocco	Senegal	Tunisia	Upper Volta

ORGANIZATION: African Air Tariff Conference

ORGANIZATION: African and Malagasy Bureau of Legislative Studies
MEMBERS:

Benin	Cameroon	Central African Rep	Congo
Gabon	Guinea	Mauritius	Niger
Rwanda	Senegal	Somalia	Togo
Upper Volta	Zaire		

Associated with OCAM.

ORGANIZATION: African and Malagasy Coffee Organisation
ACRONYM: OAMCAF   FOUNDED: 1960
HEADQUARTERS: Paris
MEMBERS:

Benin	Cameroon	Central African Rep	Congo
Gabon	Ivory Coast	Madagascar	Togo

The OAMCAF was designed to defend members' interests within the International Coffee Organization. It is associated with OCAM and it was reorganized July, 1963.

ORGANIZATION: African and Malagasy Common Organization
ACRONYM: OCAM   FOUNDED: 1964.02
HEADQUARTERS: Bangui, BP 965
MEMBERS:

Benin	Cameroon	Central African Rep	Congo
Gabon	Guinea	Mauritius	Niger
Rwanda	Senegal	Somalia	Togo

AFRICAN INTERNATIONAL ORGANIZATIONS

Upper Volta   Zaire

Mauritius joined in 1969; left in 1983. Cameroon left in 1973. Congo and Guinea left in 1972.

OCAM succeeded OAMCE. Its announced purpose was the development of international institutions. Began as UAMCE and was then OCAMM till Mauritania left the organization. It was dissolved 23 March 1985 having "achieved all its objectives." Published "Statistical Bulletin" about 3 times annually in the 1960's and 1970's. Organs: Department of Ecnomic and Financial Affairs & Transportation; Monetary and Financial Affairs; Foreign Commerce; Economic & Social Development; Statistical Service; Transportation Service; Department of Cultural and Social Affairs. See "Main Organizations" section for additional information.

ORGANIZATION: African and Malagasy Council on Higher Education
ACRONYM: CAMES   FOUNDED: 1968.02
HEADQUARTERS: Ouagadougou
MEMBERS:

Benin	Cameroon	Central African Rep	Congo
Gabon	Guinea	Mauritius	Niger
Rwanda	Senegal	Somalia	Togo
Upper Volta	Zaire		

CAMES was created by UAMCE (OCAM). There was no reported activity prior to 1979. Its purpose was to facilitate co-operation in higher education and research. It had become active by 1983.

ORGANIZATION: African and Malagasy Defense Union

Sudsidiary of UAM.

ORGANIZATION: African and Malagasy Industrial Property Office
ACRONYM: OAMPI   FOUNDED: 1962.09
HEADQUARTERS: Yaoundé
MEMBERS:

Benin	Cameroon	Central African Rep	Chad
Congo	Gabon	Ivory Coast	Madagascar
Mauritania	Niger	Senegal	Upper Volta

OAMPI was created by OAMCE (which see) with the purpose of developing common legal and administrative procedures for administering copyright and patent protection. It is associated with OCAM.

ORGANIZATION: African and Malagasy Institite of Bilingualism
MEMBERS:

Benin	Cameroon	Central African Rep	Congo
Gabon	Guinea	Mauritius	Niger
Rwanda	Senegal	Somalia	Togo
Upper Volta	Zaire		

This is associated with OCAM.

ORGANIZATION: African and Malagasy Institute of Applied Economics and Statistics
MEMBERS:

Benin	Cameroon	Central African Rep	Congo
Gabon	Guinea	Mauritius	Niger
Rwanda	Senegal	Somalia	Togo
Upper Volta	Zaire		

This is associated with OCAM.

ORGANIZATION: African and Malagasy Institute of Architecture

This is associated with OCAM.

ORGANIZATION: African and Malagasy Intellectual Property Office
HEADQUARTERS: Yaoundé

This is a subsidiary of OCAM.

ORGANIZATION: African and Malagasy Office of Industrial Property
See African and Malagasy Industrial Property Office

ORGANIZATION: African and Malagasy Organization of Economic Cooperation
ACRONYM: OAMCE   FOUNDED: 1961
HEADQUARTERS: Defunct
MEMBERS:

Benin	Cameroon	Central African Rep	Chad
Congo	Gabon	Ivory Coast	Madagascar
Mauritania	Niger	Senegal	Upper Volta

This organization had plans for a customs union, joint airline and alligned foreign policies, which was in partial reaction to the assertiveness of Ghana. Reference: Ranjeva.

ORGANIZATION: African and Malagasy Postal and Telecommunications Union
See African and Malagasy Union of Posts and Telecommunications

---

ORGANIZATION: African and Malagasy States Associated with the EEC
See Pan-African Congress
ACRONYM: CEE-EAMA

ORGANIZATION: African and Malagasy Sugar Agreement
FOUNDED: 1966
HEADQUARTERS: Ft. Lamy
MEMBERS:

Benin	Cameroon	Central African Rep	Chad
Congo	Gabon	Ivory Coast	Madagascar
Niger	Rwanda	Senegal	Togo
Upper Volta	Zaire		

The Accord was instituted as a sudsidiary of the work of OCAM. Maintenance of prices is the primary function. Policy is made by a Council which employs an Executive Director to implement its decisions.

A GUIDE TO AFRICAN INTERNATIONAL ORGANIZATIONS

ORGANIZATION: African and Malagasy Union
ACRONYM: UAM FOUNDED: 1960.12
HEADQUARTERS: Defunct
MEMBERS:

Benin	Cameroon	Central African Rep	Chad
Congo	Gabon	Ivory Coast	Madagascar
Mauritania	Niger	Rwanda	Senegal
Togo	Upper Volta		

The UAM was formed by the Brazzaville Group and was dissolved in 1964 in favor of UDEAC. It defined these areas of co-operation: defense, posts & telecommunications, and development banks. It was an extension of the Council of the Entente--a conservative alternative to the Casablanca Group. There were no intentions of union, only diplomatic co-operation. Components: (1) A & M Organization for Economic Co-operation, (2) A & M Defense Union, (3) A & M Post & Telecommunications Union, (4) Air Afrique. Its budget was CAF 300 million, which was oversubscribed. Reference: Tevoedje, 1965, *Pan-Africanism in Action: An Account of the Union Africaine et Malgache*. Cambridge: Harvard University Press.

ORGANIZATION: African and Malagasy Union for Economic and Technical Cooperation
ACRONYM: UAMCET

ORGANIZATION: African and Malagasy Union of Development Banks
See African and Mauritian Union of Development Banks

ORGANIZATION: African and Malagasy Union of Economic Cooperation
ACRONYM: UAMCE FOUNDED: 1964
HEADQUARTERS: Yaoundé
MEMBERS:

Benin	Cameroon	Chad	Congo
Gabon	Madagascar	Mauritania	Rwanda
Senegal	Togo		

Created by the Charter of Dakar, the UAMCE succeeded the UAM.

ORGANIZATION: African and Malagasy Union of Posts and Telecommunications
ACRONYM: UAMPT FOUNDED: 1961.09
HEADQUARTERS: Brazzaville, BP 44
MEMBERS:

Benin	Cameroon	Central African Rep	Congo
Gabon	Guinea	Ivory Coast	Mali
Mauritania	Niger	Rwanda	Senegal
Togo	Upper Volta	Zaire	

UAMPT provides for a uniform tariff for telecommunications usage among the members and inter-state co-operation in the use of services. Its organs are a Secretary-General, Council of Ministers, and Administrative and Technical Study Commissions.

ORGANIZATION: African and Mauritian Advanced Training Centre for Administrative Personnel
ACRONYM: CAMPC FOUNDED: 1975.12
HEADQUARTERS: Abidjan, BP 878
MEMBERS:

Benin	Central African Rep	Gabon	Ivory Coast
Mauritius	Niger	Rwanda	Senegal
Togo	Upper Volta		

Its purpose is to train executives for public and private enterprises. It is a subsiduary of OCAM.

ORGANIZATION: African and Mauritian Bilingual Institute
ACRONYM: IAMB FOUNDED: 1975
HEADQUARTERS: Port Louis
MEMBERS:

IAMB trains scholarship students in English-French translation and interpretation. It is a subsidiary of OCAM.

A GUIDE TO AFRICAN INTERNATIONAL ORGANIZATIONS

ORGANIZATION: African and Mauritian Bureau of Research and Legislative Studies
HEADQUARTERS: Bangui

A subsidiary of OCAM, its purpose is to harmonize legislation among member states as a basis for further co-operation.

ORGANIZATION: African and Mauritian Centre for Staff Improvement
HEADQUARTERS: Abidjan

As a subsidiary of OCAM, the Centre provides administrative staff training.

ORGANIZATION: African and Mauritian Cultural Institute
ACRONYM: ICAM   FOUNDED:
HEADQUARTERS: Dakar

This is a subsidiary of OCAM.

ORGANIZATION: African and Mauritian Institute of Statistics and Applied Economics
ACRONYM: IAMSEA   FOUNDED: 1975
HEADQUARTERS: Kigali, BP 1109

A subsidiary of OCAM, it provides training for statisticians.

ORGANIZATION: African and Mauritian School of Architecture and Urbanism
ACRONYM: EAMAU   FOUNDED: 1975.10
HEADQUARTERS: Lomé, BP 2067
MEMBERS:

Benin	Central African Rep	Gabon	Ivory Coast
Mauritius	Niger	Rwanda	Senegal
Togo	Upper Volta		

EAMAU offers courses for professionals in architecture and urban planning. It is a subsidiary of OCAM.

ORGANIZATION: African and Mauritian Union of Development Banks
ACRONYM: UAMBD FOUNDED: 1962.09
HEADQUARTERS: Bangui, BP 965
MEMBERS:

Benin	Cameroon	Central African Rep	Chad
Congo	Gabon	Ivory Coast	Madagascar
Niger	Senegal	Togo	Upper Volta

The Union co-ordinates activities of national development banks of the OCAM member states.

ORGANIZATION: African, Malagasy and Mauritanian Cultural Institute
See African and Mauritian Cultural Institute

ORGANIZATION: African-Malagasy Common Organization
See African and Malagasy Common Organization
Also see "Main Organizations"

ORGANIZATION: African Bureau of Educational Sciences
FOUNDED: 1973.09
HEADQUARTERS: Kisangani, BP 2014
MEMBERS:

Algeria	Angola	Benin	Botswana
Burundi	Cameroon	Central African Rep	Chad
Congo	Egypt	Ethiopia	Gabon
Ghana	Guinea-Bissau	Ivory Coast	Kenya
Liberia	Madagascar	Malawi	Mali
Mauritania	Mauritius	Morocco	Mozambique
Niger	Nigeria	Rwanda	Senegal
Sierra Leone	Sudan	Swaziland	Tanzania
Togo	Tunisia	Uganda	Upper Volta
Zaire	Zambia	Zimbabwe	

The Bureau is supported by UNESCO and the OAU. It encourages educational research, and it holds periodic conferences.

ORGANIZATION: African Caribbean Pacific Group
ACRONYM: ACP   FOUNDED: 1975.06
HEADQUARTERS: Bruxelles, Avenue Georges
MEMBERS:

Benin	Botswana	Burundi	Cameroon
Cape Verde	Central African Rep	Chad	Comoros
Congo	Djibouti	Equatorial Guinea	Ethiopia
Gabon	Gambia	Ghana	Guinea
Guinea-Bissau	Ivory Coast	Kenya	Lesotho
Liberia	Madagascar	Malawi	Mali
Mauritania	Mauritius	Niger	Nigeria
Rwanda	Sao Tome Principe	Senegal	Seychelles
Sierra Leone	Somalia	Sudan	Swaziland
Tanzania	Togo	Tunisia	Uganda
Upper Volta	Zaire	Zambia	Zimbabwe

The grouping resulting from the Yaoundé and Lomé agreements. There is a secretary general who directs the program. See "Main Organizations" section.

ORGANIZATION: African Center for Administrative Training and Research for Development
ACRONYM: CAFRAD   FOUNDED: 1964.07
HEADQUARTERS: Tangier
MEMBERS:

Algeria	Cameroon	Central African Rep	Egypt
Ghana	Ivory Coast	Libya	Mauritania
Morocco	Senegal	Somalia	Sudan
Togo	Tunisia	Zambia	

CAFRAD was established by agreement between UNESCO and Morocco. In 1980 the 20th meeting of its council was held. CAFRAD provides training for administrators of infrastructure-related government programs in Africa, gathers data related to administration of development issues. There is a translation unit. Its published statement of objecives includes the following: encourage research on administrative problems relating to development; organize cadres of public administrators; meet, analyze, and diffuse ideas regarding development. In the 1970's CAFRAD received an annual subvention from UNESCO of US$114,000.

AFRICAN INTERNATIONAL ORGANIZATIONS

ORGANIZATION: African Centre for Applied Research and Training in Social Development
ACRONYM: ACARTSOD FOUNDED: 1977
HEADQUARTERS: Tripoli
MEMBERS:

Algeria	Angola	Benin	Burundi
Cameroon	Central African Rep	Egypt	Equ. Guinea
Ethiopia	Gambia	Ghana	Guinea
Kenya	Liberia	Libya	Mali
Morocco	Senegal	Sierra Leone	Sudan
Togo	Uganda	Upper Volta	Zaire

The Centre is supported by the OAU. Its purpose is to co-ordinate research and training in the broad area of social development.

ORGANIZATION: African Centre for Monetary Studies
ACRONYM: ACMS FOUNDED: 1975
HEADQUARTERS: Dakar, BP 1791
MEMBERS:

Algeria	Benin	Cameroon	Congo
Egypt	Equatorial Guinea	Ethiopia	Gabon
Ghana	Ivory Coast	Liberia	Nigeria
Malawi	Mali	Mauritania	Mauritius
Morocco	Niger	Nigeria	Rwanda
Senegal	Seychelles	Sierra Leone	Swaziland
Tanzania	Togo	Tunisia	Upper Volta
Zaire	Zambia		

All members of the AACB belong. The Centre seeks to enable countries to coordinate their monetary policies and studies large-scale and long-term financial trends affecting Africa.

ORGANIZATION: African Civil Aviation Commission
ACRONYM: AFCAC FOUNDED: 1969.01
HEADQUARTERS: Dakar, BP 2356
MEMBERS:

Algeria	Angola	Benin	Burundi
Cameroon	Central African Rep	Chad	Congo
Egypt	Ethiopia	Gabon	Gambia

A GUIDE TO AFRICAN INTERNATIONAL ORGANIZATIONS

Ghana	Guinea	Ivory Coast	Kenya
Lesotho	Liberia	Libya	Madagascar
Malawi	Mali	Mauritania	Morocco
Niger	Nigeria	Rwanda	Senegal
Sierra Leone	Somalia	Sudan	Swaziland
Tanzania	Togo		

Convened by the OAU with support from International Civil Aviation Organization and the European Community. Membership is open to all African states. Its purposes are: (1) to encourage co-ordination and co-operation in civil aviation activities; and (2) to encourage common commercial air standards consonant with the ICAO. It is associated with the OAU. In 1974 it was substantially revised.

ORGANIZATION: African Clearing and Payments Union

ORGANIZATION: African Commercial Union
FOUNDED: 1964.05
HEADQUARTERS: Paris
MEMBERS:

Niger	Togo	Tunisia	Upper Volta

Its purpose is to "insure favorable trading conditions."

ORGANIZATION: African Commission on Agricultural Statistics
FOUNDED: 1961
HEADQUARTERS: Accra
MEMBERS:

Algeria	Benin	Botswana	Burundi
Cameroon	Central African Rep	Chad	Congo
Ethiopia	Gabon	Gambia	Ghana
Guinea	Ivory Coast	Kenya	Lesotho
Liberia	Madagascar	Malawi	Mali
Mauritania	Mauritius	Morocco	Mozambique
Niger	Nigeria	Rwanda	Senegal
Seychelles	Tanzania	Togo	Tunisia
Uganda	Upper Volta	Zaire	Zambia

The Commission was established by FAO.

ORGANIZATION: African Common Market
FOUNDED: 1980.05

Proposed by the OAU; it was to be achieved by the year 2000. The "Lagos Plan of Action" set out the details of the proposal.

ORGANIZATION: African Conference of Central African Posts and Telecommunications
HEADQUARTERS: Yaoundé

ORGANIZATION: African Consultative Council
FOUNDED: 1961.05

Related to the Casablanca Group (which see).

ORGANIZATION: African Council for the Training and Promotion of Health Sciences, Teachers & Specialists
ACRONYM: ACHSTS   FOUNDED: 1984

Its membership numbered 16 at its inception.

ORGANIZATION: African Cultural Institute
ACRONYM: ACI   FOUNDED: 1971
HEADQUARTERS: Dakar
MEMBERS:

Benin	Central African Rep	Chad	Congo
Gabon	Ghana	Ivory Coast	Mauritania
Niger	Senegal	Seychelles	Sierra Leone
Togo	Upper Volta	Zambia	

The ACI relates culture to development and conducts research in this area. Paid staff: 25.

ORGANIZATION: African Data Processing Institute
       FOUNDED: 1971
HEADQUARTERS: Libreville
       MEMBERS:

Benin	Cameroon	Central African Rep	Chad
Congo	Gabon	Ivory Coast	Niger
Senegal	Togo	Upper Volta	

This is a primarily educational organization which is a subsidiary of OCAM. It is supported by ECA.

ORGANIZATION: African Development Bank
       ACRONYM: ADB [BAD]   FOUNDED: 1963
HEADQUARTERS: Abidjan, BP 1387
       MEMBERS: 73 members; all Africa except Nambia, South Africa, and donor states

The ADB was sponsored by the ECA (UN). Its purpose is to further economic development in Africa through lending capital deposited by both African and non-African memers. It supports both private and public projects. Examples include 3.5 million UA to Togo to cover the foreign exchange costs of small and medium development projects; 8 million UA to Botswana for the foreign exchange costs of a teacher training college; and to Liberia half the cost of a manufacturing facility for glass containers. Unlike most of the organizations dealt with in this volume, the ADB publishes complete and regular annual reports which offer substantial detail about its operation. Though founded in 1963, it began operating in 1966 and approved its first loan in the next year. By 1984 it had disbursed over 500 million units of account for over 300 projects. Its 50 African members control 80% of the voting rights while 11 Western members control the remainder. See "Main Organizations" section.

ORGANIZATION: African Development Bank Group
              Also see African Development Bank
       FOUNDED: 1963
HEADQUARTERS: Abidjan

This term refers to the ADB, ADF, AIDF, and the Nigeria Trust Fund.

AFRICAN INTERNATIONAL ORGANIZATIONS

ORGANIZATION: African Development Fund
ACRONYM: ADF   FOUNDED: 1972
HEADQUARTERS: Abidjan
MEMBERS: Its membership is non-African.

The ADF was designed to provide a co-operative approach to aid to Africa. Memberhip includes non-African states. It is a lending mechanism of ADB/BAD in conjunction with external funding sources similar to IBRD/IDA. In 1982 it lent US$352 million. In 1977 it received its second replenishment of funds from its donors. It began with 16 members; it now has 25. Its terms are the same as the International Development Fund, the "soft loan" arm of World Bank). Of the 400 million UA's lent 1977-1982, one-third each went to agricultural and transportation projects, 13% went for water supply projects, and the remainer were widely dispersed.

ORGANIZATION: African Development Information Network
ACRONYM: AFDIN
HEADQUARTERS: Addis Ababa

This was created and is supported by ECA.

ORGANIZATION: African Financial Community
See Communauté Financiére Africaine

ORGANIZATION: African Forestry Commission
ACRONYM: AFC   FOUNDED: 1959
HEADQUARTERS: Accra, Box 1628 c/o FAO
MEMBERS:

Algeria	Benin	Botswana	Burundi
Cameroon	Central African Rep	Chad	Congo
Ethiopia	Gabon	Gambia	Ghana
Guinea	Ivory Coast	Kenya	Lesotho
Liberia	Madagascar	Malawi	Mali
Mauritania	Mauritius	Morocco	Niger
Nigeria	Rwanda	Senegal	Sierra Leone
Sudan	Tanzania	Togo	Tunisia
Uganda	Upper Volta	Zaire	Zambia
Zimbabwe			

AFC was created by FAO. It advises governments on the development of national forestry policy and its implementation.

ORGANIZATION: African Groundnut Council
ACRONYM: AGC FOUNDED: 1964
HEADQUARTERS: Lagos
MEMBERS:

Gambia	Mali	Niger	Nigeria
Senegal	Sudan	Zaire	

Its purpose is to ensure remunerative prices and to exchange technical information, especially with regard to alternative uses for groundnuts.

ORGANIZATION: African Industrial Development Fund
ACRONYM: AIDF
HEADQUARTERS: Abidjan

This is a subsidiary of the ADB.

ORGANIZATION: African Institute for Economic Development and Planning
ACRONYM: AIEDP FOUNDED: 1962
HEADQUARTERS: Dakar

AIEDP was created by ICA and has been supported by UNDP. At its outset it employed a paid staff of 15.

ORGANIZATION: African Institute of Informatics
ACRONYM: IAI FOUNDED: 1972
HEADQUARTERS: Libréville

IAI is a subsidiary of OCAM.

ORGANIZATION: African Institute on Information
See African Institute of Informatics.

ORGANIZATION: African Intellectual Property Organization
ACRONYM: OAPI   FOUNDED: 1962.09
HEADQUARTERS: Yaoundé
MEMBERS:

Benin	Cameroon	Central African Rep	Chad
Congo	Gabon	Ivory Coast	Madagascar
Mauritania	Niger	Senegal	Togo
Upper Volta			

This serves as the national office for member states in dealing with patents and copyrights. It succeeded OAMPI.

ORGANIZATION: African International Association
FOUNDED: 1876
HEADQUARTERS: Defunct

This was the Belgian mechanism through which the Congo was administered.

ORGANIZATION: African Liberation Committee
See Coordination Commission for Liberation Movements of Africa

---

ORGANIZATION: African Malagasy Union
See African and Malagasy Union

ORGANIZATION: African, Mauritian, and Malagasy Common Organization
ACRONYM: OCAMM
HEADQUARTERS: Defunct

In 1974 its professional staff numbered 18.

ORGANIZATION: African Ministers of Education and Planning Conference

ORGANIZATION: African National Television and Broadcasting Union
See African Union of Broadcasting

ORGANIZATION: African Parliament's Union
ACRONYM: APU   FOUNDED: 1976
HEADQUARTERS: Abidjan

Open to all parliaments of OAU members; non-parliamentary states may participate as observers.

ORGANIZATION: African Patent Document and Information Centre
ACRONYM: CADIB
HEADQUARTERS: Yaoundé, BP 887
MEMBERS:

Benin	Cameroon	Central African Rep	Chad
Congo	Gabon	Ivory Coast	Mauritania
Niger	Senegal	Togo	Upper Volta

CADIB was established by AIPO for Francophone Africa; it is managed by WIPO.

ORGANIZATION: African Postal and Telecommunications Union
ACRONYM: APU/ATU   FOUNDED: 1935
HEADQUARTERS: Pretoria
MEMBERS:

Botswana	Burundi	Lesotho	Malawi
Nambia	South Africa	Swaziland	Zaire
Zimbabwe			

As a result of political problems among the membership, it has been dormant for many years. Many members withdrew upon independence in the 1960's because of South Africa's pivotal role.

ORGANIZATION: African Postal Union
ACRONYM: AFPU FOUNDED: 1961
HEADQUARTERS: Cairo; 5, 26th July Street
MEMBERS:

Burundi	Egypt	Ghana	Guinea
Guinea-Bissau	Liberia	Libya	Mali
Mauritania	Somalia	Sudan	Zaire

AFPU was created by the Casablanca Group. It serves to facilitate postal service among its member states.

ORGANIZATION: African Posts and Telecommunications Union
ACRONYM: UAPT FOUNDED: 1961.09
HEADQUARTERS: Brazzaville
MEMBERS:

Benin	Central African Rep	Chad	Congo
Ivory Coast	Mali	Mauritius	Niger
Rwanda	Senegal	Togo	Upper Volta

UAPT was intended to develop joint communications policies among its members. It was formerly UAMPT and associated with UAM. It was reorganized in 1975.

ORGANIZATION: African Regional Center for Engineering, Design, and Manufacturing
ACRONYM: ARCDEM
HEADQUARTERS: Ibadan PMB 19

Sponsored by ECA.

ORGANIZATION: African Regional Centre for Labor Administration
ACRONYM: CRADAT

ORGANIZATION: African Regional Centre for Technology
ACRONYM: ARCT FOUNDED: 1977.11
HEADQUARTERS: Dakar, BP 2435
MEMBERS:

Algeria	Benin	Burundi	Cameroon
Egypt	Equatorial Guinea	Ethiopia	Ghana
Guinea	Kenya	Liberia	Mauritius
Mauritania	Morocco	Mozambique	Niger
Nigeria	Rwanda	Senegal	Sierra Leone
Somalia	Sudan	Tanzania	Togo
Uganda	Zaire	Zambia	

ARCT is sponsored by OAU. Its proclaimed purpose is to develop technology for use in national programs of development.

ORGANIZATION: African Regional Co-ordinating Committee for the Integration of Women in Development
HEADQUARTERS: Addis Ababa, Box 3001

Created by ECA.

ORGANIZATION: African Regional Organization for Standardization
ACRONYM: ARSO FOUNDED: 1977.01
HEADQUARTERS: Nairobi, Box 54363
MEMBERS:

Cameroon	Egypt	Ethiopia	Ghana
Guinea	Guinea-Bissau	Ivory Coast	Kenya
Liberia	Libya	Malawi	Mauritius
Niger	Nigeria	Senegal	Sudan
Tanzania	Togo	Tunisia	Uganda
Zaire	Zambia		

Its aims are industrial and consumer standardization, quality control, safety, and consumer protection.

ORGANIZATION: African Reinsurance Corporation
ACRONYM: AFRICARE FOUNDED: 1976
HEADQUARTERS: Lagos, PMB 12765
MEMBERS:

Algeria	Benin	Burundi	Cameroon
Central African Rep	Chad	Congo	Egypt
Ethiopia	Gabon	Gambia	Ghana
Guinea	Guinea-Bissau	Ivory Coast	Kenya
Liberia	Libya	Mali	Mauritania
Mauritius	Morocco	Niger	Nigeria
Senegal	Sierra Leone	Somalia	Sudan
Swaziland	Tanzania	Togo	Tunisia
Uganda	Upper Volta	Zaire	Zambia

It is open to all OAU members, and it is partially owned by the ADB. Its purpose is to promote the development of the insurance and reinsurance industry which, in turn, supports economic development in general. At its founding it had US$15 million in capital.

ORGANIZATION: African Remote Sensing Council
HEADQUARTERS: Kinshasa, BP 2092

Supported by ECA and OAU.

ORGANIZATION: African Society for the Development of the Millet-and-Sorghum-based Food Industry
ACRONYM: SADIAMIL FOUNDED: 1972
HEADQUARTERS: Niamey
MEMBERS:

Mali	Mauritania	Niger	Sudan
Upper Volta			

This was proposed by Niger. Its purpose is to promote facilities to process millet and sorghum.

ORGANIZATION: African Solidarity Fund
FOUNDED: 1978
HEADQUARTERS: Niamey, BP 382
MEMBERS:

Benin	Burundi	Central African Rep	Chad
Gabon	Ivory Coast	Mali	Mauritius
Niger	Rwanda	Senegal	Togo
Upper Volta	Zaire		

The Fund is the mode through which France provides ecomomic assistance to the members. Half its capital is provided by France. Its 1982 budget was CFA Fr 7 billion. Its objective is broadly stated as economic development.

ORGANIZATION: African States of the Casablanca Charter
See Casablanca Group

ORGANIZATION: African Telecommunications Union
ACRONYM: UAT   FOUNDED: 1961
HEADQUARTERS: Addis Ababa, Box 3243

ORGANIZATION: African Timber Organization
ACRONYM: ATO   FOUNDED: 1975.05
HEADQUARTERS: Libreville, BP 1077
MEMBERS:

Cameroon	Central African Rep	Congo	Equ. Guinea
Gabon	Ghana	Ivory Coast	Liberia
Madagascar	Nigeria	Tanzania	Zaire

Its purposes are to improve markets for timber, encourage technical co-operation, and study and co-ordinate timber markets for its members. ATO increasingly seeks to preserve tropical rainforests through conservation and prudent management. It is suppported primarily by UNDP.

ORGANIZATION: African Training and Research in Administration for Development
ACRONYM: ATRCAD   FOUNDED: 1964
HEADQUARTERS: Tangier

ATRCAD's purpose is to adapt public administration structures to development purposes. For example, in 1978 it completed a study on West African government documents with the effect of making them more widely available.

ORGANIZATION: African Union of National Radio and Television Broadcasting
See Union of National Radio and Television Broadcasters

ORGANIZATION: African Union of States
See Union of Africa

ORGANIZATION: Afro-Asian Conference of Solidarity
FOUNDED: 1957

This was not an organization, but a meeting. In the spirit of the times, it was a gathering essentially of newly-independent states expressing their newly-won independence. Following an earlier similar meeting in Bandung, it was held in Cairo. It resulted in increased competitiveness between Presidents Nasser and Nkrumah for African leadership.

ORGANIZATION: Afro-Asian Organization for Economic Cooperation
ACRONYM: AFRASEC   FOUNDED: 1958.12
HEADQUARTERS: Cairo
MEMBERS:

AFRASEC conducts annual conferences on topics of economic development.

ORGANIZATION: Afro-Asian Peoples' Solidarity Organization
FOUNDED: 1957
HEADQUARTERS: Cairo; 89, Abdul Aziz Al Saoud Manial

Its proclaimed purpose is to achieve unity in the struggle against imperialism and colonialism.

ORGANIZATION: Afro-Asian Rural Reconstruction Organization
ACRONYM: AARRO　　　　FOUNDED: 1962.03
HEADQUARTERS: New Delhi, India
MEMBERS:

Algeria	Egypt	Ethiopia	Ghana
Kenya	Liberia	Libya	Mauritius
Morocco	Sierra Leone	Sudan	Tunisia

Plus several Asian members

The purpose of AARRO is to develop understanding among members of rural welfare problems. It published "Rural Reconciliation" in the 1970's.

ORGANIZATION: Afro-Asian Solidarity Council

Not a governmental organization.

ORGANIZATION: Afro-Islamic Co-ordinating Council
FOUNDED: >1980
HEADQUARTERS: Riyadh, Saudi Arabia

The Council is sponsored by Islamic states in the Middle East for the purpose of promoting Islam in Africa.

ORGANIZATION: Afro-Malagasy Economic Cooperation Organization
ACRONYM: AMECO
HEADQUARTERS: Defunct
MEMBERS:

Benin	Cameroon	Central African Rep	Chad
Congo	Gabon	Ivory Coast	Madagascar
Mauritania	Niger	Senegal	Upper Volta

Formed by members of the Brazzaville Group.

AFRICAN INTERNATIONAL ORGANIZATIONS

ORGANIZATION: Agency for the Safety of Air Navigation in Africa and Madagascar
ACRONYM: ASECNA FOUNDED: 1959
HEADQUARTERS: Dakar, BP 3144
MEMBERS:

Benin	Cameroon	Central African Rep	Chad
Congo	Gabon	Ivory Coast	Madagascar
Mali	Mauritania	Niger	Senegal
Togo	Upper Volta		

ASECNA was revised substantially in 1974. It began as a subsidiary of OCM, and continued as an agency of OCAM.

ORGANIZATION: Air Afrique
FOUNDED: 1961
HEADQUARTERS: Abidjan
MEMBERS:

Benin	Cameroon	Chad	Cent Afr Rep
Congo	Gabon	Ivory Coast	Mauritania
Niger	Senegal	Togo	Upper Volta

Created by OCAM, [La Société] Air Afrique is a joint venture of the twelve member states. The organization also seeks to exploit the international rights of the member states with regard to air transport. Technically, Air Afrique is not an intergovernmental organization.

ORGANIZATION: All African People's Conference(s) (Organization)
ACRONYM: AAPC FOUNDED: 1958

Meetings in 1958 (Accra), 1960, 1961(Cairo). The All African Peoples' Organization, the work of which was essentially to hold the conferences, raised national consciousness among African peoples, encouraged nationalist leaders and planned independence strategies.

ORGANIZATION: All African Peoples' Organization
See above

ORGANIZATION: Arab Bank for Economic Development in Africa
ACRONYM: BADEA   FOUNDED: 1973.11
HEADQUARTERS: Khartoum, Box 2640

Created by League of Arab States, it began operations in 1975. Paid up capital: US$735 million. Recipients of loans must be non-Arab members of OAU. In 1977 it absorbed the Special Arab Assistance Fund for Africa. Its published objectives are to strengthen Arab-African ties, to further economic development and economic independence for Africa, and to increase agricultural output. Seventeen Arab states belong. By 1986 $779 million had been committed to Africa.

ORGANIZATION: Arab-African Union of States
FOUNDED: 1984.08
HEADQUARTERS: Defunct

This was an abortive attempted union betweeen Libya and Morocco. There was a proposed joint chairmanship between the two states' leaders. The announced areas of co-operation were political, defense, economic, and cultural-technical-through councils. The Union was to have been approved by a referendum in each member state.

ORGANIZATION: Architectural Institute
MEMBERS:

Benin	Botswana	Central African Rep	Congo
Gabon	Guinea	Mauritius	Niger
Rwanda	Senegal	Somalia	Togo
Upper Volta	Zaire		

This is associated with OCAM.

ORGANIZATION: Arusha Convention
FOUNDED: 1969.07
MEMBERS:

Kenya   Tanzania   Uganda
United Kingdom

This was an abortive grouping that antedated the EAC (which see).

AFRICAN INTERNATIONAL ORGANIZATIONS

ORGANIZATION: Asian-African Legal Consultative Commission
ACRONYM: AALCC   FOUNDED: 1956.11
HEADQUARTERS: New Delhi

The AALCC grew out of the Bandung Conference. With a staff of 25, its work is carried out through an advisory board of legal experts that places matters of legal interest before international bodies.

ORGANIZATION: Associated Overseas Countries of the EEC
ACRONYM: AOC

Currently PAC states (which see).

ORGANIZATION: Associated Overseas Territories
See Lomé and Yaoundé

ORGANIZATION: Associated States of Africa
FOUNDED: 1959.01

This was proposed by Liberia; there is no evidence that it ever existed.

ORGANIZATION: Association Between the EEC and the Partner States of the East African Community
See African-Caribbean-Pacific States
ACRONYM: EAMA
HEADQUARTERS: Defunct
MEMBERS:

Benin	Burundi	Cameroon	Cent Afr Rep
Chad	Congo	Gabon	Ivory Coast
Madagascar	Mali	Mauritania	Niger
Rwanda	Senegal	Somalia	Togo
Upper Volta	Zaire		

ORGANIZATION: Association for the Advancement of Agricultural Science in Africa
ACRONYM: AAASA   FOUNDED: 1968
HEADQUARTERS: Addis Ababa

AAASA promotes agricultural science, especially technical exchange among states.

ORGANIZATION: Association of African Central Banks
ACRONYM: AACB   FOUNDED: 1968.08
HEADQUARTERS: Addis Ababa
MEMBERS:

Algeria	Burundi	Cameroon	Egypt
Ethiopia	Gabon	Gambia	Ghana
Kenya	Libya	Madagascar	Malawi
Mali	Mauritius	Morocco	Nigeria
Rwanda	Sierra Leone	Somalia	Sudan
Tanzania	Tunisia	Uganda	Zaire
Zambia			

Sponsors the African Centre for Monetary Studies.

ORGANIZATION: Association of African Development Finance Institutions
FOUNDED: 1975
HEADQUARTERS: Abidjan, BP 1387 (c/o ADB)
MEMBERS:

Algeria	Benin	Burundi	Cameroon
Chad	Comoros	Congo	Egypt
Ethiopia	Gambia	Ghana	Ivory Coast
Kenya	Lesotho	Liberia	Libya
Madagascar	Mali	Mauritania	Mauritius
Morocco	Niger	Nigeria	Rwanda
Senegal	Sierra Leone	Somalia	Sudan
Swaziland	Tanzania	Togo	Tunisia
Uganda	Upper Volta	Zaire	Zambia

Sponsored and hosted by ADB, it promotes co-operation in development project design and finance. Members are national and regional financial institutions.

ORGANIZATION: Association of African Industrial Technology Organizations
ACRONYM: AAITO
FOUNDED: 1977.05
HEADQUARTERS: Lagos

The association is affiliated with STRC.

ORGANIZATION: Association of African Tax Administrators
FOUNDED: 1980
HEADQUARTERS: Addis Ababa, Box 3001

The association promotes co-operation in tax policy and its administration among its members.

ORGANIZATION: Association of African Trade Promotion Organizations
ACRONYM: AATPO
FOUNDED: 1974.01
HEADQUARTERS: Tangier, BP 23
MEMBERS:

Algeria	Burundi	Cameroon	Cent Afr Rep
Egypt	Ethiopia	Gabon	Ghana
Kenya	Liberia	Libya	Mali
Morocco	Niger	Nigeria	Rwanda
Senegal	Somalia	Sudan	Swaziland
Togo	Tunisia	Uganda	Upper Volta
Zaire	Zambia		

Its primary activity is to maintain a trade promotion center in Tangier.

ORGANIZATION: Association of Market Production, European Community/African-Caribbean-Pacific States
ACRONYM: APROMA
FOUNDED: 1982
HEADQUARTERS: Abidjan, BPV 210
MEMBERS:

Burundi	Cameroon	Ivory Coast	Senegal
Sierra Leone	also European states		

APROMA obtains and distributes information to facilitate harmonization of policies regarding market products, especially coffee, cacao, cotton, and oil seeds.

ORGANIZATION: Association of Regional and Sub-Regional Institutions for Development Financing in West Africa
    FOUNDED: 1977
    HEADQUARTERS: Lomé, c/o BOAD BP 1172
    MEMBERS:

| ADB | ASF | ECOWAS-Fund | EC-Fund |
| FOSLDEC/CEAO | OCAM-Fund | WAD | |

The sole purpose is to minimize competition in the search for development funds.

ORGANIZATION: Association of the EEC and the African and Malagasy States
    See PAC

ORGANIZATION: Bank of Central African States
    ACRONYM: BEAC   FOUNDED: 1955
    HEADQUARTERS: Yaoundé
    MEMBERS:

| Cameroon | Central African Rep | Chad | Congo |
| Gabon | | | |

BEAC collaborates with the Central African Monetary Union. Revised in 1972, it began as the issuing institute of the Equatorial African and Cameroun. Issues currency for member states and implements monetary policy. Paid-up capital: CFA francs 5 billion.

ORGANIZATION: Benin Union
    See Conseil de l'Entente

ORGANIZATION: Benin-Niger Common Organization
    ACRONYM: OCBN   FOUNDED: 1959.07
    HEADQUARTERS: Cotonou
    MEMBERS: Benin   Niger

The purpose of the organization is to manage a joint railway system.

ORGANIZATION: Brazzaville Group
FOUNDED: 1960
HEADQUARTERS: Defunct
MEMBERS:

Algeria	Egypt	Ghana	Guinea
Libya	Mali	Morocco	

ORGANIZATION: British East Africa
ACRONYM: BEA   FOUNDED: 1919
HEADQUARTERS: Defunct
MEMBERS: Kenya   Tanzania   Uganda

This served as an informal co-ordination among governors of British territories: the colonies of Kenya and Uganda; trust territory of Tanzania; Protectorate of Zanzibar. Sometimes governors of Northern and Southern Rhodesia and Nyasaland participated. It succeeded the British East Africa Protectorate, which had been established in 1895.

ORGANIZATION: British West Africa
ACRONYM: BWA   FOUNDED: 1900
HEADQUARTERS: Defunct
MEMBERS:

Gambia	Ghana	Nigeria	Sierra Leone

This was an administrative arrangement for governing British colonies in West Africa. It issued currency and stamps, among other activities. It was disbanded in 1960.

ORGANIZATION: Council on Administration of Information
MEMBERS:

Benin	Cameroon	Central African Rep	Congo
Gabon	Guinea	Mauritius	Niger
Rwanda	Senegal	Somalia	Togo
Upper Volta	Zaire		

This is associated with OCAM.

ORGANIZATION: Casablanca Group
FOUNDED: 1961.01
HEADQUARTERS: Defunct
MEMBERS:

Algeria	Egypt	Ghana	Guinea
Libya	Mali	Morocco	

This group was successor to Brazzaville Group (which see). There was "no trace after 1963." Ethiopia, Nigeria, Somalia, Sudan, Togo, India, and Indonesia refused invitations to participate in the initial meeting. It represented the more radical independent African states, in contrast to the more conservative Monrovia group and opposed foreign military bases while favoring a unified African military staff. Libya failed to participtae because of Western military bases. An African Common Market was proposed in December, 1962.

ORGANIZATION: Cattle and Meat Economic Community of the Council of the Entente States Organization
ACRONYM: CEBV
HEADQUARTERS: Ouagadougou, BP 638
MEMBERS:

Benin	Ivory Coast	Niger	Togo
Upper Volta			

CEBV encourages technical co-operation, development, and disease eradication.

ORGANIZATION: Center for Industrial Studies of the Maghreb
ACRONYM: CEIM   FOUNDED: 1967
HEADQUARTERS: Tangier, BP 235
MEMBERS:

Algeria	Morocco	Mauritania	Tunisia

CEIM provides training and conducts studies.

ORGANIZATION: Central African Bank
See Bank of Central African States

ORGANIZATION: Central African Clearing House
       FOUNDED: 1979
HEADQUARTERS: Yaoundé, BP 1917
       MEMBERS:

Cameroon	Central African Rep	Chad	Congo
Gabon	Zaire		

It operates in conjunction with BEAC (which see) and the Central Bank of Zaire. Its purpose is to encourage monetary co-operation in the region.

ORGANIZATION: Central African Customs and Economic Union
       ACRONYM: UDEAC / CACEU   FOUNDED: 1964
HEADQUARTERS: Bangui, BP 969
       MEMBERS:

Cameroon	Central African Rep	Chad	Congo
Equatorial Guinea	Gabon		

It was created by the Brazzaville Treaty, and its membership has been dynamic: Central African Rep and Chad withdrew April, 1968, and with Zambia formed the UEAC. The CAR rejoined in December, 1986. Equatorial Guinea joined in December, 1983. Its primary aim is to achieve economic integration among its members. Its interests include customs, investment codes, industrial harmonisation and transport policy. In 1968 it decided upon equal distribution of industrial locations among the members. Chad and Central African Republic--landlocked states--have complained about customs complications. Also there are differences between the needs of coastal and desert areas. UDEAC built up a history of co-operation within FEA based on geographical contiguity seeking to allocate industrial locations. "Taxe unique" was collected by exporting states and paid to importing state within the Union on manufactured goods with the intent of equalizing benefits from industrialization. The region's overall poverty prevents much development. The UDEA succeeded the UDE. It reports a permanent staff of 250 with a 1984 budget of CFA francs 250 billion. Its major organs are: Council of Heads of State (meets anually), Council of Minister (Ministers of Finance and Economic Development), and the Secretariat. The Convention on Investments was adopted January, 1966, providing for lower tariffs on food, etc. The BEAC is a subsidiary. Reference: Barbour, K.M. 1972 "Industrialization in West Africa," *Journal of Modern African Studies* 10:3, pp. 363 ff.

ORGANIZATION: Central African Economic Union
ACRONYM: UEAC   FOUNDED: 1968.04
MEMBERS:

Central African Rep   Chad   Congo   Zaire

UEAC was created by President Mobutu of Zaire to replace UDEAC. By December, 1968, the Central African Republic had returned to membership in UDEAC. Its announced purposes were to establish a common market and encourage general regional co-operation.

ORGANIZATION: Central African Federation
FOUNDED: 1953
HEADQUARTERS: Defunct
MEMBERS: Constituents: Northern Rhodesia, Nyasaland, Southern Rhodesia

This was created by the United Kingdom in a search for viable state development. It faltered on different policies put forth by settler groups, such as black political participation. It had been proposed in 1915 and again in 1927 by the Hilton Young Commission. In 1938 the Bledisloe Commission advocated amalgamation. In 1945 the Central African Council was established to coordinate services where possible. It was terminated 29 March 1963 upon self-governance in Southern Rhodesia. Reference: Somerville, 1963, "The Central African Federation" in *International Affairs* 39:3; and Hazlewood, 1967, pp. 185 ff.

ORGANIZATION: Central African Federation for Higher Education
See Higher Education Foundation in Central Africa

ORGANIZATION: Central African Mineral Resource Development Centre
HEADQUARTERS: Addis Ababa, Box 3001

This is a specialized agency of STRC.

AFRICAN INTERNATIONAL ORGANIZATIONS

ORGANIZATION: Central African Monetary Union
FOUNDED: 1972
HEADQUARTERS: Brazzaville
MEMBERS:

Cameroon	Central African Rep	Chad	Congo
Gabon			

The Union is intended to harmonize monetary policies.

ORGANIZATION: Central African Regional Labor Administration

ORGANIZATION: Central African States Development Bank
ACRONYM: CASDB
HEADQUARTERS: Brazzaville
MEMBERS:

Cameroon	Central African Rep	Chad	Congo
Gabon			

CASDB engages in standard development bank activities.

ORGANIZATION: Central Bank of West African States
ACRONYM: BCEAO   FOUNDED: 1955
HEADQUARTERS: Dakar, BP 3108
MEMBERS:

Benin	Ivory Coast	Niger	Senegal
Togo	Upper Volta		

The Bank was founded as l'Institue d'emission de l'AOF et du Togo It was reconstituted in 1962 and became the central bank of UMOA, i.e. the central bank of the member states. It operates in conjunction with WAMU (UMOA).

ORGANIZATION: Central Bank of the States of Equatorial Africa and Cameroun
FOUNDED: 1960
MEMBERS:

Cameroon	Central African Rep	Chad	Congo
Gabon	France		

This is the central bank for UDEAC states. It operates a central financial and economic data management and reporting system for the 5 African members. The currency in the CFA franc; reserves are held in French francs.

ORGANIZATION: Centre for Industrial Studies of the Maghreb
HEADQUARTERS: Tangier

ORGANIZATION: Centre for Linguistic and Historical Studies through Oral Traditions
ACRONYM: CELHTO
HEADQUARTERS: Niamey BP 878
FOUNDED: 1968
MEMBERS:

Benin	Cameroon	Cape Verde	Chad
Gambia	Ghana	Guinea	Guinea-Bissau
Ivory Coast	Mali	Mauritania	Niger
Nigeria	Senegal	Sierra Leone	Togo
Upper Volta			

CELHTO promotes and coordinates research into oral history traditions.

ORGANIZATION: Centre for Training of Cadres
MEMBERS:

Benin	Cameroon	Central African Rep	Congo
Gabon	Guinea	Mauritius	Niger
Rwanda	Senegal	Somalia	Togo
Upper Volta	Zaire		

This is associated with OCAM.

ORGANIZATION: Centre for the Coordination of Social Science Research and Documentation in Africa South of the Sahara
ACRONYM: CERDAS   FOUNDED: 1964.09
HEADQUARTERS: Kinshasa, BP 836

CERDAS promotes co-operation among social science research institutions.

ORGANIZATION: Chad Basin Commission
FOUNDED: 1964.05
HEADQUARTERS: Ndjamena
MEMBERS:

Cameroon	Chad	Niger	Nigeria

Seeks development of the Chad River basin.

ORGANIZATION: Club des Amis du Sahel
FOUNDED: 1975
HEADQUARTERS: Paris, c/o OECD, 2 rue André Pascal
MEMBERS:

Cape Verde	Chad	Gambia	Mali
Mauritania	Niger	Senegal	Upper Volta

Plus donor states

Established by the OECD as means for co-ordinating assistance for drought-induced problems, the Club co-ordinated aid flowing from OECD members that was intended to deal with the effects of drought.

ORGANIZATION: Cocoa Producers Alliance
ACRONYM: COPAL   FOUNDED: 1962.05
HEADQUARTERS: Lagos
MEMBERS:

Cameroon	Gabon	Ghana	Ivory Coast
Nigeria	Sao Tome Principe	Togo	

Plus American producing countries.

Purposes of the Alliance include exchanging information, controling production, and promoting consumption. It represents 80% of world cocoa production.

ORGANIZATION: Commercial and Development Bank for Eastern and Southern Africa
FOUNDED: 1983
HEADQUARTERS: Harare, c/o ESAPTA
MEMBERS:

Burundi	Comoros	Djibouti	Ethiopia
Kenya	Lesotho	Malawi	Mauritius
Rwanda	Somalia	Swaziland	Uganda
Zambia	Zimbabwe		

Created by members of Eastern and Southern Africa Preferential Trade Area, of which it is a subsidiary.

ORGANIZATION: Commission for Controlling the Desert Locust in Northwest Africa
FOUNDED: 1971
HEADQUARTERS: Rome, c/o FAO
MEMBERS:

Algeria	Libya	Morocco	Tunisia

It was created by the FAO.

ORGANIZATION: Commission for Technical Cooperation in Africa South of the Sahara
ACRONYM: CCTA
FOUNDED: 1954.01
HEADQUARTERS: Defunct
MEMBERS:

Benin	Cameroon	Central African Rep	Chad
Congo	Gabon	Guinea	Ivory Coast
Liberia	Madagascar	Mali	Mauritania
Niger	Nigeria	Senegal	Sierra Leone
Somalia	South Africa	Upper Volta	Zaire
Belgium	France	UK	Portugal

Federation of Rhodesia and Nyasaland

This was established by the Convention of London, it merged with the OAU in January, 1965, as STRC. It sponsored meetings dealing with industrial, commercial, and agricultural education issues; hydrobiology; statistics; research on trypanosomiasis; rural welfare;

migrant labor; and basic psychology. Its publications include erosion maps, a soil map, an inventory of economic studies, and bibliographies.

ORGANIZATION: Commission on African Animal Trypanosomiasis
FOUNDED: 1979
HEADQUARTERS: Accra
MEMBERS:

Benin	Botswana	Burundi	Cameroon
Central African Rep	Chad	Congo	Egypt
Ethiopia	Gabon	Ghana	Guinea
Kenya	Liberia	Malawi	Mali
Mozambique	Niger	Rwanda	Senegal
Sierra Leone	Somalia	Sudan	Tanzania
Togo	Upper Volta	Zaire	Zambia

Plus OECD members

It was created by FAO.

ORGANIZATION: Commission on Mediation, Conciliation and Arbitration (of the OAU)
FOUNDED: 1964
HEADQUARTERS: Addis Ababa
MEMBERS: All OAU members.

The Commission consists of 21 members elected by Assembly of Heads of State for 5-year terms; no two are to be from the same state. Its jurisdiction deals with inter-state matters only. Matters may be brought by the aggreived state. Its organs are a Council of Ministers and an Assembly.

ORGANIZATION: Committee of West African Central Banks
HEADQUARTERS: Ouagadougou, c/o ECOWAS BP 643

It supervises community payments and recommends clearing house policy.

ORGANIZATION: Committee on Inland Fisheries in Africa
See Inter-African Committee on Inland Fisheries
HEADQUARTERS: Defunct

This was a subsidiary of the EAC.

ORGANIZATION: Common Dahomey-Niger Organisation des Chemins de Fer et des Transports
See Benin-Niger Common Organization

ORGANIZATION: Common Organisation for Control of Dessert Locust and Bird Pests
ACRONYM: OCLALAV
FOUNDED: 1965.05
HEADQUARTERS: Dakar, BP 1066
MEMBERS:

Benin	Cameroon	Chad	Gambia
Ivory Coast	Mali	Mauritania	Niger
Senegal	Upper Volta		

ORGANIZATION: Common Organization for Economic Cooperation in Central Africa
ACRONYM: OCCEAC
FOUNDED: 1969
MEMBERS: Burundi   Rwanda   Zaire

ORGANIZATION: Commonwealth
FOUNDED: 1947
HEADQUARTERS: London
MEMBERS:

Botswana	Gambia	Ghana	Kenya
Lesotho	Mali	Mauritius	Nigeria
Sierra Leone	Swaziland	Tanzania	Uganda
Zambia	Zimbabwe		

Plus other former British colonies

The Commonwealth sponsors biennial meetings of heads of state, and takes decisions consensus. See also CFTC. Reference: *Europa Yearbook*, vol. 1

AFRICAN INTERNATIONAL ORGANIZATIONS

ORGANIZATION: Commonwealth Regional Health Secretariat for East, Central and Southern Africa
FOUNDED: 1974
HEADQUARTERS: Arusha, Box 1009
MEMBERS:

Botswana	Kenya	Lesotho	Malawi
Mauritius	Seychelles	Swaziland	Tanzania
Uganda	Zambia	Zimbabwe	

Promotes coordination and cooperation in the health field.

ORGANIZATION: Communauté
FOUNDED: 1959
HEADQUARTERS: Paris
MEMBERS:

Algeria	Benin	Cameroon	Cent Afr Rep
Chad	Congo	Gabon	Guinea
Madagascar	Mali	Mauritania	Niger
Senegal	Togo	Upper Volta	France

This was established at the time of independence of French Africa (and the Fifth French Republic) on the model of the British Commonwealth. The French President is the Community President; the Executive Council consists of all Presidents/Heads of State. Matters that were agreed to be considered include foreign policy, defense, justice, higher education, transportation, telecommunications, and a customs union.

ORGANIZATION: Communauté Financiere Africaine
ACRONYM: CFA   FOUNDED: 1976
HEADQUARTERS: Paris
MEMBERS:

Benin	Cameroon	Central African Rep	Congo
Guinea	Ivory Coast	Mali	Mauritania
Niger	Senegal	Togo	Upper Volta

CFA is the French-supported institution that issues and maintains the CFA Franc, the currency of its members. Plans for economic integration have not been implemented; only 10% of trade is within the community.

ORGANIZATION: Community Development Fund
ACRONYM: FCD FOUNDED: 1974
HEADQUARTERS: Ougadougou, c/o CEAO BP 643
MEMBERS:

Ivory Coast	Mali	Mauritania	Niger
Senegal	Upper Volta		

Established by CEAO, it makes payments to compensate for lost revenue under CEAO. Funds are derived from compensatory scheme.

ORGANIZATION: Community of Independent African States
FOUNDED: 1959
HEADQUARTERS: Defunct
MEMBERS: Ghana Guinea Liberia

It resulted from Saniquellie Declaration, 19 July 1959. It proposed unity without the surrender of sovereignty.

ORGANIZATION: Concerted Action for the Development of Africa
ACRONYM: ACDA FOUNDED: 1979
HEADQUARTERS: Paris, c/o Ministre des Affaires Etrangéres
MEMBERS: Non-African members only

Belgium	Canada	Federal Republic of Germany
France	UK	USA

ORGANIZATION: Conference of Administrators of Posts and Telecommunications of West Africa
ACRONYM: CAPTEAO
MEMBERS:

Benin	Ivory Coast	Libya	Mali
Niger	Senegal		

AFRICAN INTERNATIONAL ORGANIZATIONS

ORGANIZATION: Conference of African Ministers of Culture
ACRONYM: CMAC   FOUNDED: 1974
HEADQUARTERS: Dakar, BP 01 c/o ICA
MEMBERS:

Angola	Benin	Central African Rep	Chad
Comoros	Congo	Gabon	Ghana
Guinea-Bissau	Ivory Coast	Mauritania	Mauritius
Niger	Rwanda	Senegal	Seychelles
Sierra Leone	Togo	Upper Volta	Zambia

ORGANIZATION: Conference of African Ministers of Industry
HEADQUARTERS: Addis Ababa, Box 3001

There is no organization, only conferences.

ORGANIZATION: Conference of African Ministers of Trade
HEADQUARTERS: Addis Ababa Box 3001

This is not an organization, but a series of conferences.

ORGANIZATION: Conference of East and Central African States
ACRONYM: CECAS   FOUNDED: 1966
HEADQUARTERS: Defunct
MEMBERS:

Burundi	Central African Rep	Chad	Congo
Equatorial Guinea	Ethiopia	Gabon	Kenya
Malawi	Rwanda	Somalia	Sudan
Tanzania	Uganda	Zaire	Zambia

The Conference operated through meetings of heads of states and commissions. Its purpose was to co-ordinate discussions in areas of industry, energy, trade, tourism, transport, communications, and agriculture. CECAS was terminated in 1974.

ORGANIZATION: Conference of Foreign Ministers of African and Malagasy States

Meetings: 1st Lagos 1962

ORGANIZATION: Conference of Heads of African and Malagache States and Governments
FOUNDED: 1950's

4th: 1961 Tananarive [also Monrovia 1961 ?]
5th: 1962 Lagos

ORGANIZATION: Conference of Heads of State of Equatorial Africa
ACRONYM: CCEAE   FOUNDED: 1959.06
HEADQUARTERS: Bangui
MEMBERS:

| Central African Rep | Chad | Congo | Gabon |

CCEAE was to include a customs union, communications agency, posts and telecommunications, and administrative units. It shares a secretariat with UDEAC.

ORGANIZATION: Conference of Independent African States
FOUNDED: 1958.04
HEADQUARTERS: Defunct
MEMBERS:

Algeria	Cameroon	Egypt	Ethiopia
Ghana	Guinea	Liberia	Libya
Madagascar	Mali	Morocco	Nigeria
Sierra Leone	Somalia	Sudan	Tunisia

This was less an organization, and more a political consciousness-raising gathering. Its 1958 meeting was hosted by President Nkrumah in Accra. At that meeting resolutions covering the following topics were adopted: support for the United Nations; opposition to nuclear weapons; favoringthe co-ordination of economic planning; recognizing the right of the Algerian people to independence; condemning racism; favoring co-operating in resolving regional disputes; and encouraging cultural exchange among member states. At the second meeting in Monrovia the resolutions repeated many of the same themes. The final meeting at Addis Ababa in 1960 foundered on the liberal-conservative split that eventuated in the establishment of the Brazzaville and Casablanca groups (which see).

ORGANIZATION: Conference of Ministers of African Least Developed Countries
FOUNDED: 1981
HEADQUARTERS: Addis Ababa, Box 3001

The Conference coordinates development efforts under a program adopted at the Paris conference on least developed countries.

ORGANIZATION: Conference of Ministers of National Education in French-Speaking African and Malagasy States
FOUNDED: 1970
HEADQUARTERS: Defunct

Apparently only two meetings were held, both in 1970, one in Naouakchott, the other in Paris.

ORGANIZATION: Conference on Statistitians

This is associated with OCAM.

ORGANIZATION: Congress of African Peoples

Meetings: 3rd 1961 Cairo

ORGANIZATION: Conseil de l'Entente (Entente Council)
FOUNDED: 1959.05
HEADQUARTERS: Abidjan, BP 3734
MEMBERS:

Benin	Ivory Coast	Niger	Upper Volta
Togo until 1966			

This includes the Livestock and Meat Economic Community. The Council has been characterized by stustantial French influence and contact. While its primary interest is ecnomic co-ordination, it proposes to "extend its economic and financial cooperation to political matters. One of its tangible outcomes has been the creation of regional trading centers, such as the Fishmen's Trading Center in Abidjan. The Ivory Coast is the primary contributor; she agreed not to seek aid for 5 years. The Regional Commission for

Industrialization of the Entente Countries is a primary functional organ. In 1966 the Council created the Mutual Aid and Loan Guarantee Fund (which see) to support international loans. In 1970 a Road Transport Committee was established. Policy is determined at the annual meeting of the Heads of State.

ORGANIZATION: Constellation of South African States
ACRONYM: CONSAS   FOUNDED: 1979.03
MEMBERS:

| Botswana | Lesotho | South Africa | Swaziland |

Plus "autonomous" South African homelands

Proposed by South Africa, this was to be an economic unit of "inner" members--the homelands--and "outer" members--the three former High Commission Territories. It has not materialized.

ORGANIZATION: Consultative Advisory Committe on Semi-Arid Food Grain Research and Development
ACRONYM: SAFGRAD   FOUNDED:
HEADQUARTERS: Lagos, c/o OAU/STRC PMB 2459
MEMBERS:

This is a constitutent organization of STRC.

ORGANIZATION: Coordinating Committee of the Dakar-Ndjamena Highway
FOUNDED: 1974
MEMBERS:

| Cameroon | Chad | Mali | Niger |
| Nigeria | Senegal | Upper Volta | |

Its purpose is to plan, construct, and maintain a highway between the cities indicated in West Africa. It was created by ECA.

ORGANIZATION: Coordinating Committee of the Lagos-Nouakchott Highway
FOUNDED: 1974.01
HEADQUARTERS: Addis Ababa, Box 3001

Managed by ECA, it proposed to plan, improve, and maintain highway. Its secretariat is provided by TAH.

ORGANIZATION: Coordination Commission for Liberation Movements of Africa
ACRONYM: ALC   FOUNDED: 1963.05
HEADQUARTERS: Dar Es Salaam, Box 1767
MEMBERS:

Algeria	Cameroon	Congo	Egypt
Ethiopia	Ghana	Guinea	Libya
Mauritania	Morocco	Nigeria	Senegal
Somalia	Tanzania	Tunisia	Uganda
Zaire	Zambia		

Established by the OAU to further the liberation process, it instigated African Liberation Day, 25 May. Its focus was on southern Africa, especially Portuguese colonies and South Africa and Rhodesia. It has sought to bar Portugal, South Africa, and then-Rhodesia from participation in UN organs. It location and strong support by Tanzania has resulted in that state's domination. It has been more symbolic than wielding any real power;in 1971-72 it disbursed US$21,000 to liberation movements while during the same period the World Council of Churches gave US$345,000 for the same purpose. Policy is made by the Assembly of Heads of State; action administered by the Liberation Committee. Reference: Aluko.

ORGANIZATION: Council on Administration of Information
MEMBERS:

Benin	Cameroon	Central African Rep	Congo
Gabon	Guinea	Mauritius	Niger
Rwanda	Senegal	Somalia	Togo
Upper Volta	Zaire		

This is associated with OCAM.

ORGANIZATION: Customs and Economic Union of Central Africa
See Central African Customs and Economic Union

ORGANIZATION: Customs Union Agreement
FOUNDED: 1969
HEADQUARTERS: Pretoria, c/o Director-General of Industires
MEMBERS:

| Botswana | Lesotho | South Africa | Swaziland |

This was originally established in 1910 by British for High Commission Territories. It reflects South African domination of economies of these countries. Customs are collected at outside borders and distributed pro rata to its members, formerly Basutoland, Bechuanaland, and Swaziland. See also Southern African Customs Union.

ORGANIZATION: Customs Union of West Africa
See West African Customs Union

ORGANIZATION: Customs Union of West African States
ACRONYM: UDEAO   FOUNDED: 1959
HEADQUARTERS: Abidjan
MEMBERS:

| Benin | Ivory Coast | Mali | Mauritania |
| Niger | Senegal | Upper Volta | |

The UDEAO was originally established in Paris and relocated in Abidjan upon its reorganization in 1966. It has created a common external tariff and preferential trading arrangements among its members. Its primary organs are the Council of Ministers and the Council of Experts. Its primary objective is to eliminate trade barriers among its members; ironically, there is only slight commerce among the members. It led to formation of CEAO.

ORGANIZATION: Dahomey-Niger Common Organization for Railways and Transport
See Benin-Niger Common Organization for Railways

ORGANIZATION: Desert Locust Control Commission
ACRONYM: DLCO

DLCO was created by FAO as a preventive means of increasing food production.

ORGANIZATION: Desert Locust Control Organization for Eastern Africa
ACRONYM: DLCOEA   FOUNDED: 1962.08
HEADQUARTERS: Addis Ababa, Box 4255
MEMBERS:

Djibouti	Ethiopia	Kenya	Somalia
Sudan	Tanzania	Uganda	France

The DLCOEA seeks primarily to control the desert locust, but it also assists with other pests as resources permit (e.g. the army worm and tsetse fly). Its offices are in Asmara and Dire Dawa, Ethiopia; Hargeisa and Mogadiscio, Somalia, Khartoum, Sudan; and Nairobi. In 1974 its assets were Ksh 3 million. DLCOEA maintains a staff of 182 as well as vehicles and equipment, such as planes for aerial spraying. Its work has been primarily along the Red Sea. Its 19th meeting was held in Dar Es Salaam, May, 1974.

ORGANIZATION: Development Bank of the Great Lakes States
ACRONYM: BDEGL   FOUNDED: 1977
HEADQUARTERS: Goma, Zaire BP 3355
MEMBERS: Burundi   Rwanda   Zaire

Promotes economic and social development.

ORGANIZATION: ECOBANK

ECOBANK is the development bank of the ECOWAS states.

ORGANIZATION: ECOWAS Fund
FOUNDED: 1976.11
HEADQUARTERS: Lagos, 6 King George V Road
MEMBERS:

Benin	Cape Verde	Gambia	Ghana
Guinea	Guinea-Bissau	Ivory Coast	Liberia

Mali	Mauritania	Niger	Nigeria
Senegal	Sierra Leone	Togo	Upper Volta

The Fund "Promotes cooperation and development in economic activity," especially in infrastructure-related fields. Paid-up capital: US$44 million.

ORGANIZATION: East African Agriculture and Forestry Research Organization
ACRONYM: EAAFRO
HEADQUARTERS: Nairobi
MEMBERS: Kenya   Tanzania   Uganda

The EAAFRO antedated independence.

ORGANIZATION: East African Air Force
HEADQUARTERS: Defunct

This was a World War II British military unit.

ORGANIZATION: East Africa Airways
ACRONYM: EAA
HEADQUARTERS: Defunct
MEMBERS: Kenya   Tanzania   Uganda

As a component of the EAC, this was terminated with its collapse in 1979. At that time there were six planes in its fleet; two were consigned to each of the member states. A persistent problem which had faced the airline was differences of views on the role it should fulfill: Kenya saw it as a funnel for European (and American) tourists from London to Nairobi; Tanzania, on the other hand, viewed it as a commuter line for its vast territory and dispersed population; at its height it served one airport in Uganda, three or four in Kenya, but between fifteen and twenty in Tanzania.

ORGANIZATION: East African Common Market
FOUNDED: 1967.12
MEMBERS: Kenya   Tanzania   Uganda

This was the precursor to the EAC; it lasted only a few months.

ORGANIZATION: East African Common Services Organization
ACRONYM: EACSO   FOUNDED: 1961.06
HEADQUARTERS: Defunct
MEMBERS: Kenya   Tanzania   Uganda
(Tanganyika as British Trust Territory)

This replaced the EAHC preparatory to Tanganyikan independence. It was superceded by the EAC in 1967.

ORGANIZATION: East African Community
ACRONYM: EAC   FOUNDED: 1967
HEADQUARTERS: Defunct
MEMBERS: Kenya   Tanzania   Uganda

The EAC was a successor to the EACSO. Substantial steps toward a common market were taken. Numerous collaborative activities were developed--see other East African listings. Ugandan anarchy and ideological differences led to its collapse in 1979. The policy direction was provided by the Authority which consisted of the three presidents. The East African Legislative Assembly was directly elected. Its secretariat was housed at Arusha. See "Main Organizations" for a more complete description. Reference: Potholm and Fredland.

ORGANIZATION: East African Court of Appeal
FOUNDED: 1951
HEADQUARTERS: Defunct
MEMBERS: Kenya   Tanzania   Uganda

As a component of the EAC, this was no longer needed with its demise. Its role was to resolve administrative problems in the operation of the Community. It had no jurisdiction beyond Community policies. It origniated in pre-independence East Africa.

ORGANIZATION: East African Customs Union
FOUNDED: 1917
HEADQUARTERS: Defunct
MEMBERS: Kenya   Uganda
Tanzania incorporated in 1949

This was a British creation and was a precedessor to the EACSO and EAC.

ORGANIZATION: East African Development Bank
ACRONYM: EADB   FOUNDED: 1967
HEADQUARTERS: Kampala
MEMBERS: Kenya   Tanzania   Uganda

This was created by the EAC and has continued despite the latter's discontinuation. Its lending was in relation to greatest need among the three members in the following order: Tanzania, Uganda, Kenya.

ORGANIZATION: East African Examinations Council
ACRONYM: EAEC
HEADQUARTERS: Kampala
MEMBERS: Kenya   Tanzania   Uganda

The EAEC prepared and administered secondary, university, and professional examinations based upon the British system.

ORGANIZATION: East African External Telecommunications Company
HEADQUARTERS: Defunct
MEMBERS: Kenya   Tanzania   Uganda

ORGANIZATION: East African Federation
FOUNDED: 1963
HEADQUARTERS: Defunct
MEMBERS: Kenya   Tanzania   Uganda
         Plus then-independent Zanzibar

This was a bold concept which was attempted, but never achieved. It would have been, in effect, a unified polity. It was to have been built upon the East African Commission and paralleled the Central African Federation.

ORGANIZATION: East African Freshwater Fisheries Research Organization
ACRONYM: EAFFRO
HEADQUARTERS: Defunct
MEMBERS: Kenya   Tanzania   Uganda

As a component of the EAC, this is no longer operating. Its objective was to encourage fishing, primarily on Lake Victoria.

AFRICAN INTERNATIONAL ORGANIZATIONS

ORGANIZATION: East African Harbours Corporation
ACRONYM: EAHC   FOUNDED: 1963
HEADQUARTERS: Defunct
MEMBERS: Kenya   Tanzania   Uganda

This was a component of the EAC.

ORGANIZATION: East African High Commission
FOUNDED: 1948.01
HEADQUARTERS: Defunct
MEMBERS: Kenya   Tanzania   Uganda

Created by Order in Council, London, it was the administering authority for the three East African domains, the colony of Kenya, the Protectorate of Uganda, and the Trust Territory of Tanganyika, under the British Colonial Office. It was terminated in 1961.

ORGANIZATION: East African Industrial Licensing Council
MEMBERS: Kenya   Tanzania   Uganda

This was a component of the EAC.

ORGANIZATION: East African Industrial Research Organization
ACRONYM: EAIRO
HEADQUARTERS: Defunct
MEMBERS: Kenya   Tanzania   Uganda

This was a component of the EAC.

ORGANIZATION: East African Institute for Medical Research
ACRONYM: IMR   FOUNDED: 1952
HEADQUARTERS: Mwanza
MEMBERS: Kenya   Tanzania   Uganda

Formed by the merger of the East African Medical Society and the Fliarisis Research Unit, it was a component of the EAC.

A GUIDE TO AFRICAN INTERNATIONAL ORGANIZATIONS

ORGANIZATION: East African Institute of Malaria and Vector-Borne Diseases
ACRONYM: IMVBD
HEADQUARTERS: Amani, TNZ
MEMBERS: Kenya   Tanzania   Uganda

This was a component of the EAC.

ORGANIZATION: East African Marine Fisheries Research Organization
ACRONYM: MFRO
HEADQUARTERS: Zanzibar
MEMBERS: Kenya   Tanzania   Uganda

This was a component of the EAC.

ORGANIZATION: East African Medical Research Council

ORGANIZATION: East African Post and Telecommunications Corporation
ACRONYM: EAPT   FOUNDED: 1963
HEADQUARTERS: Kampala
MEMBERS: Kenya   Tanzania   Uganda

This was a component of the EAC.

ORGANIZATION: East African Railways Corporation
ACRONYM: EAR   FOUNDED: 1963
HEADQUARTERS: Defunct
MEMBERS: Kenya   Tanzania   Uganda

The primary rail line was from Kampala to Mombasa, providing the major route for Ugandan trade. Substantial problems resulted from the anarchy prevalent in Uganda in the 1970's.

ORGANIZATION: East African Railways and Harbours Administration
ACRONYM: EAR & H　　　　FOUNDED: 1967
HEADQUARTERS: Defunct
MEMBERS: Kenya　　　　Tanzania　　　　Uganda

This was a component of the EAC.

ORGANIZATION: East Africa Remote Sensing
HEADQUARTERS: Nairobi, Box 18332

ORGANIZATION: East African Tourist Travel Association
FOUNDED: 1957
MEMBERS: Kenya　　　　Tanzania　　　　Uganda

ORGANIZATION: East African Trypanosomiasis Research Organization
ACRONYM: EATRO
HEADQUARTERS: Defunct
MEMBERS: Kenya　　　　Tanzania　　　　Uganda

This was a component of the EAC.

ORGANIZATION: East African Veterinary Research Organization
ACRONYM: EAVRO
HEADQUARTERS: Defunct
MEMBERS: Kenya　　　　Tanzania　　　　Uganda

This was a component of the EAC.

ORGANIZATION: East and Central African States

It held a 5th summit April, 1969.

ORGANIZATION: Eastern African Centre for Research on Oral Traditions and African National Languages
ACRONYM: EACROTANAL   FOUNDED: 1979
HEADQUARTERS: Zanzibar, Box 600
MEMBERS:

| Burundi | Ethiopia | Madagascar | Somalia |
| Sudan | Tanzania | | |

The Centre encourages research, collection and analysis of oral traditions.

ORGANIZATION: Eastern and Southern African Compensation Office
FOUNDED: 1983

This organization was designed to mitigate the effects of trade imbalances.

ORGANIZATION: Eastern and Southern African Mineral Resources Development Centre
ACRONYM: ESAMRDC   FOUNDED: 1975
HEADQUARTERS: Dodoma, Box 1250
MEMBERS:

Botswana	Djibouti	Kenya	Lesotho
Madagascar	Malawi	Mauritius	Seychelles
Somalia	Swaziland	Zambia	Zimbabwe

This provides information on resources development and offers practical courses in geology and laboratory services.

ORGANIZATION: Eastern and Southern African Preferential Trade Area
ACRONYM: ESAPTA

ESAPTA created the Commercial and Development Bank for Eastern and Southern Africa.

ORGANIZATION: Eastern and Southern African Trade and Development Bank
FOUNDED: 1981.12
HEADQUARTERS: Lusaka
MEMBERS:

Comoros	Djibouti	Ethiopia	Kenya
Malawi	Mauritius	Somalia	Uganda
Zambia			

An organ of the Economic Community of Eastern and Southern African States, it lends only to its members.

ORGANIZATION: Economic and Customs Union of Central Africa
See Customs and Economic Union of Central Africa

ORGANIZATION: Economic Commission for Africa - UN
ACRONYM: ECA   FOUNDED: 1958.04
HEADQUARTERS: Addis Ababa, Box 3001
MEMBERS: All African states except South Africa and Namibia

The ECA serves as the co-ordinating office for all UN activities in Africa. It operates regional offices in Niamey, Tangier, and Luanda. Many non-political collaborative activities were initiated by ECA. The divisions of the ECA are Socio-Economic Research and Planning, Statistics, Population, Transportation and Communication, Social Development, Environment and Human Settlements, Agriculture, Industry, Science and Technology, Natural Resources, Energy, International Trade and Finance, Public Administration, Management and Manpower. 1986-87 budget: US$46.1 million. Reference: *Europa Yearbook*, vol. 1, annual.

ORGANIZATION: Economic Community of Central African States
ACRONYM: CEEAC   FOUNDED: 1981.10
HEADQUARTERS: Libreville, BP 546
MEMBERS:

Angola	Burundi	Cameroon	Cent Afr Rep
Chad	Congo	Equatorial Guinea	Rwanda
Sao Tome Principe	Zaire		

This resulted from the Lagos Plan of Action of 1980.

ORGANIZATION: Economic Community of Eastern Africa
ACRONYM: ECEA			FOUNDED: 1967

This was proposed by the ECA in 1967 and again in 1979, following the demise of the EAC. It is not yet in being.

ORGANIZATION: Economic Community of the Great Lakes Countries
ACRONYM: CEPGL			FOUNDED: 1976.09
HEADQUARTERS: Gisenyi, BP 58
MEMBERS: Burundi		Rwanda			Zaire

The announced purpose was to plan for a regional common market. Its second announced aim was to ensure security for its members. CEPGL cooperates with UN and regional agencies. CEPGL publishes a biennial journal.

ORGANIZATION: Economic Community of West African States
ACRONYM: ECOWAS			FOUNDED: 1975.05
HEADQUARTERS: Lagos, PM 12745
MEMBERS:

Benin	Cape Verde	Gambia	Ghana
Guinea	Guinea-Bissau	Ivory Coast	Liberia
Mali	Mauritania	Niger	Nigeria
Senegal	Sierra Leone	Togo	Upper Volta

This was a successor to the West African Economic Community (1967) and the West African Regional Group (1968). Its purpose is to "..promote co-operation and development in all fields of economic activity." A customs union is underway. CEDEAO established the Fund for Co-operation, Compensation, and Development with paid-up capital of US$38 million. Its work is accomplished primarily through its commissions: (1) Trade, Customs, Immigration, Monetary and Payments; (2) Industry, Agriculture, and Natural Resources; (3) Transport, Telecommunications, and Energy; (4) Social and Cultural Affairs. Its announced goals are to: eliminate duties, create a free trade zone, establish a common external tariff, permit the free movement of people, create a common agricultural policy, establish a joint transportation and communication infrastructure, harmonize economic policies, and create a common development fund. Only 2 percent of its international trade is internal.

ORGANIZATION: Energy Organization of the Great Lakes Countries
ACRONYM: OEPGL FOUNDED: 1974.08
HEADQUARTERS: Gisenyi, BP 58
MEMBERS: Burundi   Rwanda   Zaire

The OEPGL was integrated into the CEPGL. Its Purpose is construct a dam on the Ruzizi River, exploit methane gas of Lake Kivu, and extract peat.

ORGANIZATION: Entente Council
See Council of the Entente

ORGANIZATION: Equatorial Africa Defense Council

ORGANIZATION: Equatorial Conference of Heads of State
FOUNDED: >1970
HEADQUARTERS: Defunct
MEMBERS:

Central African Rep   Chad   Congo   Gabon

ORGANIZATION: Equatorial Customs Union
ACRONYM: UDE FOUNDED: 1959.06
HEADQUARTERS: Brazzaville
MEMBERS:

Cameroon   Central African Rep   Chad   Congo
Gabon

UDE was a subsidiary of the Conference of Heads of State of Equatorial Africa. It succeeded AEF and was succeeded by UDEAC (which see).

ORGANIZATION: Equatorial Monetary Union
ACRONYM: UME
HEADQUARTERS: Bangui
MEMBERS: Cameroon   Congo   Gabon

The UME operates as a second arm of the UMOA, the other union of central banks in central Africa. France has been an integral part of the organization.

ORGANIZATION: Equatorial Office of Posts and Telecommunications
ACRONYM: OEPT
HEADQUARTERS: Brazzaville

Subsidiary to Conference of Heads of States of Equatorial Africa.

ORGANIZATION: FAO Committee for Controlling the Desert Locust in Northwest Africa
FOUNDED: 1971.08
HEADQUARTERS: Rome, c/o FAO
MEMBERS:

Algeria   Libya   Morocco   Tunisia

The Committee seeks to control locust activity through research, active measures.

ORGANIZATION: FAO Regional Office for Africa
HEADQUARTERS: Accra

The Office operates in conjunction with ECA.

ORGANIZATION: Federation of Arab Republics
FOUNDED: 1971
HEADQUARTERS: Defunct
MEMBERS: Egypt   Libya   Syria

The proposed joint development plans were associated with the United Arab Republic.

ORGANIZATION: Federation of East African States
FOUNDED: 1960

Advocated by President Nyerere, the concept gave rise to the EAC.

ORGANIZATION: Federation of Rhodesia and Nyasaland
FOUNDED: 1953
HEADQUARTERS: Defunct
MEMBERS: Malawi   Zambia   Zimbabwe
(as colonies)

Established by the UK as an alternative to independence, the very uneven levels of development and white opposition doomed it to failure. Its Prime Minister participated in Commonwealth meetings 1938-56. Self-government for Southern Rhodesia in 1963 led the components in separate directions. Reference: Hazlewood, 1967, pp. 185ff.

ORGANIZATION: Foundation for Mutual Assistance in Africa South of the Sahara
FOUNDED: 1958

ORGANIZATION: Franc Zone
FOUNDED: 1948
HEADQUARTERS: Paris, c/o Banque de France
MEMBERS:

Benin	Cameroon	Central African Rep	Chad
Comoros	Congo	Equatorial Guinea	Gabon
Ivory Coast	Mali	Niger	Senegal
Togo	Upper Volta	France	

Former French colonies that have withdrawn include Guinea, Madagascar, Mauritania, Morocco, Tunisia. Mali was out from 1962-84. Currencies of the members are linked to the French franc and their reserves are held in that currency. Monetary policies are determined in conjunction with the French central bank. There is a guaranteed exchange of 1 French franc to 50 CFA. Regional financial organizations within the Zone: UMOA, BCEAO, BOAD, UDEAG. Reference: *Europa Yearbook*, vol. 1.

ORGANIZATION: Free Trade Area
FOUNDED: 1964
HEADQUARTERS: Defunct
MEMBERS:

Guinea   Ivory Coast   Libya   Sierra Leone

This dealt with currency problems among the member states.

ORGANIZATION: French Community
See Communauté

ORGANIZATION: French Equatorial Africa
ACRONYM: AEF   FOUNDED: 1910
HEADQUARTERS: Defunct
MEMBERS: (as French colonies)

Congo   Gabon   Central African Rep   Chad

France integrated the infrasrtucture of its African colonies (Moyen Congo, now Congo, Gabon, Oubangi-Cheri, now Central African Republic, and Chad) for administrative purposes. It established a franc zone and a common central bank. Under the Fourth Republic the area was administered by a Grand Council with elected representatives. The Loi Cadre of June, 1956, provided for universal sufferage and direct African representation in the French National Assembly. The Rassembleament Democratique Africaine, an independence-seeking party, was active throughout AEF as well as AOF. AEF was dissolved in 1958; independence came in 1960 for its constituents. Reference: Julienne in Hazelwood, 1967.

ORGANIZATION: French West Africa
ACRONYM: AOF   FOUNDED: 1895
MEMBERS: (as colonies)

| Benin | Mali | Mauritania | Guinea |
| Ivory Coast | Senegal | Upper Volta | Niger |

The executive authority lay with the French Governor-General. There was a Territorial Assembly as well as elected delegates to the French National Assembly in later years. The Loi Cadre of June, 1956, provided for increased autonomy including universal sufferage and rural agricultural collectives. A wealth redistribution scheme was included. Upon the creation of the French Community in 1960, French West Africa was dissolved. There was an autonomous railway board. Reference: Thompson and Adloff.

ORGANIZATION: Freshwater Fisheries Research Organization
See East African Freshwater Fisheries

ORGANIZATION: Front Line African States
FOUNDED: 1970's
HEADQUARTERS: Dar Es Salaam, Office of President
MEMBERS:

Angola	Botswana	Mozambique	Tanzania
Zambia	Zimbabwe		

Established to articulate the "African" position on issues relating to Southern Africa, such as Namibia and South Africa. Its members form the core of SADCC.

ORGANIZATION: Fund for Solidarity and Economic Development of the West African Community
ACRONYM: FOSIDEC   FOUNDED: 1977

ORGANIZATION: Gambia River Development Organization
ACRONYM: GRDO/OMVG   FOUNDED: 1973
HEADQUARTERS: Dakar, BP 2353
MEMBERS:

Gambia	Guinea	Guinea-Bissau	Senegal

GRDO proposed a dam on the Gambia River for hydroelectric power and irrigation. A feasibility study has been completed.

ORGANIZATION: Gambia-Senegal Confederation
See Senegambia

ORGANIZATION: Ghana-Guinea Union
FOUNDED: 1958
HEADQUARTERS: Defunct
MEMBERS: Ghana   Guinea

This was created out of an agreement between the presidents of the two countries with the intention of "...build[ing] up a free and prosperous African community in the interest of its people and world peace." It was terminated with the overthrow of President Nkrumah who, in exile, became Vice-President of Guinea. The Union was intended as a support for Guinea after it had been cast out of French Community. It was ended in 1966. See also Union of African States.

ORGANIZATION: Ghana-Guinea-Mali Union
FOUNDED: 1960.12
HEADQUARTERS: Defunct
MEMBERS: Ghana   Guinea   Mali

This was an expansion of the Ghana-Guinea Union (which see).

ORGANIZATION: Ghana-Upper Volta Customs Union
FOUNDED: 1961
HEADQUARTERS: Defunct
MEMBERS: Ghana   Upper Volta

ORGANIZATION: Government Experts of OCAM on the Problems of Film Production

This is associated with OCAM.

ORGANIZATION: Great Somalia Plan
HEADQUARTERS: Defunct

A Somalian proposal to reunite all Somali peoples presently resident in Djibouti, Ethiopia, Kenya, and Somalia, it has been strongly opposed by the surrounding states, especially Kenya and Ethiopia.

ORGANIZATION: High Commission Territories
ACRONYM: BLS
MEMBERS: Botswana   Lesotho   Swaziland

British territories administered separately from South Africa and severed into independence at different times. There is no formal organization encompassing them as such.

ORGANIZATION: Higher Education Foundation in Central Africa
ACRONYM: FESAC   FOUNDED: 1961.12
HEADQUARTERS: Brazzaville
MEMBERS:

Central African Rep   Chad   Congo   Gabon

A subsidiary of the Conference of Heads of State of Equatorial Africa, its aim is to co-ordinate higher education policies among its members. FESAC acknowledges French as the language and character of higher education in the member states. A Centre for Higher Education was established in Brazzaville, which continued an institution founded in 1958. Direction is provided by the Secretary-General of the Conference of Heads of State of Equatorial Africa. France is a member of the governing council.

ORGANIZATION: Independent African States
FOUNDED: 1958
MEMBERS:

Cameroon	Egypt	Ethiopia	Ghana
Guinea	Liberia	Libya	Morocco
Nigeria	Sudan	Tunisia	

Not a formal organization, but a series of conferences, with the first held in 1958, the second was held in 1960.

ORGANIZATION: Indian Ocean Commission
ACRONYM: IOC   FOUNDED: 1982.12
HEADQUARTERS: Port Louis
MEMBERS: Madagascar   Mauritius   Seychelles

It promotes regional co-operation among its island members.

ORGANIZATION: Industrial Property Organization for English-Speaking Africa
ACRONYM: ESARIPO   FOUNDED: 1976.12
HEADQUARTERS: Addis Ababa, Box 3001
MEMBERS:

Gambia	Ghana	Kenya	Malawi
Sierra Leone	Somalia	Sudan	Tanzania
Uganda	Zambia	Zimbabwe	

ESARIPO promotes co-operative policies regarding industrial property. It is sponsored by ECA and WIPO.

ORGANIZATION: Institute for Economic Development and Planning
HEADQUARTERS: Dakar

ORGANIZATION: Institute for Training and Demographic Research
ACRONYM: IFORD   FOUNDED: 1971
HEADQUARTERS: Yaoundé, BP 1556
MEMBERS:

Algeria	Benin	Burundi	Cameroon
Central African Rep	Chad	Comoros	Congo
Djibouti	Gabon	Guinea	Ivory Coast
Madagascar	Mali	Mauritania	Mauritius
Morocco	Niger	Rwanda	Senegal
Seychelles	Togo	Tunisia	Upper Volta
Zaire			

A meeting was held in Lomé in March, 1979. IFORD trains demographers and publishes findings.

ORGANIZATION: Institute of Sciences and Veterinary Medicine
ACRONYM: EISMV   FOUNDED: 1968.01
HEADQUARTERS: Dakar BP 5077
MEMBERS:

Benin	Cameroon	Central African Rep	Chad
Congo	Gabon	Guinea	Ivory Coast
Mauritius	Niger	Rwanda	Senegal
Somalia	Togo	Upper Volta	Zaire

This is associated with OCAM and provides training for physicians and veterinarians.

ORGANIZATION: Integrated Development Authority of the Liptako-Gourma Region
See Liptako-Gourma Integrated Development Authority

ORGANIZATION: Inter-African and Malagasy States Organization
ACRONYM: IAMO FOUNDED: 1962.12
HEADQUARTERS: Defunct

The IAMO resulted from a meeting of independent states, without the Brazzaville Group, because the Algerian Provisional Government had not been invited to participate in that group. It was subsumed by the Monrovia Group (which see).

ORGANIZATION: Inter-African Bureau for Animal Resources
FOUNDED: 1953
HEADQUARTERS: Nairobi
MEMBERS: All OAU members

The organization collects and disseminates information regarding veterinary matters and livestock health and production.

ORGANIZATION: Inter-African Bureau for Soils
FOUNDED: 1948

This was created by STRC.

ORGANIZATION: Inter-African Bureau of Animal Health
ACRONYM: IABAH

ORGANIZATION: Inter-African Bureau on Epizootic Diseases
ACRONYM: IBED

ORGANIZATION: Inter-African Coffee Organization
ACRONYM: IACO   FOUNDED: 1960.12
HEADQUARTERS: Abidjan, BPV 210
MEMBERS:

Angola	Benin	Burundi	Cameroon
Central African Rep	Congo	Equatorial Guinea	Ethiopia
Gabon	Ghana	Guinea	Ivory Coast
Kenya	Liberia	Madagascar	Malawi
Nigeria	Rwanda	Sierra Leone	Tanzania
Togo	Uganda	Zaire	Zimbabwe

The IACO seeks to ensure optimal prices for coffee exports from African producers.

ORGANIZATION: Inter-African Commission on Biological Science
HEADQUARTERS: Lagos

This was created by STRC.

ORGANIZATION: Inter-African Commission on Solar Energy

This was created by STRC.

ORGANIZATION: Inter-African Committee on African Medicinal Plants
HEADQUARTERS: Lagos

This was created by STRC.

ORGANIZATION: Inter-African Committee on Agriculture and the Mechanization of Agriculture

This was created by STRC.

ORGANIZATION: Inter-African Committee on Building Materials and Housing
HEADQUARTERS: Lagos

This was created by STRC.

ORGANIZATION: Inter-African Committee on Computer Sciences and Informatic Education
HEADQUARTERS: Lagos

This was created by STRC.

ORGANIZATION: Inter-African Committee on Earth Sciences, Geodesy
HEADQUARTERS: Lagos

This was created by STRC.

ORGANIZATION: Inter-African Committee on Fertilizers
HEADQUARTERS: Lagos

This was created by STRC.

ORGANIZATION: Inter-African Committee on Food Science and Food Technology
HEADQUARTERS: Lagos

This was created by STRC.

ORGANIZATION: Inter-African Committee on Forestry Resources
HEADQUARTERS: Lagos

This was created by STRC.

ORGANIZATION: Inter-African Committee on Geology and Mineralogy
HEADQUARTERS: Lagos

This was created by STRC.

ORGANIZATION: Inter-African Committee on Hydraulic Studies
ACRONYM: CIEH   FOUNDED: 1960
HEADQUARTERS: Ouagadougou
MEMBERS:

Benin	Cameroon	Chad	Congo
Gabon	Ivory Coast	Mali	Mauritania
Niger	Senegal	Togo	Upper Volta

CIEH fosters liaisons regarding studies of water resources and provides techinal assistance. CIEH has published a bulletin four times per year since about 1979.

ORGANIZATION: Inter-African Committee on Iron and Steel Developments
HEADQUARTERS: Lagos

This was created by STRC.

ORGANIZATION: Inter-African Committee on Natural Resources
HEADQUARTERS: Lagos

This was created by STRC.

ORGANIZATION: Inter-African Committee on Oceanography, Inland and Sea Fisheries
HEADQUARTERS: Lagos

This was created by STRC.

ORGANIZATION: Inter-African Film Production Centre
ACRONYM: CIPROFILM   FOUNDED: 1974

ORGANIZATION: Inter-African Pedological Service
HEADQUARTERS: Defunct

ORGANIZATION: Inter-African Phyto-Sanitary Council
ACRONYM: IAPSC   FOUNDED: 1954

ORGANIZATION: Inter-African Research Fund

ORGANIZATION: Inter-African Rural Economy and Soils Bureau
FOUNDED: 1950
HEADQUARTERS: Paris

ORGANIZATION: Inter-African Travel Company
ACRONYM: CIV   FOUNDED: 1963.11
HEADQUARTERS: Paris
MEMBERS:

Benin	Cameroon	Central African Rep	Chad
Congo	Gabon	Ivory Coast	Mali
Mauritania	Niger	Rwanda	Senegal
Togo	Upper Volta	Zaire	

Its one objective is to organize tours to Africa as an economic activity.

ORGANIZATION: Inter-Governmental Authority on Development and Desertification
MEMBERS:

Djibouti	Ethiopia	Kenya	Somalia
Sudan	Tanzania	Uganda	

(This appears to be the same as the next organization.)

ORGANIZATION: Inter-Governmental Authority on Drought and Development
ACRONYM: IGADO   FOUNDED: 1986
HEADQUARTERS: Djibouti, BP 26543
MEMBERS:

Djibouti	Ethiopia	Kenya	Somalia
Sudan	Uganda		

Its purpose was to formulate responses to the Sahelian drought.

ORGANIZATION: International African Migratory Locust Organization
ACRONYM: OICMA   FOUNDED: 1955.07
HEADQUARTERS: Bamako, BP 136
MEMBERS:

Cameroon	Central African Rep	Chad	Congo
Gambia	Ghana	Ivory Coast	Mali
Mauritania	Niger	Nigeria	Senegal
Sierra Leone	Togo	Uganda	Upper Volta
Zaire			

Research and action against the locust.

ORGANIZATION: International Conference of Africa on Insurance Supervision
ACRONYM: CICA   FOUNDED: 1962

ORGANIZATION: International Livestock Centre for Africa
ACRONYM: ILCA   FOUNDED: 1974
HEADQUARTERS: Addis Ababa Box 5689

The ILCA was established in conjunction with UN agencies and is supported by the OECD as well as private foundations. Its 1985 budget was US$16 million, over half of which was spent on research, and 14% on training and information. Its primary donors that year were IBRD and USAID (about half the budget). Its sole purpose is to improve and increase livestock production in Africa. Toward that end ILCA has programs in four ecological regions: the Highlands Program at its headquarters; the Humid Zone Program at Ibadan, Nigeria; the Subhumid Zone Program at Kaduna, Sudan; and the Arid and Semiarid Zone Program at Bamako, Mali. In 1985 it established the Pasture Network for Eastern and Southern Africa which incorporates 19 countries in a program to improve forage legume technology. The ILCA publishes extensively. It is supported by the Consultative Group on International Agricultureal Research.

ORGANIZATION: International Red Locust Control Organization for Central and Southern Africa
ACRONYM: IRLCO-CSA   FOUNDED: 1971
HEADQUARTERS: Ndola, Zambia, BP 240252

ORGANIZATION: Joint African and Malagasy Organization
See OCAM

ORGANIZATION: Inter-State Body for Lakes Tanganyika/Kivu Basin
FOUNDED: 1975
MEMBERS:

Burundi	Rwanda	Tanzania	Zaire
Zambia			

This organization was created by ECA to plan for co-ordinated development of the basin of the two lakes.

ORGANIZATION: Inter-State Committee for the Senegal River Basin
FOUNDED: 1963
HEADQUARTERS: Defunct

It was transformed into OERS. Reference: Gautron, J.C. 1967. *Annuaire francais du droit internationale*, pp. 690 ff.

ORGANIZATION: Inter-State Commission for the Improvement of the Senegal River Basin

---

ORGANIZATION: Inter-State Office on African Tourism
ACRONYM: OIETA   FOUNDED: 1961

This was succeeded by ODTA in 1967. OIETA was founded among individuals rather than states, and the transformation, in effect, made it an international organization.

ORGANIZATION: Inter-State School for Veterinary Science and Medicine
See Institute of Sciences and Veterinary Medicine

ORGANIZATION: Inter-State School of Rural Equipment Engineers
ACRONYM: EIER FOUNDED: 1969.01
HEADQUARTERS: Ouagadougou, Box 7023
MEMBERS:

Benin	Cameroon	Central African Rep	Chad
Congo	Gabon	Ivory Coast	Mali
Mauritania	Niger	Senegal	Togo
Upper Volta			

Subsidiary of OCAM.

ORGANIZATION: Inter-Territorial Consultative Committee on the Foot-and-Mouth Disease

---

ORGANIZATION: Inter-University Committee for East Africa
HEADQUARTERS: Defunct.
MEMBERS: Kenya Tanzania Uganda

ORGANIZATION: Joint Anti-Locust and Anti-Aviarian Organization
See Common Organization for Control of Desert Locust and Bird Pests

---

ORGANIZATION: Joint FAO/WHO/OAU Regional Food and Nutrition Commission for Africa
FOUNDED: 1963
HEADQUARTERS: Accra, Box 1628
MEMBERS:

Algeria	Angola	Benin	Botswana
Burundi	Cameroon	Cape Verde	Cent Afr Rep
Comoros	Congo	Djibouti	Egypt

Equatorial Guinea	Ethiopia	Gambia	Ghana
Guinea	Guinea-Bissau	Kenya	Lesotho
Liberia	Madagascar	Malawi	Mali
Mauritius	Morocco	Mozambique	Niger
Nigeria	Rwanda	Sao Tome Principe	Senegal
Sierra Leone	Somalia	Sudan	Swaziland
Tanzania	Tunisia	Uganda	Upper Volta
Zaire	Zambia	Zimbabwe	

ORGANIZATION: Jurist Experts

This is associated with OCAM.

ORGANIZATION: Kagera River Basin Organization
See Organization for the Management and Development of the Kagera River Basin

ORGANIZATION: Lake Chad Basin Commission
ACRONYM: CBLT   FOUNDED: 1964.05
HEADQUARTERS: Ft. Lamy
MEMBERS:

Cameroon	Chad	Niger	Nigeria

This organization was initiated by STRC. Its jurisdiction includes navigation, resource exploitation, and planning. There is an executive secretary. In 1969 its budget was CFA francs 42 million.

ORGANIZATION: Lake Victoria Fisheries Commission
FOUNDED: 1967
MEMBERS: Kenya   Tanzania   Uganda

It protects and safeguards the lake's fish resources. Incorporated into EAC; dissolved when the EAC dissolved; reestablished in 1981.

ORGANIZATION: Lakes Tanganyika and Kivu Basin Commission
FOUNDED: 1975.05
HEADQUARTERS: Addis Ababa, Box 3001
MEMBERS:

| Burundi | Rwanda | Tanzania | Zaire |

Zambia

Supported by ECA.

ORGANIZATION: Liberation Committee of OAU
See Coordination Commission for Liberation Movements

ORGANIZATION: Libyan-Moroccan Uniopn
FOUNDED: 1984.09
MEMBERS: Libya   Morocco

This effort was announced in August, 1984, and subsequently ratified by both parliaments.

ORGANIZATION: Liptako-Gourma Integrated Development Authority
ACRONYM: LGA   FOUNDED: 1970.12
HEADQUARTERS: Ouagadougou, BP 619
MEMBERS: Mali   Niger   Upper Volta

Proposed by UNDP, the LGA is intended to facilitate integrated development of the region. Its 1975 budget was CFA francs 47 million. In 1984 its budget was US$185,000. It has concentrated on agro-industry, mining, and energy projects.

ORGANIZATION: Lomé I
FOUNDED: 1975.02

The Lomé agreements expand upon the original Yaoundé agreement which created the relationship between the members of the European Community and their former colonies in Africa. 3,466 million ECU's were distributed in aid. A price stabilization scheme, "Stabex," was introduced. Reference: *Africa South of the Sahara, Europa Yearbook*.

ORGANIZATION: Lomé II
FOUNDED: 1979.10
MEMBERS:

Angola	Benin	Botswana	Burundi
Cameroon	Cape Verde	Central African Rep	Chad
Comoros	Congo	Djibouti	Equ. Guinea
Ethiopia	Gabon	Gambia	Ghana
Guinea	Guinea-Bissau	Ivory Coast	Kenya
Lesotho	Liberia	Libya	Madagascar
Malawi	Mali	Mauritania	Mauritius
Niger	Nigeria	Rwanda	Sao Tome Pr
Senegal	Seychelles	Sierra Leone	Somalia
Sudan	Swaziland	Tanzania	Togo
Uganda	Upper Volta	Zaire	Zambia
Zimbabwe			

This built upon the two Yaoundé agreements as well as Lomé I. It implemented aid and trade terms for EC-PAC countries. Funds for distribution: 5,512 million ECU's. Reference: Asante, 1981, "The Lomé Convention: Towards Perpetuation of Dependence or Promotion of Interdependence?" *Third World Quarterly*, 3:4.

ORGANIZATION: Lomé III
FOUNDED: 1985.12

This was a continuation of the Yaoundé and Lomé I and II agreements with some additional provisions. It included a provision for ECU 7.5 billion in aid. (See Yaoundé and Lomé I, II.)

ORGANIZATION: Lomé IV
FOUNDED: 1990
HEADQUARTERS: Bruxelles

As this is being prepared, negotiations are underway for the successor arrangement to the Yaoundé and Lomé agreements.

A GUIDE TO AFRICAN INTERNATIONAL ORGANIZATIONS

ORGANIZATION: Maghreb Permanent Consultative Committee
ACRONYM: CPCM   FOUNDED: 1964.10
HEADQUARTERS: Tunis

Committees:
Maghreb Committee on Insurance and Reinsurance
Maghreb Transportation and Communications Commission
Maghreb Coordinating Committee on Postal Services and Telecommunications (Tunis)
Maghreb Commissioon Shipping (Tunis)
Maghreb Commission for Air Transportation (Rabat)
Maghreb Commission for Road Transport (Algiers)
Maghreb Tourist Commission (Tripoli)
Maghreb Esparto Grass Service (Algiers)
Industrial Study Center (Tripoli) (with assistance of UNDP)
The Maghreb Council of Ministers provides policy guidance. The stated objective is to study problems of economic co-operation.

ORGANIZATION: Maghreb Regional Economic Organization
ACRONYM: MREO   FOUNDED: 1964
MEMBERS:

| Algeria | Libya | Morocco | Tunisia |

ORGANIZATION: Maghrebin Charter
FOUNDED: 1945.05
HEADQUARTERS: Defunct
MEMBERS: Morocco   Tunisia (independence parties)
Algeria later

The document proclaimed the unity of the region, but no political or institutional action was taken in its name.

ORGANIZATION: Mali Federation
FOUNDED: 1960.04
HEADQUARTERS: Defunct
MEMBERS:

| Benin | Mali | Senegal | Upper Volta |

This was propsed as a union of the states of former French West Africa. The Federation disintegrated shortly after inception with the prompt withdrawal of Dahomey and Upper Volta (August, 1960). At the time of the federation, present-day Mali was was known as Soudan.

ORGANIZATION: Mali Federation
FOUNDED: 1959
MEMBERS: Mali   Senegal

The Federation was proposed as a union of states of former French West Africa. The proposal was approved by only two potential members, and the union dissolved in August, 1960.

ORGANIZATION: Mano River Union
ACRONYM: MRU   FOUNDED: 1973.10
HEADQUARTERS: Freetown, PM Bag 133
MEMBERS: Guinea   Liberia   Sierra Leone

The Union began as a customs union, but its goals have expanded. The document which created this organization was the Mano River Declaration. It announced purposes include the encouragement of trade, harmonization of tariff and trade policies, and to secure a fair distribution of benefits for all members. Its primary policy-making body is the Ministerial Council; there are also functional committees.

ORGANIZATION: Merchant Fleet

This is associated with OCAM.

ORGANIZATION: Ministerial Conference of West and Central African States on Maritime Transport
ACRONYM: MCWCS   FOUNDED: 1975.05
HEADQUARTERS: Abidjan, BP V 257
MEMBERS:

Angola	Benin	Cameroon	Cape Verde
Central African Rep	Chad	Congo	Equ. Guinea
Gabon	Gambia	Ghana	Guinea
Guinea-Bissau	Ivory Coast	Liberia	Mali
Mauritania	Niger	Nigeria	Sao Tome Pr
Senegal	Sierra Leone	Togo	Upper Volta

Zaire

The organization attempts to maximize its members' leverage with regard to maritime matters, such as joint negotiating. It operates through several committees, such as Problmes of Land-Locked States.

ORGANIZATION: Monetary Union of Equatorial Africa and Cameroun
ACRONYM: UMAEC   FOUNDED: 1962
MEMBERS:

| Cameroon | Central African Rep | Chad | Congo |

Gabon

ORGANIZATION: Monetary Union of the States of West Africa
FOUNDED: 1962
MEMBERS:

| Benin | Ivory Coast | Mauritania | Niger |
| Senegal | Upper Volta | | |

Mali and Togo later

With an initial capital contribution from France, this Union was created by BCEAO.

ORGANIZATION: Monrovia Group
FOUNDED: 1961
MEMBERS:

| Ethiopia | Liberia | Nigeria | Sierra Leone |
| Somalia | Togo | Zaire | |

Plus UAM

Formed by the Charter of the Interafrican and Malagasy Organisation. It was absorbed into the OAU.

ORGANIZATION: Multilateral Development Council
FOUNDED: 1982

ORGANIZATION: Mutual Aid and Loan Guarantee Fund of the Council of the Entente States
ACRONYM: FEGE FOUNDED: 1966.06
HEADQUARTERS: Abidjan
MEMBERS:

| Benin | Ivory Coast | Niger | Senegal |
| Togo | Upper Volta | | |

The purpose of the Fund is to guarantee international loans. Its 1983 budget was CFA francs 1.2 billion. CFA francs 14.5 billion in loans have been guaranteed. The Fund has a paid staff of 38. Replenishment is provided by contributions of 1% of members' customs receipts. With external aid the Fund supports development activity--CFA francs 29.4 billion by the end of 1981.

ORGANIZATION: National Congress of British West Africa
FOUNDED: 1920.03
HEADQUARTERS: Defunct

The Congress held four sessions from 1920 to 1929 (Accra, Freetown, Bathurst, Lagos) and made representations to the British Colonial Office on behalf of the residents of BWA. The Congress was founded in Accra by Joseph Casely-Hayford with the intention of supporting African intellectuals.

ORGANIZATION: Network of Educational Innovation for Development in Africa
ACRONYM: NEIDA FOUNDED: 1977

ORGANIZATION: Niger Basin Authority
ACRONYM: NBA FOUNDED: 1968
HEADQUARTERS: Niamey BP 729
MEMBERS:

Benin	Cameroon	Chad	Guinea
Ivory Coast	Mali	Niger	Nigeria
Upper Volta			

The announced objective of the NBA is to "harmonize and co-ordinate development policies and activities." See also Niger River Commission. There are several publications.

ORGANIZATION: Niger River Commission
ACRONYM: CFN FOUNDED: 1963
HEADQUARTERS: Defunct
MEMBERS:

Benin	Guinea	Ivory Coast	Mali
Niger	Nigeria	Upper Volta	
Chad until 1964			

Created by Act of Niamey, the CFN became the Niger Basin Authority February, 1968.

ORGANIZATION: Niger-Nigeria Joint Commission for Cooperation
HEADQUARTERS: Niamey
MEMBERS: Niger   Nigeria

Its primary focus is on economic co-operation, for example, a UNIDO study of shared iron deposits.

ORGANIZATION: Nonaligned Countries Working Group on Southern Africa
MEMBERS:

| Angola | Botswana | Chad | Guinea |
| Liberia | Nigeria | Sudan | |

Plus other non-aligned states.

ORGANIZATION: Office for Research on African Food and Nutrition
ACRONYM: ORANA FOUNDED: 1956
HEADQUARTERS: Dakar, BP 2089
MEMBERS:

Benin	Ivory Coast	Mali	Mauritania
Niger	Senegal	Togo	Upper Volta
France			

ORANA collects and processes data on food and nutrition matters as well as conducts research. Membership is concomitant with OCCGE.

ORGANIZATION: Organization Commune Africaine et Malgache
See Main Organizations: OCAM

ORGANIZATION: Oganization of Senegal River States
ACRONYM: OERS　　　　　　　FOUNDED: 1964.03
HEADQUARTERS: Defunct
MEMBERS: Guinea　　　　　　Senegal

Now OMVS. This was a creation of President Senghor who wanted Francophonie to be elemental in the organization. It countered the Entente Council, and was resisted by President Touré. Lack of the proposed common currency by 1971 led to disaffection. It replaced the Senegal River States Committee, and claims the following objectives: co-operation and peace, economic development through co-ordinated planning and increased mobility of people and goods; and common trade and fiscal policies. Its members favored African unity and adopted a co-operative agreement with UNIDO intended to further integrated development. Its 1970 budget was CFA francs 76 million. Few activities were reported. It foundered over hostility between Guinea and Senegal and was ended in March, 1972. Reference: Bornstein, 1972, *Journal of Modern African Studies*.

ORGANIZATION: Organization for Afro-Asian Peoples' Solidarity
See Afro-Asian Conference of Solidarity

ORGANIZATION: Organization for Coordination and Cooperation in the Control of Major Endemic Diseases
ACRONYM: OCCGE　　　　　　FOUNDED: 1960.04
HEADQUARTERS: Bobo-Dioulasso, Burkina Fasso
MEMBERS:

Benin	Guinea	Ivory Coast	Mali
Mauritania	Niger	Senegal	Togo
Upper Volta	France		

The OCCGE focusses on trypanosomiasis, leprosy, trepanomatosis, malaria, onchocecosis, bilharziosis, trachoma, tuberculosis, measles.

ORGANIZATION: Organization for Meat Marketing
HEADQUARTERS: Niamey
MEMBERS:

Benin	Cameroon	Central African Rep	Congo
Gabon	Guinea	Mauritius	Niger
Rwanda	Senegal	Somalia	Togo
Upper Volta	Zaire		

This is associated with OCAM.

ORGANIZATION: Organization for West African Economic Cooperation
FOUNDED: 1960's
HEADQUARTERS: Freetown

ORGANIZATION: Organization for the African Community
ACRONYM: OAC   FOUNDED: 1961
HEADQUARTERS: Defunct

This was proposed by Nigeria; however, no concrete action was ever taken.

ORGANIZATION: Organization for the Coordination in Control of Endemic Diseases in Central Africa
ACRONYM: OCCGEAC   FOUNDED: 1963.08
HEADQUARTERS: Yaoundé, BP 288
MEMBERS:

Cameroon	Central African Rep	Chad	Congo
Equatorial Guinea	Gabon		

It focusses on the same diseases as OCCGE (above).

ORGANIZATION: Organization for the Development of African Tourism
ACRONYM: ODTA   FOUNDED: 1967.11
HEADQUARTERS: Yaoundé
MEMBERS:

Benin	Cameroon	Central African Rep	Chad

AFRICAN INTERNATIONAL ORGANIZATIONS

Congo	Gabon	Ivory Coast	Mali
Mauritania	Niger	Rwanda	Senegal
Togo	Upper Volta	Zaire	

ODTA succeeded OIETA. Its two missions were to assess the touristique resources available in the member states and solicit tourists to utilize the facilities. A Secretary-General and General Assembly provide direction.

ORGANIZATION: Organization for the Development of Tourism in Africa
FOUNDED: 1973
MEMBERS:

Benin	Cameroon	Central African Rep	Congo
Gabon	Guinea	Mauritius	Niger
Rwanda	Senegal	Somalia	Togo
Upper Volta	Zaire		

This is associated with OCAM.

ORGANIZATION: Organization for the Development of the Senegal River
ACRONYM: OMVS   FOUNDED: 1972.03
HEADQUARTERS: Dakar, BP 3152
MEMBERS: Mali   Mauritania   Senegal

Construction of 2 major dams, Diama and Manantali, were undertaken. OMVS also provides agricultural training courses for farmers. Its long-term goal is broad economic co-operation among the members. A 40-year plan has been adopted.

ORGANIZATION: Organization for the Management and Development of the Kagera River Basin
ACRONYM: KBO / OBK   FOUNDED: 1977.08
HEADQUARTERS: Kigali, BP 297
MEMBERS:

Burundi	Rwanda	Tanzania	Uganda

This organization seeks cooperative development of the resources of the Kagera River basin. It is intended to achieve integrated development of the river basin area, including hydro and telecommunications.

ORGANIZATION: Organization of African and Malagasy States
FOUNDED: 1961
MEMBERS:

Ethiopia	Liberia	Libya	Nigeria
Sierra Leone	Somalia	Togo	Tunisia
Plus Brazzaville Group			

A conference and subsequent informal organization of the more conservative states of independenet Africa in the immediate post-independence period. It was subsumed by the OAU. This should not be confused with other organizations with similar names, such as OCAM.

ORGANIZATION: Organization of African Unity
ACRONYM: OAU   FOUNDED: 1963
HEADQUARTERS: Addis Ababa
MEMBERS:

Algeria	Angola	Benin	Botswana
Burundi	Cameroon	Cape Verde	Cent Afr Rep
Chad	Comoros	Congo	Djibouti
Egypt	Equatorial Guinea	Ethiopia	Gabon
Gambia	Ghana	Guinea	Guinea-Bissau
Ivory Coast	Kenya	Lesotho	Liberia
Libya	Madagascar	Malawi	Mali
Mauritania	Mauritius	Morocco	Mozambique
Niger	Nigeria	Rwanda	Sao Tome Pr
Senegal	Seychelles	Sierra Leone	Somalia
Sudan	Swaziland	Tanzania	Togo
Tunisia	Uganda	Upper Volta	Zaire
Zambia	Zimbabwe		

This is the most broadly-based international organization on the continent; it has been appropriately compared to the United Nations. It annual sessions tend to focus upon political issues, but through STRC it has supported technical initiatives akin to UN specialized agencies. See elsewhere in this volume for a full description. Reference: Yassin El-Ayouty, 1975, *The OAU after Ten Years: A Comparative Perspective*.

ORGANIZATION: Organization of Senegal Riparian States
See Organization for the Development of the Senegal River

ORGANIZATION: Organization of Senegal River States
FOUNDED: 1968.03
MEMBERS:

| Guinea | Mali | Mauritania | Senegal |

This organization proposed joint development of the river basin as well as economic integration among its members.

ORGANIZATION: Organization of the Riverine States of the Senegal River
See Organization for the Development of the Senegal River

ORGANIZATION: Organization of Wood Producing and Exporting African Countries
FOUNDED: 1975.05
MEMBERS:

Cameroon	Central African Rep	Congo	Equ. Guinea
Gabon	Ghana	Ivory Coast	Liberia
Madagascar	Nigeria	Tanzania	Zaire

ORGANIZATION: Pan-African Congress(es)
ACRONYM: PAC   FOUNDED: 1919
MEMBERS:

Meetings of private individuals from Africa and the diaspora were held to raise their common consciousness and political awareness.
Sessions:
  1900 London (Protest Congress)
  1919 1st Paris
  1921 2nd London, Bruxelles, and Paris
  1923 3rd London and Lisbon
  1927 4th New York
  1945 5th Manchester
  1974 6th Dar Es Salaam

ORGANIZATION: Pan-African Cultural Festival
ACRONYM: FESTAC   FOUNDED: 1969

This was a political-cultural event which was held originally in Algiers to bring together artists and politicians from Africa and the black diaspora. A second festival occurred in Lagos in Feburary, 1977; a later one also was held in Lagos.

ORGANIZATION: Pan-African Federation
FOUNDED: 1944
HEADQUARTERS: Defunct
MEMBERS: African support groups in U.K.

This convened 5th Pan-African Congress.

ORGANIZATION: Pan-African Freedom Movements for East, Central and Southern Africa
ACRONYM: PAFMECSA   FOUNDED: 1960.10
HEADQUARTERS: Defunct
MEMBERS:

| Ethiopia | Tanzania | Kenya | Somalia |

A regional unit of All African Peoples' Organization, PAFMECSA incorporated both states and independence movements. It was formerly PAFMECA--which see. It favored East African Federation. It was terminated in 1963. Reference: Cox, 1964, *Pan-Africanism in Practice: an East African Study*.

ORGANIZATION: Pan-African Institute for Development
ACRONYM: PAID   FOUNDED: 1964
HEADQUARTERS: Douala, BP 4056

PAID trains rural development officers at four regional institutes (Douala; Ouagadougou; Buea, Cameroon; Kabwe, Zambia).

ORGANIZATION: Pan-African Movement for Eastern and Central Africa
ACRONYM: PAFMECA   FOUNDED: 1958.09
HEADQUARTERS: Defunct
MEMBERS: (as colonies)

Burundi	Ethiopia	Ivory Coast	Kenya
Rwanda	Somalia	Tanzania	Uganda
Zambia			

The Organization was expanded into PAFMECSA in 1960. PAFMECA proclaimed the "Freedom Charter," advocating democracy and anti-colonialism, and called for African independence by 1965 by non-violent means. Its membership consisted of representatives of 21 political parties in the region. It was seen by its leaders as an East African attempt to curtail the influence of Nkrumah and Touré.

ORGANIZATION: Pan-African News Agency
ACRONYM: PANA   FOUNDED: 1979.07
HEADQUARTERS: Dakar, BP 4056
MEMBERS:

Algeria	Angola	Burundi	Cameroon
Cape Verde	Congo	Egypt	Ethiopia
Gabon	Gambia	Guinea	Guinea-Bissau
Madagascar	Mali	Mauritania	Mozambique
Niger	Nigeria	Rwanda	Sao Tome Pr
Senegal	Sierra Leone	Sudan	Tanzania
Togo	Tunisia	Uganda	Upper Volta
Zaire	Zambia	Zimbabwe	

PANA resulted from a 1979 resolution of the OAU in connection with the New World Information Order. Its announced objectives lie in areas of professional, political, corrective, and didactic. It is similar to other Third World regional news organizations. PANA is a loose network of national news agencies that collects stories from participating agencies (40 or more), synthesizes, and refiles them. Staff is borrowed from national agencies which creates problems with continuity. Work is in English, French and some Arabic. PANA has been supported by UNESCO, but there have been chronic budget shortages. Its 1985 budget was US$3.5 million. Offices are located in Lagos, Tripoli, Khartoum, Kinshasa, Lusaka with bureaus in Addis covering the OAU and in Harare to cover South African activity.

ORGANIZATION: Pan-African Postal Union
ACRONYM: PAPU   FOUNDED: 1980.01
HEADQUARTERS: Arusha, BP 6026
MEMBERS:

Algeria	Angola	Benin	Botswana
Burundi	Cameroon	Central African Rep	Chad
Comoros	Congo	Egypt	Equ. Guinea
Ethiopia	Gabon	Gambia	Ghana
Guinea	Ivory Coast	Kenya	Liberia
Libya	Madagascar	Mali	Morocco
Mozambique	Niger	Nigeria	Senegal
Sierra Leone	Somalia	Sudan	Swaziland
Tanzania	Togo	Tunisia	Uganda
Upper Volta	Zimbabwe		

Established by OAU merging PAPU and PATU, its purpose is to extend postal cooperation and imporve service. It is a specialized agency of the OAU.

ORGANIZATION: Pan-African Telecommunications Network
ACRONYM: PANAFTEL   FOUNDED: 1973
HEADQUARTERS: Addis Ababa, Box 3243

Created by International Telecommunications Union to disseminate news regarding African issues, it is a subsidiary of OAU.

ORGANIZATION: Pan-African Telecommunications Union
ACRONYM: PATU   FOUNDED: 1978.02
HEADQUARTERS: Kinshasa
MEMBERS: All OAU members.

This resulted from the Pan-African Telecommunications Network (which see). It was supported by the OAU and UNESCO. Its purpose is to provide an exchange of information in the communications field. The 1986 OAU meeting ordered PATU and PAPU to merge.

ORGANIZATION: Pan-Africanist Manifesto
FOUNDED: 1959

This document was adopted at the inaugural conference of the Pan-African Congress, April, 1959. The spirit is captured by the sentence: "The militant progressive forces of African nationalism are bound to crush the reactionary forces of white domination."

ORGANIZATION: Permanent Consultative Committee of the Maghreb
ACRONYM: PCCM   FOUNDED: 1964
HEADQUARTERS: Tunis, 14 rue Yahia Ibn Omar
MEMBERS:

| Algeria | Mauritania | Morocco | Tunisia |

Though there were larger hopes, one of its few concrete accomplishments was sanctioning the establishment of Air Maghreb in 1971. Many study committees were established.

ORGANIZATION: Permanent Inter-African Bureau for Tsetse and Trypanosomiasis
FOUNDED: 1949

Its work has been taken over by STRC.

ORGANIZATION: Permanent Interstate Drought Control Committee for the Sahel
ACRONYM: CILSS   FOUNDED: 1973.09
HEADQUARTERS: Ouagadougou, BP 7049
MEMBERS:

Cape Verde	Chad	Gambia	Guinea-Bissau
Mali	Mauritania	Niger	Senegal
Upper Volta			

CILSS proposes to co-ordinate Sahelian development programs in co-operation with the UN Sahelian office, focusing particularly on drought. It operates the Centre for Agrometeorology and Operational Hydrology.

ORGANIZATION: Preferential Exchange Zone
ACRONYM: ZEP   FOUNDED: 1981.12
MEMBERS:

Burundi	Comoros	Djibouti	Ethiopia
Kenya	Lesotho	Mali	Mauritius
Uganda	Rwanda	Somalia	Swaziland
Tanzania	Zambia	Zimbabwe	

ZEP proposes a sub-regional common market by 1992 and an African Economic Community by 2000. See Eastern and Southern African Preferential Trade Area.

ORGANIZATION: Preferential Trade Area for East and Southern Africa
ACRONYM: PTA   FOUNDED: 1981.11
HEADQUARTERS: Lusaka
MEMBERS:

Angola	Botswana	Burundi	Comoroes
Djibouti	Ethiopia	Kenya	Lesotho
Malawi	Mauritius	Mozambique	Rwanda
Seychelles	Somalia	Swaziland	Tanzania
Uganda	Zambia	Zimbabwe	

PTA seeks to co-ordinate regional development and traiff reduction. A trade and development bank has been proposed. In 1989, common travelers' checks were issued by the member states denominated in Special Drawing Rights. Reference: Butete, "PTA: Toward an African Common Market," *Africa Report*, 30:1 (1985)

ORGANIZATION: Rand Monetary Area
FOUNDED: 1974
MEMBERS:

Botswana	Lesotho	South Africa	Swaziland

ORGANIZATION: Regional Centre for Book Promotion in Africa
See UNESCO Regional

ORGANIZATION: Regional Centre for Demographic Research and Training in Africa
HEADQUARTERS: Addis Ababa, Box 3001

ORGANIZATION: Regional Centre for Services in Surveying, Mapping and Remote Sensing
FOUNDED: 1975
HEADQUARTERS: Nairobi, Box 18118
MEMBERS:

Comoros	Kenya	Lesotho	Malawi
Somalia	Swaziland	Uganda	Zambia

This provides cartographic services and training.

ORGANIZATION: Regional Centre for Solar Energy Research and Development
ACRONYM: CRES   FOUNDED: 1979.11
HEADQUARTERS: Addis Ababa, Box 3243
MEMBERS:

Ivory Coast	Mali	Mauritania	Niger
Senegal	Upper Volta		

CREA develops global energy policy for members of WAEC.

ORGANIZATION: Regional Centre for Training in Aerial Surveys
FOUNDED: 1972.01
HEADQUARTERS: Ile-Ife, PMB 5545
MEMBERS:

Benin	Ghana	Mali	Nigeria
Senegal	Upper Volta		

ORGANIZATION: Regional Trust Fund for the Protection of West and Central Africa
FOUNDED: 1982

ORGANIZATION: Road Transport Committee of the Entente Council
ACRONYM: CSTT   FOUNDED: 1970.07
HEADQUARTERS: Abidjan, BP 3734
MEMBERS:

Benin	Ivory Coast	Niger	Togo
Upper Volta			

CSTT cooperates with ECOWAS.

ORGANIZATION: Sahel-Benin Union

ORGANIZATION: Science Education Programme for Africa
ACRONYM: SEPA   FOUNDED:
MEMBERS:

Botswana	Ethiopia	Gambia	Kenya
Lesotho	Liberia	Sierra Leone	Swaziland
Tanzania	Uganda	Zambia	

ORGANIZATION: Scientific, Technical and Research Committee of OAU
ACRONYM: STRC   FOUNDED: 1965.01
HEADQUARTERS: Lagos, PMB 2359
MEMBERS: All OAU members

This is an umbrella organization for various specialized groups within its purview. It holds periodic conferences on topics of interest to the scientific community focusing on specific technical issues. It succeeded CCTA (which see).

ORGANIZATION: Senegambia, Union of
FOUNDED: 1982.01
HEADQUARTERS: Banjul, 4 Marina Street
MEMBERS: Gambia   Senegal

The proposal was for an integrated military, economic union, and co-ordinated foreign policy. Sovereignty was to be retained by each member state. The Senegalese President is President of the Union; the Gambian President is Vice-President. Its origins were in a 1961 United Nations-sponsored study. It also recalled the 1765-83 British colony that occupied the entire territory. While a cabinet consisting of five Senegalese and four Gambians was announced in 1982, little has come of the union. It was precipitated by deposed Gambian President Jawara's calling upon the Senegalese military to restore him to power. It was strengthened in 1982.

ORGANIZATION: Shelter Afrique
FOUNDED: 1982.12
HEADQUARTERS: Nairobi, Box 52617
MEMBERS:

Burundi	Congo	Djibouti	Egypt
Gabon	Gambia	Kenya	Liberia
Malawi	Mauritius	Morocco	Sao Tome Pr
Sierra Leone	Somalia	Uganda	Zambia

This organization finances private housing development. It is funded 25% by the ADB.

ORGANIZATION: Solidarity and Intervention Fund (of CEAO)
ACRONYM: FOSIDEC   FOUNDED: 1977.12

It subsidizes community development projects. With initial capital of 5 billion CFA francs, it was to receive 1.5 billion CFA franc augmentation annually.

ORGANIZATION: South African Customs Union
FOUNDED: 1910
HEADQUARTERS: Defunct
MEMBERS: (as British colonies)

Botswana	Lesotho	South Africa	Swaziland

This was created by the British colony of South Africa and the three protectorates, Bechuanaland, Basutoland, and Swaziiland. It was succeeded by the Southern African Customs Agreement.

ORGANIZATION: Southern Africa Regional Tourism Council
ACRONYM: SARTOC   FOUNDED: 1973.03
HEADQUARTERS: Blantryre, Box 564
MEMBERS: Malawi   South Africa   Swaziland

SARTOC's aim is to develop tourism.

ORGANIZATION: Southern African Common Market

It was advocated by Prime Minister Verwoerd of South Africa, but it never materialized.

ORGANIZATION: Southern African Customs Union
FOUNDED: 1969.12
HEADQUARTERS: Pretoria
MEMBERS:

| Botswana | Lesotho | South Africa | Swaziland |

The Agreement provides for protection for infant industries in the three poorer states while making a flexible distribution of collected duties. This was a revision of the South African Customs Union.

ORGANIZATION: Southern African Development Bank
FOUNDED: 1982

South Africa plus "independent" homelands

ORGANIZATION: Southern African Development Coordination Conference
ACRONYM: SADCC   FOUNDED: 1980.04
HEADQUARTERS: Gaberone, PB 0095
MEMBERS:

Angola	Botswana	Lesotho	Malawi
Mozambique	Swaziland	Tanzania	Zambia
Zimbabwe			

SADCC promotes regional self-sufficiency to reduce dependency on South Africa. It was an outgrowth of the Front Line States. It has proposed hundreds of projects to be funded by Western donors, all in line with its proposed objectives. See Main Organizations chapter for additional information.

ORGANIZATION: Southern African Regional Commission for the Consevation and Utilization of the Soil
ACRONYM: SARCCUS   FOUNDED: 1950.06
HEADQUARTERS: Pretoria, PB X116
MEMBERS:

Botswana	Lesotho	Malawi	Nambia
South Africa	Swaziland		

SARCCUS promotes regional co-operation regarding soil issues, operating through ten specialized committees.

ORGANIZATION: Southern African Transport and Communications Commission
ACRONYM: SATCC   FOUNDED: 1980
HEADQUARTERS: London, c/o Tanzanian High Commission
MEMBERS:

Angola	Botswana	Lesotho	Malawi
Mozambique	Swaziland	Tanzania	Zambia
Zimbabwe			

A subsidiary of SADCC, it coordinates existing network and plans future development.

ORGANIZATION: Special Commonwealth African Assistance Plan
ACRONYM: SCAAP   FOUNDED: 1960
HEADQUARTERS: London, c/o Comnmonwealth Secretariat

Created by Commonwealth Prime Ministers' conference, SCAAP functions as a series of bilateral programs between the UK on one hand and a former British African colony on the other.

ORGANIZATION: Standing Commission of the OAU and the League of Arab States
FOUNDED: 1977.03
HEADQUARTERS: Tunis, c/o League of Arab States

Task forces are set up as necessary to deal with common problems. There is an Ad Hoc Court of Arbitration and Conciliation. Triennial conferencs are held.

ORGANIZATION: Tanzania-Zambia Railway Authority
ACRONYM: TAZARA   FOUNDED: 1968.03
HEADQUARTERS: Dar Es Salaam, Box 2834
MEMBERS: Tanzania   Zambia   China

Created to administer the railway constructed by the Chinese which connects Zambian copper field with the Tanzanian port of Dar Es Salaam. The authority, with Chinese consultation, deals with technical matters. The Railway links Zambian copper fields with the port of Dar Es Salaam. Its more than 1800 km are the same gauge as other railways in southern Africa.

ORGANIZATION: Trans-African Highway Coordinating Commission [A]
ACRONYM: TAH [A]   FOUNDED: 1971
MEMBERS:

| Algeria | Mali | Niger | Nigeria |

Tunisia

Formerly Comité de la Liaison Trans-Saharienne.

ORGANIZATION: Trans-African Highway Coordinating Commission [B]
ACRONYM: TAH [B]   FOUNDED: 1971.06
HEADQUARTERS: Addis Ababa
MEMBERS:

| Cameroon | Central African Rep | Kenya | Lesotho |
| Nigeria | Uganda | Zaire | |

It was to develop the Lagos-Mombasa Highway and connect with other regional highways. A new agreement in 1978 created the TAM Authority. It is supported by UNDP (See also TAH [B]).

ORGANIZATION: Trans-East African Highway Authority
HEADQUARTERS: Addis Ababa, Box 3001
MEMBERS:

Burundi	Congo	Djibouti	Egypt
Ethiopia	Kenya	Malawi	Rwanda
Sudan	Swaziland	Uganda	Zambia
Zimbabwe			

It plans to develop the Cairo-Gaberones Highway.

ORGANIZATION: Transequatorial Communications Agency
ACRONYM: ATEC   FOUNDED: 1959.06
HEADQUARTERS: Pointe-Noire
MEMBERS:

Central African Rep   Chad   Congo   Gabon

ATEC is an arm of UDEAC. Its primary responsibility is transportation planning, particularly ports.

ORGANIZATION: Trans-Sahara Liaison Committee
See Trans-African Highway Coordinating Commission [A]

ORGANIZATION: UAR-Libyan-Sudanese Economic Integration
FOUNDED: 1970.04
HEADQUARTERS: Defunct
MEMBERS: Egypt   Libya   Sudan

This proposed agreements of standard customs union types.

ORGANIZATION: UDEAC Solidarity Fund
FOUNDED: 1964
HEADQUARTERS: Bangui, c/o UDEAC

Established by CACEU (UDEAC), it is the successor to the UDE Solidarity Fund. It proposes to reduce inequality among UDEAC members with particular attention to the relative advantages of coastal states versus landlocked ones.

ORGANIZATION: UNESCO Regional Book Centre for Africa South of the Sahara
ACRONYM: CREPLA   FOUNDED: 1962
HEADQUARTERS: Yaoundé, BP 1646

CREPLA supports textbook production.

ORGANIZATION: UNESCO Regional Office for Education in Africa
ACRONYM: UNESCO/BRE   FOUNDED: 1970
HEADQUARTERS: Dakar, c/o UNESCO

It encourages African participation in relevant organizations.

ORGANIZATION: Union Africaine et Malgache de Defense
ACRONYM: UAMD   FOUNDED:

This is a subsidiary of UAM.

ORGANIZATION: Union of African Parliaments
ACRONYM: UAP   FOUNDED: 1976
HEADQUARTERS: Abidijan, BP 1381
MEMBERS:

Algeria	Cameroon	Egypt	Gabon
Ivory Coast	Lesotho	Liberia	Mauritania
Mauritius	Morocco	Senegal	Sierra Leone
Sudan	Tunisia	Zaire	

Its purpose is to strengthen parliamentary institutions. The agenda for its second conference suggested there were no pressing issues before it.

ORGANIZATION: Union of African Railways
ACRONYM: UAR   FOUNDED: 1972
HEADQUARTERS: Kinshasa, BP 687
MEMBERS:

Algeria	Angola	Cameroon	Congo
Djibouti	Egypt	Ethiopia	Gabon
Ghana	Guinea	Ivory Coast	Kenya
Liberia	Libya	Malawi	Mali
Morocco	Mozambique	Niger	Nigeria
Senegal	Sudan	Swaziland	Tanzania
Togo	Tunisia	Zaire	Zambia

The Union promotes opening routes to isolated regions as well as infrastructure integration.

ORGANIZATION: Union of African States
ACRONYM: UEA (UAS) FOUNDED: 1961.04
HEADQUARTERS: Defunct
MEMBERS: Ghana   Guinea   Mali

This was proposed as the core of a United States of Africa by the presidents of the three states. It was a precursor to the Ghana-Guinea-Mali Union. It was created by the Charter of African Unity signed by the first two members.

ORGANIZATION: Union of Central African Republics
ACRONYM: URAC   FOUNDED: 1959.01
HEADQUARTERS: Defunct
MEMBERS: Central African Rep   Chad   Congo

This grouping consisted of four French colonies at the time of independence. A solidarity fund was established by the states of former French West Africa.

ORGANIZATION: Union of Central African States
See Central African Ecnomic Union

ORGANIZATION: Union of Independent African States [A]
ACRONYM: UIAS   FOUNDED: 1958.04
HEADQUARTERS: Defunct
MEMBERS:

Egypt	Ethiopia	Ghana	Guinea
Liberia	Libya	Morocco	Sudan
Tunisia			

This was a manifestation of pan-Africanism as espoused by George Padmore and Kwame Nkrumah. It announced an intention to determine common defense policy and to expand to include all African states. Other organs were to be the Union Economic Council and the Union Bank.

ORGANIZATION: Union of Independent African States [B]
ACRONYM: UEIA FOUNDED: 1958.11
MEMBERS: Ghana Guinea

There were to be a common bank, economic council, and management by a heads of state conference. It was to be the incipient United States of Africa.

ORGANIZATION: Union of National Radio and Television Broadcasters
ACRONYM: URTNA FOUNDED: 1962.09
HEADQUARTERS: Dakar, BP 3237
MEMBERS:

Algeria	Angola	Benin	Botswana
Cameroon	Cape Verde	Central African Rep	Chad
Comoros	Congo	Djibouti	Egypt
Ethiopia	Gabon	Gambia	Ghana
Guinea	Guinea-Bissau	Ivory Coast	Kenya
Liberia	Libya	Madagascar	Malawi
Mali	Mauritania	Mauritius	Morocco
Niger	Nigeria	Rwanda	Senegal
Seychelles	Sierra Leone	Somalia	Sudan
Tanzania	Togo	Tunisia	Uganda
Upper Volta	Zaire	Zambia	Zimbabwe

URTNA facilitates co-operation in the production of radio and television programs as well as supporting all other aspects of activity in these fields.

ORGANIZATION: Union of Nile States
HEADQUARTERS: Defunct
MEMBERS: Egypt Sudan

This collaborative effort ended in 1955.

ORGANIZATION: Union of the Republics of Central Africa
FOUNDED: 1960.05
MEMBERS: Central African Rep Chad Congo

The members planned for co-ordination of posts and telecommunications, defense, currency, foreign affairs, and similar matters.

ORGANIZATION: United Arab Maghreb
FOUNDED: 1962.01

Proposed by Morocco, it was to be open to the four states of the Maghreb. A commission was named to draft a charter in 1962.

ORGANIZATION: United Arab Republic
ACRONYM: UAR
FOUNDED: 1969.12
HEADQUARTERS: Defunct
MEMBERS: Egypt   Libya
Later included Syria

The Union resulted from the Pact of Tripoli. It was renewed in 1972, but was dissolved a few years later.

ORGANIZATION: United Nations Development Programme
ACRONYM: UNDP   FOUNDED:

The UNDP maintains offices in the following locations: Algiers, Cotonou, Gaberones, Bujumbura, Yaoundé, Bangui, Ndjamena, Brazzaville, Cairo, Malabo, Addis Ababa, Libréville, Banjul, Accra, Conakry, Bissau, Abidjan, Nairobi, Maseru, Monrovia, Tripoli, Tananarive, Zomba, Bamako, Nouakchott, Port Louis, Rabat, Niamey, Lagos, Kigali, Dakar, Freetown, Mogadishu, Khartoum, Mbabane, Dar Es Salaam, Lomé, Tunis, Kampala, Ougadougou, Kinshasa, Lusaka, Harare.

ORGANIZATION: United Nations Economic Commission for Africa
See Economic Commission for Africa

ORGANIZATION: United States of Central Africa
FOUNDED: 1968.04
MEMBERS: Central African Rep   Chad   Zaire

These states proposed economic and defense co-operation. The groups became the Union of Central African States after a single day with the former name.

ORGANIZATION: Universal Negro Improvement Association
(Also known as United Negro Improvement Association)
ACRONYM: UNIA FOUNDED: 1914
HEADQUARTERS: Defunct
MEMBERS: Individuals

It was founded by Jamaican Marcus Garvey to further the interests of blacks, both in Africa and elsewhere. It split with the NAACP, which was too conservative. It advocated "Africa for the Africans." UNIA held 8 conventions from 1920 to 1938 in New York (5 times), Jamaica (twice), and Canada.

ORGANIZATION: University of East Africa
FOUNDED: 1961
HEADQUARTERS: Defunct
MEMBERS: Kenya Tanzania Uganda

ORGANIZATION: West African Common Market
FOUNDED: 1966.10
MEMBERS:

Benin	Ghana	Ivory Coast	Liberia
Mali	Mauritania	Niger	Nigeria
Senegal	Sierra Leone	Togo	Upper Volta

An agreement was signed, supported by the ECA.

ORGANIZATION: West African Union
See Union of Independent African States

ORGANIZATION: West Africa Currency Board
ACRONYM: WACB

AFRICAN INTERNATIONAL ORGANIZATIONS

ORGANIZATION: West Africa Rice Development Association
ACRONYM: WARDA FOUNDED: 1970.09
HEADQUARTERS: Monrovia, Box 1019
MEMBERS:

Benin	Cameroon	Chad	Gambia
Ghana	Guinea	Guinea-Bissau	Ivory Coast
Liberia	Mali	Mauritania	Niger
Nigeria	Senegal	Sierra Leone	Togo
Upper Volta			
Gabon applied			

WARDA fosters a co-operative relationship among rice-producing states in the region. Its treaty provides for its termination if the membership drops below 5. Its announced purpose is to promote and increase rice production. In a recent year its budget was US$8 million, and its staff numbered 252. Publishes quarterly newsletter, annual statistics.

ORGANIZATION: West African Clearing House
ACRONYM: WACH FOUNDED: 1975.06
HEADQUARTERS: Freetown, BP 218
MEMBERS:

Gambia	Ghana	Guinea	Guinea-Bissau
Liberia	Mali	Mauritania	Nigeria
Sierra Leone			

This was created by the central banks of the member states to facilitate regional trade. Its purpose is to promote balanced development among members.

ORGANIZATION: West African Customs Union
ACRONYM: UDAO FOUNDED: 1959
HEADQUARTERS: Defunct
MEMBERS:

Benin	Mali	Mauritania	Niger
Togo	Upper Volta		

UDAO is also known as the Customs Union of West Africa. It became UDEAO in 1966.

ORGANIZATION: West African Development Bank
    ACRONYM: WADB [BOAD]   FOUNDED: 1973.11
HEADQUARTERS: Lomé, BP 1172
    MEMBERS:

Benin   Ivory Coast   Niger   Senegal
Togo   Upper Volta

Membership is automatic for members of WAMU and BCEAO. Its shares are held by BCEEAO and the European Investment Bank. Its capital is from France and FGR. Paid-up capital was 7500 million CFA francs at inception.

ORGANIZATION: West African Economic Community
    ACRONYM: CEAO   FOUNDED: 1970.05
HEADQUARTERS: Ouagadougou, BP 643
    MEMBERS:

Benin   Ivory Coast   Mali   Mauritania
Niger   Senegal   Upper Volta
Guinea and Togo as observers

This was formerly Customs Union of West African States (which see). It was proposed for several years, but its meetings were postponed several times. The subsidiaries it has established include the Community Development Fund (which see), and it encourages intra-community trade in manufactured goods. Its primary functions are in the area of trade and regional economic programs (e.g., a fish purchasing and marketing company). This is the principle group of Francophone states. There was a corruption scandal uncovered by President Sankara of Burkina Fasso in 1985. Reference: *Europa Yearbook,* vol. 1.

ORGANIZATION: West African Economic Community Development Fund
    FOUNDED: 1973
HEADQUARTERS: Ouagadougou, c/o CEAO

This is a component of the West African Economic Community. It provides industrial development funds, but it is hampered by overdue contributions.

ORGANIZATION: West African Examinations Council
ACRONYM: WAEC   FOUNDED: 1951.12
HEADQUARTERS: Accra, Box 125
MEMBERS:

Gambia   Ghana   Liberia   Nigeria
Sierra Leone

Established by Cambridge and Oxford Universities along with West African Education Ministries, WAEC conducts various educational, vocational, and professional examinations.

ORGANIZATION: West African Health Community
ACRONYM: WAHC   FOUNDED: 1972.05
HEADQUARTERS: Lagos, PMB 2023
MEMBERS:

Gambia   Ghana   Liberia   Nigeria
Sierra Leone

It was revised by the treaty of 25 Oct 78. WAHC provides health training programs and sharing of information in the health area. Its 1985-86 biennial budget was 2.279 Naira.

ORGANIZATION: West African Insurance Consultative Association
ACRONYM: WAICA   FOUNDED: 1978
HEADQUARTERS: Monrovia, Box 2551
MEMBERS:

Gambia   Ghana   Liberia   Nigeria
Sierra Leone

WAICA established the West African Insurance Institute for training in the area of insurance. It compiles and publishes relevant data.

ORGANIZATION: West African Insurance Institute
FOUNDED: 1978
HEADQUARTERS: Monrovia, Box 2551
MEMBERS:

Gambia   Ghana   Liberia   Nigeria
Sierra Leone

Established with assistance of the West African Insurance Consultative Asociation, the Institute provides training.

    ORGANIZATION: West African Monetary Union
         ACRONYM: UMOA   FOUNDED: 1962.05
    HEADQUARTERS: Dakar, BP 3159
         MEMBERS:

Benin	Ivory Coast	Mali	Mauritania
Niger	Senegal	Togo	Upper Volta
Mauritania in 1972	Mali left in 1983, rejoined in 1984		

A new treaty was signed 14 November 1973. UMOA is an organ of BCEAO. It was created to manage the common currency of the member states. There is a single central bank. Reference: IMF Occasional Paper #35 (1985).

    ORGANIZATION: West African Regional Group
         FOUNDED: 1968.04
    HEADQUARTERS: Defunct
         MEMBERS:

Gambia	Ghana	Guinea	Liberia
Mali	Mauritania	Nigeria	Senegal
Upper Volta			

This Group was created by the Monrovia Protocol. No activity was reported. It led to the West African Economic Community (which see).

    ORGANIZATION: West African Remote Sensing
    HEADQUARTERS: Ouagadougou, BP 1762

    ORGANIZATION: Yaoundé I (Association)
         FOUNDED: 1963.07
    HEADQUARTERS: London
         MEMBERS:

Benin	Burundi	Cameroon	Cent Afr Rep
Chad	Congo	Gabon	Ivory Coast
Malawi	Mali	Mauritania	Niger

Rwanda	Senegal	Somalia	Togo
Upper Volta	Zaire		

Pursuant to the 1957 Treaty of Rome, the association following from conferences in Yaoundé and later Lomé was designed to sustain ties between former colonies and metropolitan states. Trade and import advantages were offered by the European powers in exchange for preferred access for exports. It took effect 1 June 1964. See also Lomé agreements.

ORGANIZATION: Yaoundé II
FOUNDED: 1969.07
MEMBERS: Same as Yaoundé I

$918 million in aid was promised. Regional organizations were encouraged. It took effect 1 June 1971.

INDIVIDUALS IN THE LEADERSHIP OF AFRICAN INTERNATIONAL ORGANIZATIONS

NAME: Abbas, Ferhat 1899-
NATIONALITY: Algerian
SOURCE OF INFORMATION: Segal
Abbas is noted for founding the Algerian Moslem Student Union in Paris in the 1920's. In 1943 he was imprisoned for publishing the Algerian People's Manifesto. He was elected to both the French and Algerian National Assemblies. He openly and eagerly supported a proposed union with Tunisia. His worldview was reflected in his comment, "This country does not exist. We are the product of a new world born out of the spirit and the efforts of the French." Professsionally he was a chemist, but he also wrote "La Nuit Coloniale," and "Le Jeune Algériene."

NAME: Abselwahab
SOURCE OF INFORMATION: ADB annual report
President, African Development Bank, 1970-75.

NAME: Adedeji, Adebayo 1930-
NATIONALITY: Nigeria
He was educated at Ibadan, Leicester, Harvard Universities, and then filled civil service positions for the Nigerian government. He became Executive Secretary of ECA in 1975. He has been a professor and wrote several books.

NAME: Adjei, Ako
NATIONALITY: Ghana
Foreign Minister, Ghana

NAME: Allaf, Ely Ould 1937-
NATIONALITY: Mauritania
SOURCE OF INFORMATION: ACP, Who's Who
Allaf is a civil engineer, politician, and civil servant. In 1979 he was Seretary General of OMVS.

NAME: Alomenu, H. S.
NATIONALITY: Ghana
Director-General, OICMA, 1985.

NAME: Amin, Samir 1931-
NATIONALITY: Egypt
SOURCE OF INFORMATION: ACP, Who's Who
He was Director, AIEDP, 1970-1979. Amin was educated in Paris as an economist and has written and taught in the field.

NAME: Appiah, Joe 1918-
NATIONALITY: Ghana
Appiah shared a room with Kwame Nkrumah in London and shared in his African nationalist sentiments and activities as well. However, being more conservative, he split with Nkrumah. Nonetheless, he was detained by the British in 1966. He studied law in England. In 1946 he had married the daughter of the British Chancellor of the Exchequer, Sir Stafford Cripps. Elected to parliament in Ghana, he later became Ghana's delegate to the UN.

NAME: Atante, Philip
NATIONALITY: Botswana
Parliamentary opposition leader 1966. Born in South Africa, as a member of parliament he has espoused the ideals of Kwame Nkrumah and Pan-Africanism.

NAME: Ayari, Chedly 1933-
NATIONALITY: Tunisia
President/Chairman, BADEA, 1975-
Formerly with IBRD and CERES, Ayari has been his country's Ambassador to Belgium as well as Minister of National Economy. He also served on the staff of the United Nations.

NAME: Beheiry, Mamoun Ahmed 1925-
NATIONALITY: Sudan
SOURCE OF INFORMATION: ADB annual report, Who's Who
Educated in England, he became a banker. Among his posts was IMF Governor for Sudan. He was President of the African Development Bank 1964-70. He later became Sudanese Minister of Finance.

NAME: Blyden, Dr. Edward Wilmot 1832-1912
NATIONALITY: Virgin Islands-Sierra Leone
SOURCE OF INFORMATION: *African Affairs* 7/74
Author of African Life and Culture. Blyden advocated migration to Liberia for American blacks. He struggled for an autonomous African church while vigorously opposing "mongrelization." He claimed Ibo ancestry. Coming to the United States, he made an attempt to enroll at Rutgers Theological Seminary; discrimination kept him out. Eventually he went to Liberia where he learned several local languages, he became a teacher of Greek and Latin despite having only completed secondary school. From the faculty of Liberia College he went on to become president. To further his views he established a newspaper.

He was brought into the government as Foreign Minister and in 1877 became Ambassador to the U.K. He received honorary degrees from several U.S. institutions. Nnamde Azikiwe termed him the father of African nationalism. He advocated a "Christian African empire," with an African essence but European civilization.

NAME: **Blumeris, Frederick Arthur**
NATIONALITY: Zimbabwe
Executive Secretary, SADCC, 1983.

NAME: **Bonaventura, Kidwingira**
SOURCE OF INFORMATION: ACP
Secretary General, CEDGL, 1979.

NAME: **Brumby, P. J.**
Director General, ICCA, 1985.

NAME: **Cabou, Daniel** 1929-
NATIONALITY: Senegal
SOURCE OF INFORMATION: Who's Who
Secretary General, BCEAO 1977-, Cabou was educated in Senegal and France and served in the French civil service in West Africa. Following independence he held positions in the Senegalese cabinet.

NAME: **Caiore, Augustus**
Secretary General, Mano River Organization.

NAME: **Carpenter, Muhamadu A.**
NATIONALITY: Nigeria
Executive Secretary, Lake Chad Basin Commission

NAME: **Carrington, Edwin**
Carrington became Secretary General of PAC in 1988.

NAME: **Casely-Hayford, Joseph** 1867-1930
NATIONALITY: Gold Coast
Founder of the National Congress of British West Africa, for 13 years he served in the Gold Coast Legislative Assembly.

NAME: **Cudjoe, Seth Dzifanu** 1910-
NATIONALITY: Ghana
SOURCE OF INFORMATION: Who's Who
In 1949 he wrote an influential pamphlet, "Aids to African Autonomy," as well as "Self-Reliance and the Colonial Mentality" which raised political consciousness in British West Africa. By training Cudjoe was a physician, having been trained in Scotland and England.

NAME: **Dehinde, A.E.**
SOURCE OF INFORMATION: ACP
Executive Secretary, RNC, 1979.

NAME: **Delany, Martin R.**
His biography is: "African Dream and the Emergence of Pan-African Thought," 1975, by C.E.Griffith, Pennsylvania State University Press.

NAME: **Diaby-Ouattara, Aboubacar**
NATIONALITY: Ivory Coast
Secretary General, ECOWAS, 1979-

NAME: **Diallo, Aliou Samba** 1934-
NATIONALITY: Senegal
He became Director General of CAFRAD in 1985. He was educated in Dakar and Paris in Medicine and taught in the field.

NAME: **Diallo-Telli, Boubacar** 1925-1973
NATIONALITY: Guinea
Secretary-General of the OAU 1964-1972, Diallo-Telli began his career as a civil servant in French West Africa, finally becoming Secretary-General of the Grand Council of French West Africa. After independence, he became Guinea's Ambassador to the United States and the United Nations and was elected Vice-President of the United Nations General Assembly in 1963. Subsequently he served as President of the UN Special Committee on Apartheid. Following his return to Guinea he was arrested as a political threat, and he died in prison.

NAME: **Diori, Hamani** 1916-
NATIONALITY: Niger
Chairman of ECOWAS 1971 and 1973 and of OCAM in 1971, Diori was President of Niger 1960-1974. From 1967 to 1974 he was President of the Council of the Entente. He was ousted in a coup. Prior to independence he had served in the French National Assembly. He was educated both in Dakar and in Paris; he spent some time teaching African languages in Paris. This experience in France led to his staunch support of the French Community as well as OCAM. By reputation he was a respected conciliator.

NAME: **DuBois, William E. B.** 1869-1963
NATIONALITY: USA
SOURCE OF INFORMATION: Dissertation Abstracts, 31A,1183
One of the earliest black intellectuals in the United States, DuBois received a Ph.D. from Harvard University in 1895. He studied further in Berlin and then received an appointment to the faculty of Atlanta University where he served 1897-1910 and 1933-1944. In 1909 he participated in the founding of the NAACP, editing that organization's magazine "Crisis" 1910-1932. In his view, pan-Africanism was anti-racist and anti-imperialist. In 1919 he convened the first Pan-African Congress in Paris in 1919. In 1926 he visited the USSR and adopted communism as his mode of political expression. He ultimately became a citizen of Ghana, but he spent his later years residing in the Soviet Union, and died there in 1963.

NAME: **Dzakpasu, Cornelius K.**
In 1985 he was the Secretary General of the African Association of Public Affairs and Management.

NAME: **Eastman, T. Ernest** 1933-
NATIONALITY: Liberia
SOURCE OF INFORMATION: Who's Who
Secretary General, Mano River Union, 1979, Eastman served in several diplomatic posts for Liberia.

NAME: **Eboucha-Babackas, M.**
NATIONALITY: Congo
He was President of UDE in 1964.

NAME: **Ekangaki, Nzo** 1934-
NATIONALITY: Cameroun
Secretary General OAU 1972-74. He was educated in Nigeria at Oxford University and in Germany. He served as a member of parliament and in the cabinet of Cameroun.

NAME: **El-Fouly, M.**
Acting Secretary General, AAASA, 1985.

NAME: **Eteki, William-Aurélian** 1933-
NATIONALITY: Cameroun
He was educated in Paris and served as Secretary General of the OAU 1974-1978. He has also served as President of UNESCO and in Cameroun as Special Adviser to the President as well as Minister of Foreign Affairs.

NAME: **Eton, Vincent**
SOURCE OF INFORMATION: ACP
Secretary General, UDEAC, 1979

NAME: **Fall, Cheikh Ibrahima**   1930-
NATIONALITY: Senegal
SOURCE OF INFORMATION: ACP, Who's Who
Secty General, CEAO 1973-76, Fall served in several major Senegalese diplomatic positions, particularly in UN agencies. He was educated in Dakar and Paris.

NAME: **Fanon, Franz**   1925-1961
NATIONALITY: Algeria (born in Martinique)
His most influential work was "Wretched of the Earth." Trained as a psychiatrist, he became an articulate voice of African nationalism and anti-imperialism in the 1950's. He was an influential figure in the Algerian revolution, and his writings have been widely read in Africa and beyond. His view of negritude was that it was a cultural, not a nationalist, phenomenon.

NAME: **Felleke, Zawdu**
He was Secretary General of the African Regional Organization for Standardization

NAME: **Foalem, Ambroise**
NATIONALITY: Cameroun
Secretary General, UDEAC

NAME: **Fordwor, Kwame D.**   1933-
NATIONALITY: Ghana
SOURCE OF INFORMATION: ACP, Who's Who
Fordwor was educated in England and was President of ADB, 1976-79. His tenure was cut short by political disagreements with the Board of Governors, all of which is reported in his book, *The African Development Bank; Problems of International Cooperation*. He was previously an economist with the IFC and has published in the field of economics.

NAME: **Ganou, Silimane**
NATIONALITY: Niger
Secretary General, Liptako-Gourma Region.

BIOGRAPHICAL DATA

NAME: **Gardiner, Robert Kweku Atta**   1914-
NATIONALITY: Ghana
Gardiner studied economics at Cambridge and Oxford Universities in England. He was Executive Secretary of the ECA 1963-1975; he was Deputy Executive Secretary 1959-61 and has filled numerous positions for the Nigerian and Ghanain governments as well as the UN.

NAME: **Garvey, Marcus**   1887-1940
NATIONALITY: Jamaica
SOURCE OF INFORMATION: J.H. Clarke, *Marcus Garvey and the Vision of Africa*
1974, Random House
Founder of the Universal Negro Improvement Association, Garvey was trained as a printer, and at an early age espoused a United States of Africa. In 1920 he convened a conference at which was issued the "Declaration of the Rights of Negro Peoples of the World." The U.S. Postal Service charged him with fraud in 1922 and he was indicted. Black leaders turned against him, and he was finally convicted. Out of jail, he struck a deal with the Liberian government for some land for resettlement purposes, but the Liberians reneged. Garvey is widely recognized as a leader of pan-African thought. He received international attention when he petitioned the League of Nations in 1928 on behalf of black peoples, to no avail.

NAME: **Gillet, Jean-François**   1923-
Secretary-General, Conference of Heads of State of Equatorial Africa, 1964.

NAME: **Gueye, Dieumb Ojibail**
NATIONALITY: Senegal
SOURCE OF INFORMATION: ACP
Executive Secretary, AGC, 1979. He was educated in France.

NAME: **Haile Selassie, I**   1892-1975
NATIONALITY: Ethiopia
Born Ras Tafari Makonnen, Haile Selassie became Emperor of Ethiopia in 1930. As regent he had abolished slavery in 1924 and later promulgated Ethiopia's first constitution. When Ethiopia was attacked by Italy in 1936, Selassie appealed to the League of Nations in vain. He lived in exile in England 1936-40. Haile Selassie was a major figure in the founding of the OAU and chaired the First Conference of African Heads of State.

NAME: **Hassan, Hassan M.**
NATIONALITY: Egypt
Secretary-General, AAHO.

NAME: **Horton, James Africanus Beale**   1835-1883
NATIONALITY: Sierra Leone
A surgeon-major in the British Medical Corps, he graduated from Fourah Bay College and the University of Edinburg. He wrote widely, including *The Political Economy of British West Africa* in 1965 and *West African Countries and Peoples* in 1868. He also wrote for Edward Blyden's newspaper.

NAME: **Houphouët-Boigny, Félix**   1905-
NATIONALITY: Ivory Coast
SOURCE OF INFORMATION: Who's Who
As President of the Ivory Coast, he convened the Abidjan Conference which led to the founding of the UAM. He was an early advocate of unity and participated in the founding of the Council of the Entente. He also participated in the establishment of OCAM. He was trained in France as a physician.

NAME: **Jagne, Alieu B.**
NATIONALITY: The Gambia
Executive Secretary, WARDA, 1985.

NAME: **John, Malick**
High Commissioner, OMVG, 1985.

NAME: **Johnson, James**   1836-1917
NATIONALITY: Sierra Leone
SOURCE OF INFORMATION: Biography by E.A.Ayandele, 1970

NAME: **Joudiou, Christian**
SOURCE OF INFORMATION: ACP
Director General, BEAC, 1979

NAME: **Kane, Falilou**   1938-
NATIONALITY: Senegal
SOURCE OF INFORMATION: Who's Who
Secretary General of OCAM, 1968-72, Kane was educated at the University of Dakar. In his public career he was a minister and diplomat.

NAME: **Kanza, Thomas R.**
Director General, CAFRAD, 1985, and a professor.

BIOGRAPHICAL DATA

NAME: **Karefa-Smart, Dr. John Musselman**   1915-
NATIONALITY: Sierra Leone
SOURCE OF INFORMATION: Who's Who
Assistant Director-General of WHO 1965-70, he later became a Professor at Harvard University. He was educated in Canada and the USA. His career included professional service with WHO, government minister and author.

NAME: **Kaunda, Kenneth**   1924-
NATIONALITY: Zambia
SOURCE OF INFORMATION: Who's Who
His career included involvement as a teacher and political organizer. He was a founder of PAFMESA as well as Chairman of the OAU. He has been President of Zambia since independence, and has written several books.

NAME: **Kaya, Paul**   1933-
NATIONALITY: Congo
SOURCE OF INFORMATION: Who's Who
Secretary General of the Entente Council, 1979-. Kane was educated in France as an economist, he has been a United Nations consultant.

NAME: **Keita, Drissa**
NATIONALITY: Mali
Secretary-General, CEAO 1986

NAME: **Keita, Founéké**
NATIONALITY: Mali
Secretary General, OMVS

NAME: **Keita, Modibo**   1915-
NATIONALITY: Mali
Keita led Mali into union with Ghana and Guinea in 1961. He received the Lenin Peace Prize in 1962.

NAME: **Kenyatta, Jomo**   1891-1978
NATIONALITY: Kenya
President of Kenya; founder of PAFMECA and the EAC, Kenyatta was one of the leaders of post-independence Africa. As leader of pre- and post-independence Kenya, he was instrumental in the founding of PAFMECA, PAFMECSA, and the EAC. He had gone to England in the 1940's (where he took an English wife) and argued for self-government. During the Mau Mau uprising, he was imprisoned and tried by the British for complicity. Trained as an anthropologist, Kenyatta wrote several books about the Kikuyu and Kenya.

NAME: **Kodjo, Edem** 1938-
NATIONALITY: Togo
SOURCE OF INFORMATION: Who's Who
Secretary General of the OAU 1978- , he also held offices in BCEAO. He was educated in France in economics. He served as Togolese Minister of Finance and as a member of the boards of the IMF and ADB.

NAME: **Konaté, Tiéoulé**
Secretary General, ACP, 1979-

NAME: **Kotso Nathaniels, E.K.**
NATIONALITY: Togo
Secretary General, CAMES, 1983

NAME: **Kouyaté, Garan**
NATIONALITY: Sudan
Seen as a Free French sympathizer, Kouyaté was shot by the Nazis in France during the Second World War.

NAME: **Landeroin, Ms**
Secretary-General, Entente Council, 1965

NAME: **Mahamane, Brah**
Executive Secretary, CILSS, 1985

NAME: **Makonnen, Ras**
He is the author of: *Pan-Africanism from Within*, Oxford University Press, 1973.

NAME: **Makoni, Simbarashe** 1950-
NATIONALITY: Zimbabwe
SOURCE OF INFORMATION: Who's Who
Executive Secretary, SADCC. He was educated in England and served as a member of the Zimbabwean parliament as well as a government minister.

NAME: **Mamadou Samb, Mour**
NATIONALITY: Senegal
Executive Secty, AGC, 1985.

BIOGRAPHICAL DATA

NAME: **Materu, M. E. A.**
Director General, International Red Locust Organization, 1985.

NAME: **Mazrui, Ali** 1933-
NATIONALITY: Kenya
SOURCE OF INFORMATION: Who's Who
Professor of Political Science at Makerere University, he fled Idi Amin's Uganda. He is Director, World Order Models Project-Africa. Mazrui is the author of numerous books on political topics and is probably the best known professional figure in contemporary Africa. He was educated in England and the United States. Upon his exile from Uganda under General Amin, he held teaching posts in several American universities. In the mid-1980's he produced a popular television series, "The Africans."

NAME: **Mbita, Hashim Iddi** 1933-
NATIONALITY: Tanzania
SOURCE OF INFORMATION: Who's Who
Executive Secretary, OAU-Liberation Committee, 1972-present. He was educated in England and the USA as a journalist. He has spent time in the military service.

NAME: **Mboumoua, William Etexi**
Secretary General, OAU, 1979

NAME: **Minhas, B. S.**
Secretary General, AARRO, 1985.

NAME: **Mondjanagni, A. C.**
Secretary General, PAID, 1985

NAME: **Moutia, Sidney** 1932-
NATIONALITY: Mauritius
SOURCE OF INFORMATION: ACP, Who's Who
Secretary-General of OCAM, 1974-79, Moutia is known as both an agriculturalist and as an author. He was educated in England and India.

NAME: **Mung'omba, Wila d'Israeli** 1939-
NATIONALITY: Zambia
SOURCE OF INFORMATION: Who's Who, ADB annual report
Executive President and Chairman, ADB 1980-1985, he was educated in Uganda and England as a barrister and served in the Zambian diplomatic service.

NAME: **Munu, Momodou** 1938-
NATIONALITY: Sierra Leone
Executive Secretary, ECOWAS, January, 1985-. He was previously a civil servant and lawyer.

NAME: **N'Diaye, Babacar** 1937-
NATIONALITY: Senegal
Executive President/Chairman, ADB, May, 1985-. He joined the Bank in 1965.

NAME: **Nduwayo, Alieu M. B.**
NATIONALITY: Burundi
Executive Secretary, CEPGL, 1985

NAME: **Ngom, Moussa**
NATIONALITY: Senegal
Secretary General, CEAO, 1976-. He attended universities in Dakar and Paris before entering the civil service.

NAME: **N'Jie, Pierre Saar** 1909-
NATIONALITY: The Gambia
SOURCE OF INFORMATION: Who's Who
He was educated in England as a barrister and has been prominent in Gambian public life.

NAME: **Nkrumah, Kwame** 1909-1972
NATIONALITY: Ghana
Prime Minister and then President of Ghana, Nkrumah was educated as a teacher in the United States and England. In 1945 he participated in the Pan-African Congress. That led to his editorship of the "New African" from 1945 till 1947. He was seen as a subversive by the British and imprisoned. He was elected Leader of Government for the Gold Coast colony and then Prime Minister and President of Ghana 1952-1966. His major writing was "Neo-Imperialism." He sought an African leadership role and convened in 1958 the first Conference of Independent African States. His leadership soured and he was exiled in 1966. He was offered the Co-Presidency of Guinea (1966-1972) by fellow radical, Sekou Touré. He died in Conakry in relative obscurity. Despite his poor administration and subsequent disgrace, he is widely recognized as the preeminent voice of Pan-Africanism, especially in conjunction with the independence era.

NAME: **Nomvete, Bax**
Secretary General, Preferential Trade, South Africa, 1985

NAME: **Nyerere, Julius Kambarage**   1922-
NATIONALITY: Tanzania
Prime Minister and then President of Tanganyika/Tanzania, Nyerere was educated at Makerere University as a teacher; he later studied at Edinburg University. He founded the Tanganyika African Union and published a party paper. He became Prime Minister, then President of Tanganyika, 1961-1985. His operating policy to achieve development was termed "Ujamaa," selfhood. He proposed the Arusha Declaration in 1976 which lead to the establishment of the East African Community. He postponed independence for Tanganyika so that Kenya and Uganda could simultaneously emerge. He presided over the Tanganyika-Zanzibar union, forming Tanzania. Nyerere's adamant refusal to collaborate with Idi Amin precipitated the demise of the EAC in 1979. He voluntarily relinquished the Presidency of Tanzania in 1985, though he retains leadership of the party. His expressed pan-African view was that, "African unity must take priority over all other associations." Outside his political pursuits Nyerere translated several of Shakespeare's plays into Swahili.

NAME: **Obote, Milton**   1924-
NATIONALITY: Uganda
SOURCE OF INFORMATION: Who's Who
Obote was educated at Makerere University and was a founder of KAU. At independence he was elected to Parliament ultimately becoming Prime Minister. He was overthrown by Idi Amin, and after several years' exile in Tanzania he was restored to power with assistance from the Tanzania military. His unpopularity led to his unseating and a return to exile.

NAME: **Okelo-Odongo, Thomas**
NATIONALITY: Kenya
He was a Director of ADP and subsequently became Secretary General of ACP.

NAME: **Olatunde-Oshinibi, Ayotunde**
Secretary General, African Cocoa Alliance

NAME: **Olufolabi, F. Olufemi**
SOURCE OF INFORMATION: ACP
Secretary General, CBC, 1979

NAME: **Onu, Peter**
NATIONALITY: Nigeria
Secretary General, OAU, and Assistant Secretary General OAU

NAME: **Ould Soueid Ahmed, Abdullah**
Director General, OCLALAV.

NAME: Oumarou, Ide   1937-
NATIONALITY: Niger
Secretary General, OAU 1985-. He was educated in Paris and then became a civil servant, including Minister of Foreign Affairs.

NAME: Padmore, George
He was a political adviser to President Nkrumah of Ghana. As a moderate anti-colonialist, he sought US aid against communism. He wrote the book, "Pan-Africanism or Communism."

NAME: Philip, Prof. Kjeld   1912-
NATIONALITY: Danish
He was Chairman of the UN Commission on East Africa 1965-67. As an economic consultant, Kjeld propsed the EAC. He has been an economics professor at several Danish and Swedish universities. In 1965 he was economics adviser to the President of Somalia.

NAME: Quaison-Sackey, Alex   1924-
NATIONALITY: Ghana
SOURCE OF INFORMATION: Who's Who
He was educated in England as a barrister. His service in the Ghanian diplomatic corps included representing the country at the United Nations. He was President of the United Nations General Assembly, 1964-65. He was arrested in 1966, but soon released.

NAME: Seydou, Amadou   1928-
NATIONALITY: Niger
Educated in Algiers, Cairo and Paris, Seydou was a Director of UNESCO 1967-74.

NAME: Simpore, Mamadou
Secretary General, APTU

NAME: Sired, Ismail Amri
NATIONALITY: Rwanda
Secretary General, OCAM

NAME: Sory Balde, Ibrahim
NATIONALITY: Guinea
Executive Secretary, Niger Basin Authority, 1985.

NAME: Sylvester-Williams, Henry
-see Williams

NAME: Tanganika, Gahuranyi
Secretary General, ATO, 1985.

NAME: Taylor, Alwyn B.
NATIONALITY: Sierra Leone
SOURCE OF INFORMATION: *New York Times*
In 1987, he was Director General, African Center for Monetary Studies. He had been a civil servant since 1964.

NAME: Tchanque, Pierre   1925-
NATIONALITY: Cameroun
SOURCE OF INFORMATION: ACP, Who's Who
Director-General of the BDEAC, 1979; Secretary-General of UDEAC 1970-77. He was educated in France, and has a background in finance.

NAME: Tevoedjre, Albert   1929-
NATIONALITY: Benin
SOURCE OF INFORMATION: Who's Who
Educated in Switzerland and the USA in economics, he pursued a career as a teacher and writer. He was employed by the ILO before becoming Secretary-General of the UAM, 1961-63.

NAME: Touré, Bakary
SOURCE OF INFORMATION: ACP
Director General of the Liptako-Gourma Region, 1979

NAME: Touré, Ahmed Sekou   1922-1984
NATIONALITY: Guinea
SOURCE OF INFORMATION: Who's Who
His early career was as a labor union leader. (At age 15 he organized a strike against the food at his boarding school.) As a postal clerk he organized a union and strike. He rose to leadership of the communist-supported Confederation General de Travailleurs and later travelled in East Europe. When he became Secretary-General of UGTAN, he broke from French communist unions. In 1946 he co-founded (with Houphouet-Boigny) the Rassemblement Democratique Afrique. Toure' was elected to the extraterritorial assembly in 1953. By 1957 he had become a member of the Grand Council of French West Africa. He led the campaign against DeGaulle's proposed Communauté; Guinea was the only colony to reject participation; the vote was 1.1 million against, 57,000 for. President DeGaulle did all he could to destroy Guinea; Touré sought assistance from the Soviet Union. His forced dependence upon the Eastern bloc diminished his pan-African leadership, and poor health in his last years removed him from the international scene.

NAME: Traoré, Diawa-Mory
NATIONALITY: Guinea
Executive Secretary, Niger Basin Authority in 1983. In 1984 he became Prime Minister of Guinea; he was also Minister of Education.

NAME: Tsiranana, Philip   1910-
NATIONALITY: Madagascar
He was educated in France and was engaged in teaching. Upon independence he was the first President of Madagascar. Prior to the creation of OCAM he was a staunch advocate of a Francophone union.

NAME: Tubman, Robert C.   1939-
NATIONALITY: Liberia
SOURCE OF INFORMATION: Who's Who
Managing Director, ECOWAS-Fund, 1974-1985, he was educated at the London School of Economics, University of Edinburg and Harvard Law School. He headed the Liberian delegation to Law of the Sea Conference and served as Minister of Justice. His father was President of Liberia.

NAME: Wacha, D. S. O.
Executive Seretary, Kagera River Basin Organization

NAME: Wako, D. M.
NATIONALITY: Kenya
Director General, Desert Locust Organization, 1985.

NAME: Williams, A.O.
Executive Secretary, STRC.

NAME: Williams, Henry Sylvester   1869-1911
NATIONALITY: Trinidad
SOURCE OF INFORMATION: Biography by J.R. Hooker, 1975; another 1976.
He organized the first Pan-African Congress, London, 1900. Upon completing secondary school he became a teacher. Unhappy with the pay, he went to New York, then Halifax. He enrolled at Dalhousie University to study law; he remained only one year. In 1895 he went to London and spent a year at King's College, Cambridge. In 1897 he formed the Pan-African Association to secure rights for Africans, prompted by stories of conditions for laborers in South Africa. He married a white English woman; they had 5 children. Supported by Booker T. Washington, he convened the first Pan-African Congress in Westminster Hall, London. Thirty delegates from North America, Africa, and the Caribbean came. A petition to Queen Victoria was formulated regarding working conditions in South Africa. The Pan-African Association was dissolved about 1903,

weakened by a dispute between Williams and DuBois. Having become a lawyer, Williams went to South Africa. He returned to London and became the agent for the African National Congress. He joined the Fabian Society and won a seat on his borough council. Declining health limited his activities in his last years.

NAME: **Windapo, Adesoye**
NATIONALITY: Nigeria
Executive Secretary, WACH, 1985

NAME: **Worku, Arega**
NATIONALITY: Ethiopia
Secretary General, IACO 1979-1984.

SOURCES NOTED:

ACP Yearbook 1980-81, 1st edition.
Segal, Ronald. 1962. *African Profiles*, Baltimore: Penguin Books
Who's Who in Africa, by John Dickie and Alan Rake. London: African Development, 1973.

CHRONOLOGY

SIGNIFICANT DATES RELATING TO INTERNATIONAL ORGANIZATIONS IN AFRICA

1884-5	Berlin Conference: Africa partitioned by colonial powers
1885	French West Africa created
1900	African Protest Congress (London)
1908	Union of South Africa established
1910	French Equatorial Africa created Establishment of South African Customs Union
1914	Founding of UNIA
1919	Establishment of British East Africa 1st Pan-African Congress (Paris)
1920	March, National Congress of British West Africa
1921	2nd Pan-African Congress (London, Bruxelles, Paris)
1923	3rd Pan-African Congress (London, Lisbon)
1927	4th Pan-African Congress (New York)
1935	Emperor Haile Selassi of Ethiopia appealed unsuccessfully for League of Nations aid against Italian invasion
1945	October, Fifth Pan-African Congress (Manchester)
1953	December, Sixth Pan-African Congress (Accra)
1957	March, Independence of Gold Coast-Ghana beginning the rush to independence.
1958	April, Establishment of UN ECA April, Conference of Independent African States, Accra September, Establishment of PAFMECA December, Establishment of French Community December, All-African People's Congress, Accra

1959	Establishment of UDAO
April, Adoption of Pan-Africanist Manifesto
May, Founding of Council of the Entente
June, Establishment of UDE
1960	Independence for 16 French colonies.
Mali Federation
June, United Nations forces enter Congo (Zaire)
June, Second Conference of Independent African States, Addis Ababa
1960	October, Establishment of PAFMECSA
December, Establishment of UAM
1961	January, Establishment of Casablanca Group
April, UAS founded
May, South Africa left British Commonwealth
May, Monrovia Group established
June, Establishment of EACSO
1962	May, Establishment of UMOA
1963	May, Founding of Organization of African Unity.
Establishment of OAU Scientific,Technical and Research Committee
August, Founding of African Development Bank
Independence for Kenya, Tanganyika, Uganda
1964	December, Founding of Central African Customs and Economic Union
1966	June, Establishment of OCAM
1967	June, Establishment of East African Community
1968	April, Founding of UEAC
December, Creation of Tazara
1969	April, Lusaka Manifesto
1970	April, Founding of UAR
May, Establishment of CEAO
September, Establishment of WARDA
Demise of WACU
1971	World Court ruled Namibia was illegally held by South Africa
1972	March, Organization for the Development of the Senegal River created
1973	June, Economic Community of West Africa formed
November, Establishment of WADB

1974	CEAO founded; replaced UDEAC Pan-African Congress (Dar Es Salaam)
1975	February, Lomé I Convention May, ECOWAS treaty
1977	UN created Contact Group of 5 to deal with Namibia
1979	July, Demise of the East African Community. October, Lomé II Convention
1980	April, Establishment of SADCC November, Niger Basin Authority established
1983	May, Establishment of Pan-African News Agency
1985	Demise of OCAM.
1986	January, Lomé III Convention
1989	November, Pre-independence election in Namibia; UN auspices Lomé IV negotiations

APPENDICES

1.	A Note on Kenya and International Organizations	183
2.	Alphabetical Listing of Acronyms	185
3.	Founding Dates of African International Organizations	191
4.	Countries and Number of Memberships	199
5.	Individual Country Memberships	201
6.	Number of Memberships by Groups	267

APPENDIX 1

ONE COUNTRY'S MEMBERSHIP IN INTERNATIONAL ORGANIZATIONS

Kenya Budget for International Organizations
(Amounts in Kenyan Shillings)

ORGANIZATION	ESTIMATES APPROVED 85/86	86/87
OAU Liberation Council	50,000	100,000
OAU Secretariat	560,000	600,799
African Training & Research Center in Administration for Development	15,830	15,830
Pan African News Agency	40,000	51,370
Council for Development of Economic and Social Research in Africa	1,420	1,420
Pan African Cultural Festival	1,200	1,200
African Regional Center for Engineering Design and Manufacturing	16,680	200,000
International African Institute	300	300
African Institute for Development Planning	7,000	7,000
African Civil Aviation Commission (AFCAC)	3,700	7,230
African Council for Communication and Education	150	150
Union of National Radio and TV (URNTA)	2,760	200,000
African Association of Industrial Research Orgs.	2,080	2,080
African Institute for Higher Research	69,000	69,080
Outward Bound School	5,000	5,000
Preferential Trade Area (PTA)	361,296	480,990
African Regional Centre for Technology	35,360	35,360
Science Education Programme for Africa	4,300	4,300
African Social Studies Programme	2,130	7,930
African Curriculum Organization	4,200	4,200
African Centre for Applied Research and Training	60,000	70,000
Eastern and Southern African Management Institute	40,000	64,200
Organization of African Trade Union Unity	13,000	13,000
African Association for Public Administration Management	10,400	10,400
African Regional Labour Administration Centre	10,400	10,400
Eastern African Statistical Training Centre *	25,000	25,000
African Institute for Economic Development and Planning	70,000	100,000
African Regional Organization for Standardization	23,465	23,465
International Organization for Standardization (ISO)	27,437	27,437
International Org. of Legal Metrology	6,378	6,378
English Speaking Africa Regional Industrial Organization	50,000	80,000
CIRDA Africa	44,000	85,230
IEC	8,016	8,016
Intergovernmental Authority on Drought and Development (IGADD)	--------	125,340
	1,570,502	2,443,105

A GUIDE TO AFRICAN INTERNATIONAL ORGANIZATIONS

* This is the only organization listed with an "East African" name, suggesting that Kenya is not supporting any of the East African Community subsidiaries (see section on East Africa).

This is drawn from only a single page of the Kenyan budget, suggesting that there may be more to this budget category; it is indicative of the publicized obligations of one state. Several of the organizations are not considered in this volume because they are not intergovernmental.

APPENDIX 2

ALPHABETICAL LISTING OF ACRONYMS

AAASA	Association for the Advancement of Agricultural Science in Africa
AAC	African Accounting Council
AACB	Association of African Central Banks
AACC	African Agricultural Credit Commission
AAITO	Association of African Industrial Technology Organizations
AALCC	Asian-African Legal Consultative Commission
AAPC	All African Peoples' Conference (s)
AARRO	Afro-Asian Rural Reconstruction Organization
AATPO	Association of African Trade Promotion Organizations
ACARTSOD	African Centre for Applied Research and Training in Social Development
ACDA	Concerted Action for the Development of Africa
ACHSTS	African Council for the Training and Promotion of Health Sciences, Teachers and Specialists
ACI	African Cultural Institute
ACMS	African Center for Monetary Studies
ACP	African Caribbean Pacific Group
ADB	African Development Bank
ADF	African Development Fund
AEF	French Equatorial Africa
AFC	African Forestry Commission
AFCAC	African Civil Aviation Commission
AFDIN	African Development Information Network
AFPU	African Postal Union
AFRASEC	Afro-Asian Organization for Economic Cooperation
AFRICARE	African Reinsurance Corporation
AGC	African Groundnut Council
AIDF	African Industrial Development Fund
AIEDP	African Institute for Economic Development and Planning
ALC	Coordination Commission for Liberation Movements of Africa
AMECO	Afro-Malagasy Economic Cooperation Organization
AOC	Associated Overseas Countries of the EEC
AOF	French West Africa
APROMA	Association of Market Production, European Community/African-Caribbean-Pacific States
APU	African Parliament's Union
APU	African Postal and Telecommunications Union
ARCDEM	African Regional Center for Engineering, Design, and Manufacturing
ARCT	African Regional Centre for Technology
ARSO	African Regional Organization for Standardisation
ASECNA	Agency for the Safety of Air Navigation in Africa and Madagascar
ATEC	Transequatorial Communications Agency
ATO	African Timber Organization
ATRCAD	African Training and Research in Administration for Development

A GUIDE TO AFRICAN INTERNATIONAL ORGANIZATIONS

ATU	African Postal and Telecommunications Union
BAD	African Development Bank
BADEA	Arab Bank for Economic Development in Africa
BCEAO	Central Bank of West African States
BDEGL	Development Bank of the Great Lakes States
BEA	British East Africa
BEAC	Bank of Central African States
BLS	High Commission Territories
BOAD	West African Development Bank
BWA	British West Africa
CACEU	Central African Customs and Economic Union
CADIB	African Patent Document and Information Centre
CAFRAD	African Center for Administrative Training and Research for Development
CAMES	African and Malagasy Council on Higher Education
CAMPC	African and Mauritian Advanced Training Centre for Administrative Personnel
CAPTEAO	Conference of Administrators of Posts and Telecommunications of West Africa
CASDB	Central African States Development Bank
CBLT	Lake Chad Basin Commission
CCEAE	Conference of Heads of State of Equatorial Africa
CCTA	Commission for Technical Cooperation in Africa South of the Sahara
CEAO	West African Economic Community
CEBV	Cattle and Meat Economic Community of the Council of the Entente States Organization
CECAS	Conference of East and Central African States
CEE-EAMA	African and Malagasy States Associated with the EEC
CEEAC	Economic Community of Central African States
CEIM	Center for Industrial Studies of the Maghreb
CELHTO	Centre for Linguistic and Historical Studies through Oral Traditions
CEPGL	Economic Community of the Great Lakes Countries
ERDAS	Centre for the Coordination of Social Science Research and Documentation in Africa South of the Sahara
CFA	Communauté Financiere Africaine
CFN	Niger River Commission
CICA	International Conference of Africa on Insurance Supervision
CIEH	Inter-African Committee on Hydraulic Studies
CILSS	Permanent Interstate Drought Control Committee for the Sahel
CIPROFILM	Inter-African Film Production Centre
CIV	Inter-African Travel Company
CMAC	Conference of African Ministers of Culture
CMCPT	Maghreb Committee on Postal and Telecommunications Coordination
COMALFA	Maghreb Esparto Bureau
CONSAS	Constellation of South African States
COPAL	Cocoa Producers Alliance
CPCM	Maghreb Permanent Consultative Committee
CRADAT	African Regional Centre for Labor Administration

APPENDIX 2

CREPLA	UNESCO Regional Book Centre for Africa South of the Sahara
CRES	Regional Centre for Solar Energy Research and Development
CSTT	Road Transport Committee of the Entente Council
DLCO	Desert Locust Control Commission
DLCOEA	Desert Locust Control Organization for Eastern Africa
EAA	East Africa Airways
EAAFRO	East African Agriculture and Forestry Research Organization
EAC	East African Community
EACROTANAL	Eastern African Centre for Research on Oral Traditions and African National Languages
EACSO	East African Common Services Organization
EADB	East African Development Bank
EAEC	East African Examinations Council
EAFFRO	East African Freshwater Fisheries Research Organization
EAHC	East African Harbours Corporation
EAIRO	East African Industrial Research Organization
EAMAU	African and Mauritian School of Architecture and Urbanism
EAPT	East African Post and Telecommunications Corporation
EAR	East African Railways Corporation
EAR & H	East African Railways and Harbours Administration
EATRO	East African Trypanosomiasis Research Organization
EAVRO	East African Veterinary Research Organization
ECA	Economic Commission for Africa - UN
ECEA	Economic Community of Eastern Africa
ECOWAS	Economic Community of West African States
EIER	Inter-State School of Rural Equipment Engineers
EISMV	Institute of Sciences and Veterinary Medicine
ESAMRDC	Eastern and Southern African Mineral Resources Development Centre
ESAPTA	Eastern and Southern African Preferential Trade Area
ESARIPO	Industrial Property Organization for English-Speaking Africa
FCD	Community Development Fund
FESAC	Higher Education Foundation in Central Africa
FESTAC	Pan-African Cultural Festival
FOSIDEC	Fund for Solidarity and Economic Development
FOSIDEC	Solidarity and Intervention Fund
GRDO	Gambia River Development Organization
IABAH	Inter-African Bureau of Animal Health
IACO	Inter-African Coffee Organization
IAI	African Institute of Informatics
IAMB	African and Mauritian Bilingual Institute
IAMO	Inter-African and Malagasy States Organization
IAMSEA	African and Mauritian Institute of Statistics and Applied Economics
IAPSC	Inter-African Phyto-Sanitary Council
IBED	Inter-African Bureau on Epizootic Diseases
ICAM	African, Malagasy and Mauritania Cultural Institute
IFORD	Institute for Training and Demographic Research
IGADO	Inter-Governmental Authority on Drought and Development

ILCA	International Livestock Centre for Africa
IMR	East African Institute for Medical Research
IMVBD	East African Institute of Malaria and Vector-Borne Diseases
IOC	Indian Ocean Commission
IRLCO-CSA	International Red Locust Control Organization for Central and Southern Africa
KBO	Organization for the Management and Development of the Kagera River Basin
LGA	Liptako-Gourma Integrated Development Authority
MCWCS	Ministerial Conference of West and Central African States on Maritime Transport
MFRO	East African Marine Fisheries Research Organization
MREO	Maghreb Regional Economic Organization
MRU	Mano River Union
NBA	Niger Basin Authority
NEIDA	Network of Educational Innovation for Development in Africa
OAC	Organization for the African Community
OAMCAF	African and Malagasy Coffee Organisation
OAMCE	African and Malagasy Organization of Economic Cooperation
OAMPI	African and Malagasy Industrial Property Office
OAPI	African Intellectual Property Organization
OAU	Organization of African Unity
OBK	Organization for the Management and Development of the Kagera River Basin
OCAM	African and Malagasy Common Organization
OCAMM	African Mauritian, and Malagasy Common Organization
OCBN	Benin-Niger Common Organization
OCCEAC	Common Organization for Economic Cooperation in Central Africa
OCCGE	Organization for Coordination and Cooperation in the Control of Major Endemic Diseases
OCCGEAC	Organization for the Coordination in Control of Endemic Diseases in Central Africa
OCDN	Common Dahomey-Niger Organization des Chemins de Fer et des Transports
OCLALAV	Common Organization for the Control of Dessert Locust and Bird Pests
ODTA	Organization for the Development of African Tourism
OEPGL	Energy Organization of the Great Lakes Countries
OEPT	Equatorial Office of Posts and Telecommunications
OERS	Oganization of Senegal River States
OICMA	International African Migratory Locust Organization
OIETA	Interstate Office on African Tourism
OMVG	Gambia River Development Organization
OMVS	Organization for the Development of the Senegal River
ORANA	Office for Research on African Food and Nutrition
PAC	Pan-African Congress(es)
PAFMECA	Pan-African Movement for Eastern and Central Africa

APPENDIX 2

PAFMECSA	Pan-African Freedom Movements for East, Central and Southern Africa
PAID	Pan-African Institue for Development
PANA	Pan-African News Agency
PANAFTEL	Pan-African Telecommunications Network
PAPU	Pan-African Postal Union
PATU	Pan-African Telecommunications Union
PCCM	Permanent Consultative Committee of the Maghreb
PTA	Preferential Trade Area for Eastern and Southern Africa
RAN	Abidjan-Niger Railway Regime
SADCC	Southern African Development Coordination Conference
SADIAMIL	African Society for the Development of the Millet-and-Sorghum-based Food Industry
SAFGRAD	Consultative Advisory Committe on Semi-Arid Food Grain Research and Development
SARCCUS	Southern African Regional Commission for the Consevation and Utilisation of the Soil
SARTOC	Southern Africa Regional Tourism Council
SATCC	Southern African Transport and Communications Commission
SCAAP	Special Commonwealth African Assistance Plan
SEPA	Science Education Programme for Africa
STRC	Scientific, Technical and Research Committee of OAU
TAH [A]	Trans-African Highway Coordinating Commission [A]
TAH [B]	Trans-African Highway Coordinating Commission [B]
TAZARA	Tanzania-Zambia Railway Authority
UAM	African and Malagasy Union
UAMBD	African and Mauritian Union of Development Banks
UAMBD	African and Malagasy Union of Development Banks
UAMCE	African and Malagasy Union of Economic Cooperation
UAMCET	African and Malagasy Union for Economic and Technical Cooperation
UAMD	Union Africaine et Malgache de Defense
UAMPT	African and Malagasy Union of Posts and Telecommunications
UAP	Union of African Parliaments
UAPT	African Posts and Telecommunications Union
UAR	Union of African Railways
UAR	United Arab Republic
UAS	Union of African States
UAT	African Telecommunications Union
UDAO	West African Customs Union
UDE	Equatorial Customs Union
UDEAC	Central African Customs and Economic Union
UDEAO	Customs Union of West African States
UEA	Union of African States
UEAC	Central African Economic Union
UEAC	Union of Central African States
UEIA	Union of Independent African States
UIAS	Union of Independent African States
UMAEC	Monetary Union of Equatorial Africa and Cameroun

UME	Equatorial Monetary Union
UMOA	West African Monetary Union
UNDP	United Nations Development Programme
UNESCO/BRE	UNESCO Regional Office for Education in Africa
UNIA	Universal Negro Improvement Association
URAC	Union of Central African Republics
URTNA	Union of National Radio and Television Broadcasters
WACB	West Africa Currency Board
WACH	West African Clearing House
WADB	West African Development Bank
WAEC	West African Examinations Council
WAHC	West African Health Community
WAICA	West African Insurance Consultative Association
WARDA	West Africa Rice Development Association
ZEP	Preferential Exchange Zone

FRENCH ACRONYMS WITH ENGLISH EQUIVALENTS

French	**English**
CEDEAO	ECOWAS
OECE	OECD
ONU	UN
OUA	OAU

NON-AFRICAN ACRONYMS

EC	European Community
EEC	European Economic Community (the EC is in earlier years)
FAO	Food and Agriculture Organization (a UN specialized agency)
ICAO	International Civil Aviation Organization (a UN specialized agency)
OCED	Organization for Economic Co-operation and Development (industrialized states collaboration for, e.g., economic development assistance)
UNESCO	United Nations Education, Scientific, and Cultural Organization (a UN specialized agency)
UNDP	United Nations Development Programme
USAID	United States Agency for International Development
WHO	World Health Organization (a UN specialized agency)

APPENDIX 3

FOUNDING DATES OF AFRICAN INTERNATIONAL ORGANIZATIONS
(Decimals refer to months)

1950's	Conference of Heads of African and Malagache States and Governments
1957	East African Tourist Travel Association
1960's	African Malagasy Union
1960's	Organization for West African Economic Cooperation
1970's	Front Line African States
1876	African International Association
1895	French West Africa
1900	British West Africa
1910	French Equatorial Africa
1910	South African Customs Union
1914	Universal Negro Improvement Association
1917	East African Customs Union
1919	British East Africa
1919	Pan-African Congress(es)
1920.03	National Congress of British West Africa
1935	African Postal and Telecommunications Union
1944	Pan-African Federation
1945.05	Maghrebin Charter
1947	Commonwealth
1948	Franc Zone
1948	Inter-African Bureau for Soils
1948.01	East African High Commission
1949	Permanent Inter-African Bureau for Tsetse and Trypamosomiasis
1950	Inter-African Rural Economy and Soils Bureau
1950.06	Southern African Regional Commission for the Consevation and Utilisation of the Soil
1951	East African Court of Appeal
1951.12	West African Examinations Council
1952	East African Institute for Medical Research
1953	Central African Federation
1953	Federation of Rhodesia and Nyasaland
1953	Inter-African Bureau for Animal Resources
1954	Inter-African Phyto-Sanitary Council
1954.01	Commission for Technical Cooperation in Africa South of the Sahara
1955	Bank of Central African States
1955	Central Bank of West African States
1955.07	International African Migratory Locust Organization
1956	Office for Research on African Food and Nutrition
1956.11	Asian-African Legal Consultative Commission
1957	Afro-Asian Conference of Solidarity
1957	Afro-Asian Peoples' Solidarity Organization

1958	All African People's Conference (s)
1958	Foundation for Mutual Assistance in Africa South of the Sahara
1958	Ghana-Guinea Union
1958	Independent African States
1958.04	Conference of Independent African States
1958.04	Economic Commission for Africa - UN
1958.04	Union of Independent African States
1958.09	Pan-African Movement for Eastern and Central Africa
1958.11	Union of Independent African States
1958.12	Afro-Asian Organization for Economic Cooperation
1959	African Forestry Commission
1959	Agency for the Safety of Air Navigation in Africa and Madagascar
1959	Communauté
1959	Community of Independent African States
1959	Customs Union of West African States
1959	Mali Federation
1959	Pan-Africanist Manifesto
1959	West African Customs Union
1959.01	Associated States of Africa
1959.01	Union of Central African Republics
1959.05	Conseil de l'Entente
1959.06	Conference of Heads of State of Equatorial Africa
1959.06	Equatorial Customs Union
1959.06	Transequatorial Communications Agency
1959.07	Benin-Niger Common Organization
1960	Abidjan-Niger Railway Regime
1960	African and Malagasy Coffee Organisation
1960	Brazzaville Group
1960	Central Bank of the States of Equatorial Africa and Cameroun
1960	Federation of East African States
1960	Inter-African Committee on Hydraulic Studies
1960	Special Commonwealth African Assistance Plan
1960.04	Mali Federation
1960.04	Organization for Coordination and Cooperation in the Control of Major Endemic Diseases
1960.05	Union of the Republics of Central Africa
1960.10	Pan-African Freedom Movements for East, Central and Southern Africa
1960.12	African and Malagasy Union
1960.12	Ghana-Guinea-Mali Union
1960.12	Inter-African Coffee Organization
1961	African and Malagasy Organization of Economic Cooperation
1961	African and Malagasy Union of Development Banks
1961	African Commission on Agricultural Statistics
1961	African Postal Union
1961	African Telecommunications Union
1961	Air Afrique
1961	Central African Federation for Higher Education
1961	Ghana-Upper Volta Customs Union

APPENDIX 3

1961	Interstate Office on African Tourism
1961	Monrovia Group
1961	Organization for the African Community
1961	Organization of African and Malagasy States
1961	University of East Africa
1961.01	Casablanca Group
1961.04	Union of African States
1961.05	African Consultative Council
1961.06	East African Common Services Organization
1961.09	African and Malagasy Union of Posts and Telecommunications
1961.09	African Posts and Telecommunications Union
1961.12	Higher Education Foundation in Central Africa
1962	African and Malagasy Office of Industrial Property
1962	African Institute for Economic Development and Planning
1962	African Union of National Radio and Television Broadcasting
1962	International Conference of Africa on Insurance Supervision
1962	Monetary Union of Equatorial Africa and Cameroun
1962	Monetary Union of the States of West Africa
1962	UNESCO Regional Book Centre for Africa South of the Sahara
1962.01	United Arab Maghreb
1962.03	Afro-Asian Rural Reconstruction Organization
1962.05	Cocoa Producers Alliance
1962.05	West African Monetary Union
1962.08	Desert Locust Control Organization for Eastern Africa
1962.09	African and Mauritian Union of Development Banks
1962.09	African and Malagasy Industrial Property Office
1962.09	African Intellectual Property Organization
1962.09	Union of National Radio and Television Broadcasters
1962.12	Inter-African and Malagasy States Organization
1963	African Development Bank
1963	African Development Bank Group
1963	East African Federation
1963	East African Post and Telecommunications Corporation
1963	East African Railways Corporation
1963	East African Harbours Corporation
1963	Inter-state Committee for the Senegal River
1963	Joint FAO/WHO/OAU Regional Food and Nutrition Commission for Africa
1963	Niger River Commission
1963	Organization of African Unity
1963.05	Coordination Commission for Liberation Movements of Africa
1963.07	Yaoundé I (Association)
1963.08	Organization for the Coordination in Control of Endemic Diseases in Central Africa
1963.11	Inter-African Travel Company
1964	African and Malagasy Union of Economic Cooperation
1964	African Groundnut Council
1964	African Training and Research in Administration for Development

1964	Central African Customs and Economic Union
1964	Chad Basin Commission
1964	Commission on Mediation, Conciliation and Arbitration (of OAU)
1964	Customs and Economic Union of Central Africa
1964	Free Trade Area
1964	Maghreb Committee on Postal and Telecommunications Coordination
1964	Maghreb Regional Economic Organization
1964	Pan-African Institue for Development
1964	Permanent Consultative Committee of the Maghreb
1964	UDEAC Solidarity Funnd
1964.02	African and Malagasy Common Organization
1964.03	Oganization of Senegal River States
1964.05	African Commercial Union
1964.05	Lake Chad Basin Commission
1964.07	African Center for Administrative Training and Research for Development
1964.09	Centre for the Coordination of Social Science Research and Documentation in Africa South of the Sahara
1964.10	Maghreb Permanent Consultative Committee
1965	Common Organization for the Control of Dessert Locust and Bird Pests
1965.01	Scientific, Technical and Research Committee of OAU
1965.05	Joint Anti-Locust and Anti-Aviarian Organization
1966	African and Malagasy Sugar Agreement
1966	Conference of East and Central African States
1966.06	Mutual Aid and Loan Guarantee Fund of the Council of the Entente States
1966.09	African Agricultural Credit Commission
1966.10	West African Common Market
1967	Center for Industrial Studies of the Maghreb
1967	East African Community
1967	East African Development Bank
1967	Economic Community of Eastern Africa
1967	Lake Victoria Fisheries Commission
1967.11	Organization for the Development of African Tourism
1967.12	East African Common Market
1968	Association for the Advancement of Agricultural Science in Africa
1968	Central African Economic Union
1968	Centre for Linguistic and Historical Studies through Oral Traditions
1968	Niger Basin Authority
1968.01	Institute of Sciences and Veterinary Medicine
1968.02	African and Malagasy Council on Higher Education
1968.03	Organization of Senegal River States
1968.03	Tanzania-Zambia Railway Authority
1968.04	Union of Central African States
1968.04	United States of Central Africa
1968.04	West African Regional Group
1968.08	Association of African Central Banks
1969	Common Organization for Economic Cooperation in Central Africa

APPENDIX 3

1969	Customs Union Agreement
1969	Pan-African Cultural Festival
1969.01	African Civil Aviation Commission
1969.01	Inter-State School of Rural Equipment Engineers
1969.04	Lusaka Manifesto
1969.07	Arusha Convention
1969.07	Yaoundé II
1969.12	Southern African Customs Union
1969.12	United Arab Republic
1970	Equatorial Conference of Heads of State
1970	Conference of Ministers of National Education in French-Speaking African and Malagasy States
1970	UNESCO Regional Office for Education in Africa
1970.04	UAR-Libyan-Sudanese Economic Integration
1970.05	West African Economic Community
1970.07	Road Transport Committee of the Entente Council
1970.09	West Africa Rice Development Association
1970.12	Integrated Development Authority of the Liptako-Gourma Region
1970.12	Liptako-Gourma Integrated Development Authority
1971	African Cultural Institute
1971	African Data Processing Institute
1971	Commission for Controlling the Desert Locust in Northwest Africa
1971	Federation of Arab Republics
1971	Institute for Training and Demographic Research
1971	International Red Locust Control Organization for Central and Southern Africa
1971	Trans-African Highway Coordinating Commission [A]
1971.06	Trans-African Highway Coordinating Commission [B]
1971.08	FAO Committee for Controlling the Deasrt Locust in Northwest Africa
1972	African Development Fund
1972	African Institute of Informatics
1972	African Society for the Development of the Millet-and-Sorghum-based Food Industry
1972	Central African Monetary Union
1972	Union of African Railways
1972.01	Regional Centre for Training in Aerial Surveys
1972.03	Organization for the Development of the Senegal River
1972.05	West African Health Community
1973	Gambia River Development Organization
1973	Organization for the Development of Tourism in Africa
1973	Pan-African Telecommunications Network
1973	West African Economic Community Development Fund
1973.03	Southern Africa Regional Tourism Council
1973.09	African Bureau of Educational Sciences
1973.09	Permanent Interstate Drought Control Committee for the Sahel
1973.10	Mano River Union
1973.11	Arab Bank for Economic Development in Africa
1973.11	West African Development Bank

1974	Commonwealth Regional Health Secretariat for East, Central and Southern Africa
1974	Community Development Fund
1974	Conference of African Ministers of Culture
1974	Coordinating Committee of the Dakar-Ndjamena Highway
1974	Inter-African Film Production Centre
1974	International Livestock Centre for Africa
1974	Rand Monetary Area
1974.01	Association of African Trade Promotion Organizations
1974.01	Coordinating Committee of the Lagos-Nouakchott Highway
1974.08	Energy Organization of the Great Lakes Countries
1975	African and Mauritian Bilingual Institute
1975	African and Mauritian Institute of Statistics and Applied Economics
1975	African Center for Monetary Studies
1975	Association of African Development Finance Institutions
1975	Club des Amis du Sahel
1975	Eastern and Southern African Mineral Resources Development Centre
1975	Inter-State Body for Lakes Tanganyika/Kivu Basin
1975	Regional Centre for Services in Surveying, Mapping and Remote Sensing
1975.02	Lomé I
1975.05	African Timber Organization
1975.05	Economic Community of West African States
1975.05	Lakes Tanganyika and Kivu Basin Commission
1975.05	Ministerial Conference of West and Central African States on Maritime Transport
1975.05	Organization of Wood Producing and Exporting African Countries
1975.06	African Caribbean Pacific Group
1975.06	West African Clearing House
1975.10	African and Mauritian School of Architecture and Urbanism
1975.12	African and Mauritian Advanced Training Centre for Administrative Personnel
1976	African Parliament's Union
1976	African Reinsurance Corporation
1976	Communauté Financiere Africaine
1976	Union of African Parliaments
1976.09	Economic Community of the Great Lakes Countries
1976.11	ECOWAS Fund
1976.12	Industrial Property Organization for English-Speaking Africa
1977	African Centre for Applied Research and Training in Social Development
1977	Association of Regional and Sub-Regional Institutions for Development Financing in W. Africa
1977	Development Bank of the Great Lakes States
1977	Fund for Solidarity and Economic Development
1977	Network of Educational Innovation for Development in Africa
1977.01	African Regional Organization for Standardisation
1977.03	Standing Commission of the OAU and the League of Arab States
1977.05	Association of African Industrial Technology Organizations

1977.08	Organization for the Management and Development of the Kagera River Basin
1977.11	African Regional Centre for Technology
1977.12	Solidarity and Intervention Fund
1978	African Centre for Monetary Studies
1978	African Solidarity Fund
1978	West African Insurance Consultative Association
1978	West African Insurance Institute
1978.02	Pan-African Telecommunications Union
1979	Central African Clearing House
1979	Commission on African Animal Trypanosomiasis
1979	Concerted Action for the Development of Africa
1979	Eastern African Centre for Research on Oral Traditions and African National Languages
1979.03	Constellation of South African States
1979.10	African Accounting Council
1979.10	Lomé II
1979.11	Regional Centre for Solar Energy Research and Development
1980	Afro-Islamic Co-ordinating Council
1980	Association of African Tax Administrators
1980	Southern African Transport and Communications Commission
1980.01	Pan-African Postal Union
1980.04	Southern African Development Coordination Conference
1980.05	African Common Market
1981	Conference of Ministers of African Least Developed Countries
1981.10	Economic Community of Central African States
1981.11	Preferential Trade Area for Eastern and Southern Africa
1981.12	Eastern and Southern African Trade and Development Bank
1981.12	Preferential Exchange Zone
1982	Association of Market Production, European Community/African-Caribbean-Pacific States
1982	Multilateral Development Council
1982	Regional Trust Fund for the Protection of West and Central Africa
1982	Southern African Development Bank
1982.01	Senegambia, Union of
1982.12	Indian Ocean Commission
1982.12	Shelter Afrique
1983	Commercial and Development Bank for Eastern and Southern Africa
1983	Eastern and Southern African Compensation Office
1983.05	Pan-African News Agency
1984	African Council for the Training and Promotion of Health Sciences, Teachers and Specialists
1984.08	Arab-African Union of States
1984.09	Libyan-Moroccan Union
1985.12	Lomé III
1986	Inter-Governmental Authority on Drought and Development

APPENDIX 4

COUNTRIES AND NUMBER OF MEMBERSHIPS
(By Number of Memberships)

Senegal	111	Zambia	46
Niger	109	Burundi	46
Burkina Fasso	105	Sudan	44
Cameroon	97	Gambia	44
Congo	96	Morocco	41
Benin	96	Madagascar	41
Central African Rep	92	Algeria	41
Gabon	91	Tunisia	40
Ivory Coast	90	Libya	40
Togo	88	Egypt	40
Mali	86	Malawi	37
Chad	79	Swaziland	35
Tanzania	77	Lesotho	32
Kenya	74	Botswana	31
Mauritania	73	Zimbabwe	25
Uganda	72	Guinea-Bissau	24
Zaire	70	Equatorial Guinea	23
Guinea	70	Angola	22
Ghana	65	Djibouti	20
Rwanda	63	Comoros	18
Nigeria	60	Seychelles	16
Somalia	54	Cape Verde	16
Liberia	52	Mozambique	15
Sierra Leone	51	Sao Tome Principe	14
Mauritius	48	South Africa	10
Ethiopia	47	Nambia	2

COUNTRIES AND NUMBER OF MEMBERSHIPS
(In Alphabetical Order)

Algeria	41	Malawi	37
Angola	22	Mali	86
Benin	96	Mauritania	73
Botswana	31	Mauritius	48
Burundi	46	Morocco	41
Cameroon	97	Mozambique	15
Cape Verde	16	Nambia	2
Central African Rep	92	Niger	109
Chad	79	Nigeria	60
Comoros	18	Rwanda	63
Congo	96	Sao Tome Principal	14
Djibouti	20	Senegal	111
Egypt	40	Seychelles	16
Equatorial Guinea	23	Sierra Leone	51
Ethiopia	47	Somalia	54
Gabon	91	South Africa	10
Gambia	44	Sudan	44
Ghana	65	Swaziland	35
Guinea	70	Tanzania	77
Guinea-Bissau	24	Togo	88
Ivory Coast	90	Tunisia	40
Kenya	74	Uganda	72
Lesotho	32	Upper Volta	105
Liberia	52	Zaire	70
Libya	40	Zambia	46
Madagascar	41	Zimbabwe	25

APPENDIX 5

INDIVIDUAL COUNTRY MEMBERSHIPS

ALGERIA

African Accounting Council
African Agricultural Credit Commission
African Bureau of Educational Sciences
African Center for Administrative Training and Research for Development
African Center for Monetary Studies
African Centre for Applied Research and Training in Social Development
African Centre for Monetary Studies
African Civil Aviation Commission
African Commission on Agricultural Statistics
African Development Bank
African Forestry Commission
African Regional Centre for Technology
African Reinsurance Corporation
Afro-Asian Rural Reconstruction Organization
Association of African Central Banks
Association of African Development Finance Institutions
Association of African Trade Promotion Organizations
Brazzaville Group
Casablanca Group
Center for Industrial Studies of the Maghreb
Commission for Controlling the Desert Locust in Northwest Africa
Communauté
Conference of Independent African States
Coordination Commission for Liberation Movements of Africa
Economic Commission for Africa-UN
FAO Committee for Controlling the Desert Locust in Northwest Africa
Institute for Training and Demographic Research
Inter-African Bureau for Animal Resources
Joint FAO/WHO/OAU Regional Food and Nutrition Commission for Africa
Maghreb Regional Economic Organization
Maghrebin Charter
Organization of African and Malagasy States
Organization of African Unity
Pan-African News Agency
Pan-African Postal Union
Pan-African Telecommunications Union
Permanent Consultative Committee of the Maghreb
Trans-African Highway Coordinating Commission [A]
Union of African Parliaments
Union of African Railways
Union of National Radio and Television Broadcasters

A GUIDE TO AFRICAN INTERNATIONAL ORGANIZATIONS

ANGOLA

    African Accounting Council
    African Bureau of Educational Sciences
    African Centre for Applied Research and Training in Social Development
    African Civil Aviation Commission
    African Development Bank
    Conference of African Ministers of Culture
    Economic Community of Central African States
    Front Line African States
    Inter-African Coffee Organization
    Inter-African Bureau for Animal Resources
    Joint FAO/WHO/OAU Regional Food and Nutrition Commission for Africa
    Lomé II
    Ministerial Conference of West and Central African States on Maritime Transport
    Non-aligned Countries Working Group on Southern Africa
    Organization of African Unity
    Pan-African News Agency
    Pan-African Postal Union
    Pan-African Telecommunications Union
    Southern African Development Coordination Conference
    Southern African Transport and Communications Commission
    Union of African Railways
    Union of National Radio and Television Broadcasters

BENIN

    African Accounting Council
    African and Malagasy Common Organization
    African and Malagasy Council on High Education
    African Bureau of Educational Sciences
    African Caribbean Pacific Group
    African Centre for Applied Research and Training in Social Development
    African Centre for Monetary Studies
    African Civil Aviation Commission
    African Commission on Agricultural Statistics
    African Cultural Institute
    African Data Processing Institute
    African Development Bank
    African Forestry Commission
    African Intellectual Property Organization
    African Malagasy Union
    African Patent Document and Information Centre
    African Posts and Telecommunications Union
    African Regional Centre for Technology
    African Reinsurance Corporation

African Solidarity Fund
African Union of National Radio and Television Broadcasting
African and Malagasy Bureau of Legislative Studies
African and Malagasy Coffee Organisation
African and Malagasy Common Organization
African and Malagasy Industrial Property Office
African and Malagasy Institite of Bilingualism
African and Malagasy Institute of Applied Economics and Statistics
African and Malagasy Office of Industrial Property
African and Malagasy Organization of Economic Cooperation
African and Malagasy Sugar Agreement
African and Malagasy Union
African and Malagasy Union of Economic Cooperation
African and Malagasy Union of Posts and Telecommunications
African and Mauritian Advanced Training Centre for Administrative Personnel
African and Mauritian School of Architecture and Urbanism
African and Mauritian Union of Development Banks
Afro-Malagasy Economic Cooperation Organization
Agency for the Safety of Air Navigation in Africa and Madagascar
Air Afrique
Architectural Institute
Association of African Development Finance Institutions
Benin-Niger Common Organization
Cattle and Meat Economic Community of the Council of the Entente States Organization
Central Bank of West African States
Centre for Linguistic and Historical Studies through Oral Traditions
Centre for Training of Cadres
Commission for Technical Cooperation in Africa South of the Sahara
Commission on African Animal Trypanosomiasis
Communauté
Communauté Financiere Africaine
Conference of Administrators of Posts and Telecommunications of West Africa
Conference of African Ministers of Culture
Conseil de l'Entente
Council on Administration of Information
Customs Union of West African States
ECOWAS Fund
Economic Commission for Africa
Economic Community of West African States
Franc Zone
French West Africa
Institute for Training and Demographic Research
Institute of Sciences and Veterinary Medicine
Inter-African Bureau for Animal Resources
Inter-African Coffee Organization
Inter-African Committee on Hydraulic Studies
Inter-African Travel Company

Inter-State School of Rural Equipment Engineers
Joint Anti-Locust and Anti-Aviarian Organization
Joint FAO/WHO/OAU Regional Food and Nutrition Commission for Africa
Lomé II
Mali Federation
Ministerial Conference of West and Central African States on Maritime Transport
Monetary Union of the States of West Africa
Monrovia Group
Mutual Aid and Loan Guarantee Fund of the Council of the Entente States
Niger Basin Authority
Niger River Commission
Office for Research on African Food and Nutrition
Organization for Coordination and Cooperation in the Control of Major Endemic Diseases
Organization for Meat Marketing
Organization for the Development of African Tourism
Organization for the Development of Tourism in Africa
Organization of African Unity
Pan-African Postal Union
Pan-African Telecommunications Union
Regional Centre for Training in Aerial Surveys
Road Transport Committee of the Entente Council
Union of National Radio and Television Broadcasters
West African Common Market
West Africa Rice Development Association
West African Customs Union
West African Development Bank
West African Economic Community
West African Monetary Union
Yaoundé I (Association)
Yaoundé II (Association)

BOTSWANA

African Bureau of Educational Sciences
African Caribbean Pacific Group
African Commission on Agricultural Statistics
African Development Bank
African Forestry Commission
African Postal and Telecommunications Union
Architectural Institute
Commission on African Animal Trypanosomiasis
Commonwealth
Commonwealth Regional Health Secretariat for East, Central and Southern Africa
Constellation of South African States
Customs Union Agreement

APPENDIX 5

Eastern and Southern African Mineral Resources Development Centre
Economic Commission for Africa
Front Line African States
High Commission Territories
Inter-African Bureau for Animal Resources
Joint FAO/WHO/OAU Regional Food and Nutrition Commission for Africa
Lomé II
Non-aligned Countries Working Group on Southern Africa
Organization of African Unity
Pan-African Postal Union
Pan-African Telecommunications Union
Rand Monetary Area
Science Education Programme for Africa
South African Customs Union
Southern African Customs Union
Southern African Development Coordination Conference
Southern African Regional Commission for the Consevation and Utilisation of the Soil
Southern African Transport and Communications Commission
Union of National Radio and Television Broadcasters

BURUNDI

African Accounting Council
African Bureau of Educational Sciences
African Caribbean Pacific Group
African Center for Monetary Studies
African Centre for Applied Research and Training in Social Development
African Civil Aviation Commission
African Commission on Agricultural Statistics
African Development Bank
African Forestry Commission
African Postal Union
African Postal and Telecommunications Union
African Regional Centre for Technology
African Reinsurance Corporation
African Solidarity Fund
Association of African Central Banks
Association of African Development Finance Institutions
Association of African Trade Promotion Organizations
Association of Market Production, European Community/African-Caribbean-Pacific States
Commercial and Development Bank for Eastern and Southern Africa
Commission on African Animal Trypanosomiasis
Common Organization for Economic Cooperation in Central Africa
Conference of East and Central African States

Development Bank of the Great Lakes States
Eastern African Centre for Research on Oral Traditions and African National Languages
Economic Commission for Africa
Economic Community of Central African States
Economic Community of the Great Lakes Countries
Energy Organization of the Great Lakes Countries
Institute for Training and Demographic Research
Inter-African Bureau for Animal Resources
Inter-African Coffee Organization
Inter-State Body for Lakes Tanganyika/Kivu Basin
Joint FAO/WHO/OAU Regional Food and Nutrition Commission for Africa
Lakes Tanganyika and Kivu Basin Commission
Lomé II
Organization for the Management and Development of the Kagera River Basin
Organization of African Unity
Pan-African Movement for Eastern and Central Africa
Pan-African News Agency
Pan-African Postal Union
Pan-African Telecommunications Union
Preferential Exchange Zone
Shelter Afrique
Trans-East African Highway Authority
Yaoundé I (Association)
Yaoundé II (Association)

CAMEROON

African and Malagasy Common Organization
African and Malagasy Council on High Education
African Bureau of Educational Sciences
African Caribbean Pacific Group
African Center for Administrative Training and Research for Development
African Center for Monetary Studies
African Centre for Applied Research and Training in Social Development
African Centre for Monetary Studies
African Civil Aviation Commission
African Commission on Agricultural Statistics
African Data P.ocessing Institute
African Development Bank
African Forestry Commission
African Intellectual Property Organization
African Malagasy Union
African Patent Document and Information Centre
African Regional Centre for Technology
African Regional Organization for Standardisation

APPENDIX 5

African Reinsurance Corporation
African Timber Organization
African Union of National Radio and Television Broadcasting
African and Malagasy Bureau of Legislative Studies
African and Malagasy Coffee Organisation
African and Malagasy Common Organization
African and Malagasy Industrial Property Office
African and Malagasy Institite of Bilingualism
African and Malagasy Institute of Applied Economics and Statistics
African and Malagasy Office of Industrial Property
African and Malagasy Organization of Economic Cooperation
African and Malagasy Sugar Agreement
African and Malagasy Union
African and Malagasy Union of Economic Cooperation
African and Malagasy Union of Posts and Telecommunications
African and Mauritian Union of Development Banks
Afro-Malagasy Economic Cooperation Organization
Agency for the Safety of Air Navigation in Africa and Madagascar
Air Afrique
Association of African Central Banks
Association of African Development Finance Institutions
Association of African Trade Promotion Organizations
Association of Market Production, European Community/African-Caribbean-Pacific States
Bank of Central African States
Central African Clearing House
Central African Customs and Economic Union
Central African Monetary Union
Central African States Development Bank
Central Bank of the States of Equatorial Africa and Cameroun
Centre for Linguistic and Historical Studies through Oral Traditions
Centre for Training of Cadres
Cocoa Producers Alliance
Commission for Technical Cooperation in Africa South of the Sahara
Commission on African Animal Trypanosomiasis
Communauté
Communauté Financiere Africaine
Conference of Independent African States
Coordinating Committee of the Dakar-Ndjamena Highway
Coordination Commission for Liberation Movements of Africa
Council on Administration of Information
Customs and Economic Union of Central Africa
Economic Commission for Africa
Economic Community of Central African States
Equatorial Customs Union
Equatorial Monetary Union
Franc Zone
Independent African States

Institute for Training and Demographic Research
Institute of Sciences and Veterinary Medicine
Inter-African Bureau for Animal Resources
Inter-African Coffee Organization
Inter-African Committee on Hydraulic Studies
Inter-African Travel Company
Inter-State School of Rural Equipment Engineers
International African Migratory Locust Organization
Joint Anti-Locust and Anti-Aviarian Organization
Joint FAO/WHO/OAU Regional Food and Nutrition Commission for Africa
Lake Chad Basin Commission
Lomé II
Ministerial Conference of West and Central African States on Maritime Transport
Monetary Union of Equatorial Africa and Cameroun
Monrovia Group
Niger Basin Authority
Organization for Meat Marketing
Organization for the Coordination in Control of Endemic Diseases in Central Africa
Organization for the Development of African Tourism
Organization for the Development of Tourism in Africa
Organization of African Unity
Organization of Wood Producing and Exporting African Countries
Pan-African News Agency
Pan-African Postal Union
Pan-African Telecommunications Union
Trans-African Highway Coordinating Commission [B]
Union of African Parliaments
Union of African Railways
Union of National Radio and Television Broadcasters
West Africa Rice Development Association
Yaoundé I (Association)
Yaoundé II (Association)

CAPE VERDE

African Caribbean Pacific Group
African Development Bank
Centre for Linguistic and Historical Studies through Oral Traditions
Club des Amis du Sahel
ECOWAS Fund
Economic Commission for Africa
Economic Community of West African States
Inter-African Bureau for Animal Resources
Joint FAO/WHO/OAU Regional Food and Nutrition Commission for Africa
Lomé II
Ministerial Conference of West and Central African States on Maritime Transport

APPENDIX 5

Organization of African Unity
Pan-African News Agency
Pan-African Telecommunications Union
Permanent Interstate Drought Control Committee for the Sahel
Union of National Radio and Television Broadcasters

CENTRAL AFRICAN REPUBLIC

African Accounting Council
African and Malagasy Common Organization
African and Malagasy Council on High Education
African Bureau of Educational Sciences
African Caribbean Pacific Group
African Center for Administrative Training and Research for Development
African Centre for Applied Research and Training in Social Development
African Civil Aviation Commission
African Commission on Agricultural Statistics
African Cultural Institute
African Data Processing Institute
African Development Bank
African Forestry Commission
African Intellectual Property Organization
African Malagasy Union
African Patent Document and Information Centre
African Posts and Telecommunications Union
African Reinsurance Corporation
African Solidarity Fund
African Timber Organization
African Union of National Radio and Television Broadcasting
African and Malagasy Bureau of Legislative Studies
African and Malagasy Coffee Organisation
African and Malagasy Common Organization
African and Malagasy Industrial Property Office
African and Malagasy Institite of Bilingualism
African and Malagasy Institute of Applied Economics and Statistics
African and Malagasy Office of Industrial Property
African and Malagasy Organization of Economic Cooperation
African and Malagasy Sugar Agreement
African and Malagasy Union
African and Malagasy Union of Posts and Telecommunications
African and Mauritian Advanced Training Centre for Administrative Personnel
African and Mauritian School of Architecture and Urbanism
African and Mauritian Union of Development Banks
Afro-Malagasy Economic Cooperation Organization
Agency for the Safety of Air Navigation in Africa and Madagascar
Air Afrique

Architectural Institute
Association of African Trade Promotion Organizations
Bank of Central African States
Central African Clearing House
Central African Customs and Economic Union
Central African Economic Union
Central African Federation for Higher Education
Central African Monetary Union
Central African States Development Bank
Central Bank of the States of Equatorial Africa and Cameroun
Centre for Training of Cadres
Commission for Technical Cooperation in Africa South of the Sahara
Commission on African Animal Trypanosomiasis
Communauté
Communauté Financiere Africaine
Conference of African Ministers of Culture
Conference of East and Central African States
Conference of Heads of State of Equatorial Africa
Council on Administration of Information
Customs and Economic Union of Central Africa
Economic Commission for Africa
Economic Community of Central African States
Equatorial Conference of Heads of State
Equatorial Customs Union
Franc Zone
French Equatorial Africa
Higher Education Foundation in Central Africa
Institute for Training and Demographic Research
Institute of Sciences and Veterinary Medicine
Inter-African Bureau for Animal Resources
Inter-African Coffee Organization
Inter-African Travel Company
Inter-State School of Rural Equipment Engineers
International African Migratory Locust Organization
Joint FAO/WHO/OAU Regional Food and Nutrition Commission for Africa
Lomé II
Ministerial Conference of West and Central African States on Maritime Transport
Monetary Union of Equatorial Africa and Cameroun
Monrovia Group
Organization for Meat Marketing
Organization for the Coordination in Control of Endemic Diseases in Central Africa
Organization for the Development of African Tourism
Organization for the Development of Tourism in Africa
Organization of African Unity
Organization of Wood Producing and Exporting African Countries
Pan-African Postal Union
Pan-African Telecommunications Union
Trans-African Highway Coordinating Commission [B]

APPENDIX 5

Transequatorial Communications Agency
Union of Central African Republics
Union of the Republics of Central Africa
United States of Central Africa
Yaoundé I (Association)
Yaoundé II (Association)

CHAD

African Bureau of Educational Sciences
African Caribbean Pacific Group
African Civil Aviation Commission
African Commission on Agricultural Statistics
African Cultural Institute
African Data Processing Institute
African Development Bank
African Forestry Commission
African Intellectual Property Organization
African Patent Document and Information Centre
African Posts and Telecommunications Union
African Reinsurance Corporation
African Solidarity Fund
African Union of National Radio and Television Broadcasting
African and Malagasy Industrial Property Office
African and Malagasy Organization of Economic Cooperation
African and Malagasy Sugar Agreement
African and Malagasy Union
African and Malagasy Union of Economic Cooperation
African and Mauritian Union of Development Banks
Afro-Malagasy Economic Cooperation Organization
Agency for the Safety of Air Navigation in Africa and Madagascar
Air Afrique
Association of African Development Finance Institutions
Bank of Central African States
Central African Clearing House
Central African Customs and Economic Union
Central African Federation for Higher Education
Central African Monetary Union
Central African States Development Bank
Central Bank of the States of Equatorial Africa and Cameroun
Centre for Linguistic and Historical Studies through Oral Traditions
Chad Basin Commission
Club des Amis du Sahel
Commission for Technical Cooperation in Africa South of the Sahara
Commission on African Animal Trypanosomiasis
Common Organization for the Control of Dessert Locust and Bird Pests

211

Communauté
Conference of African Ministers of Culture
Conference of East and Central African States
Conference of Heads of State of Equatorial Africa
Coordinating Committee of the Dakar-Ndjamena Highway
Economic Commission for Africa
Economic Community of Central African States
Equatorial Conference of Heads of State
Equatorial Customs Union
Franc Zone
French Equatorial Africa
Higher Education Foundation in Central Africa
Institute for Training and Demographic Research
Institute of Sciences and Veterinary Medicine
Inter-African Bureau for Animal Resources
Inter-African Committee on Hydraulic Studies
Inter-African Travel Company
Inter-State School of Rural Equipment Engineers
International African Migratory Locust Organization
Joint Anti-Locust and Anti-Aviarian Organization
Lake Chad Basin Commission
Lomé II
Ministerial Conference of West and Central African States on Maritime Transport
Monetary Union of Equatorial Africa and Cameroun
Monrovia Group
Niger Basin Authority
Non-aligned Countries Working Group on Southern Africa
Organization for the Coordination in Control of Endemic Diseases in Central Africa
Organization for the Development of African Tourism
Organization of African Unity
Pan-African Postal Union
Pan-African Telecommunications Union
Permanent Interstate Drought Control Committee for the Sahel
Transequatorial Communications Agency
Union of Central African Republics
Union of Central African States
Union of National Radio and Television Broadcasters
Union of the Republics of Central Africa
United States of Central Africa
West Africa Rice Development Association
Yaoundé I (Association)
Yaoundé II (Association)

APPENDIX 5

COMOROS

    African Caribbean Pacific Group
    African Development Bank
    Association of African Development Finance Institutions
    Commercial and Development Bank for Eastern and Southern Africa
    Conference of African Ministers of Culture
    Eastern and Southern African Trade and Development Bank
    Economic Commission for Africa
    Franc Zone
    Institute for Training and Demographic Research
    Inter-African Bureau for Animal Resources
    Joint FAO/WHO/OAU Regional Food and Nutrition Commission for Africa
    Lomé II
    Organization of African Unity
    Pan-African Postal Union
    Pan-African Telecommunications Union
    Preferential Exchange Zone
    Regional Centre for Services in Surveying, Mapping and Remote Sensing
    Union of National Radio and Television Broadcasters

CONGO

    African Accounting Council
    African and Malagasy Common Organization
    African and Malagasy Council on High Education
    African Agricultural Credit Commission
    African Bureau of Educational Sciences
    African Caribbean Pacific Group
    African Centre for Monetary Studies
    African Civil Aviation Commission
    African Commission on Agricultural Statistics
    African Cultural Institute
    African Data Processing Institute
    African Development Bank
    African Forestry Commission
    African Intellectual Property Organization
    African Malagasy Union
    African Patent Document and Information Centre
    African Posts and Telecommunications Union
    African Reinsurance Corporation
    African Timber Organization
    African Union of National Radio and Television Broadcasting
    African and Malagasy Bureau of Legislative Studies
    African and Malagasy Coffee Organisation
    African and Malagasy Common Organization

African and Malagasy Industrial Property Office
African and Malagasy Institite of Bilingualism
African and Malagasy Institute of Applied Economics and Statistics
African and Malagasy Office of Industrial Property
African and Malagasy Organization of Economic Cooperation
African and Malagasy Sugar Agreement
African and Malagasy Union
African and Malagasy Union of Economic Cooperation
African and Malagasy Union of Posts and Telecommunications
African and Mauritian Union of Development Banks
Afro-Malagasy Economic Cooperation Organization
Agency for the Safety of Air Navigation in Africa and Madagascar
Air Afrique
Architectural Institute
Association of African Development Finance Institutions
Bank of Central African States
Central African Clearing House
Central African Customs and Economic Union
Central African Economic Union
Central African Federation for Higher Education
Central African Monetary Union
Central African States Development Bank
Central Bank of the States of Equatorial Africa and Cameroun
Centre for Training of Cadres
Commission for Technical Cooperation in Africa South of the Sahara
Commission on African Animal Trypanosomiasis
Communauté
Communauté Financiere Africaine
Conference of African Ministers of Culture
Conference of East and Central African States
Conference of Heads of State of Equatorial Africa
Coordination Commission for Liberation Movements of Africa
Council on Administration of Information
Customs and Economic Union of Central Africa
Economic Commission for Africa
Economic Community of Central African States
Equatorial Conference of Heads of State
Equatorial Customs Union
Equatorial Monetary Union
Franc Zone
French Equatorial Africa
Higher Education Foundation in Central Africa
Institute for Training and Demographic Research
Institute of Sciences and Veterinary Medicine
Inter-African Bureau for Animal Resources
Inter-African Coffee Organization
Inter-African Committee on Hydraulic Studies
Inter-African Travel Company

APPENDIX 5

    Inter-State School of Rural Equipment Engineers
    International African Migratory Locust Organization
    Joint FAO/WHO/OAU Regional Food and Nutrition Commission for Africa
    Lomé II
    Ministerial Conference of West and Central African States on Maritime Transport
    Monetary Union of Equatorial Africa and Cameroun
    Monrovia Group
    Organization for Meat Marketing
    Organization for the Coordination in Control of Endemic Diseases in Central Africa
    Organization for the Development of African Tourism
    Organization for the Development of Tourism in Africa
    Organization of African Unity
    Organization of Wood Producing and Exporting African Countries
    Pan-African News Agency
    Pan-African Postal Union
    Pan-African Telecommunications Union
    Shelter Afrique
    Trans-East African Highway Authority
    Transequatorial Communications Agency
    Union of African Railways
    Union of Central African Republics
    Union of National Radio and Television Broadcasters
    Union of the Republics of Central Africa
    Yaoundé I (Association)
    Yaoundé II (Association)

DJIBOUTI

    African Caribbean Pacific Group
    African Development Bank
    Commercial and Development Bank for Eastern and Southern Africa
    Desert Locust Control Organization for Eastern Africa
    Eastern and Southern African Mineral Resources Development Centre
    Eastern and Southern African Trade and Development Bank
    Economic Commission for Africa
    Institute for Training and Demographic Research
    Inter-African Bureau for Animal Resources
    Inter-Governmental Authority on Drought and Development
    Intergovernmental Authority on Development and Desertification
    Joint FAO/WHO/OAU Regional Food and Nutrition Commission for Africa
    Lomé II
    Organization of African Unity
    Pan-African Telecommunications Union
    Preferential Exchange Zone
    Shelter Afrique
    Trans-East African Highway Authority

Union of African Railways
Union of National Radio and Television Broadcasters

EGYPT

African Bureau of Educational Sciences
African Center for Administrative Training and Research for Development
African Center for Monetary Studies
African Centre for Applied Research and Training in Social Development
African Centre for Monetary Studies
African Civil Aviation Commission
African Development Bank
African Postal Union
African Regional Centre for Technology
African Regional Organization for Standardisation
African Reinsurance Corporation
African Union of National Radio and Television Broadcasting
Afro-Asian Rural Reconstruction Organization
Association of African Central Banks
Association of African Development Finance Institutions
Association of African Trade Promotion Organizations
Brazzaville Group
Casablanca Group
Commission on African Animal Trypanosomiasis
Conference of Independent African States
Coordination Commission for Liberation Movements of Africa
Economic Commission for Africa
Federation of Arab Republics
Inter-African Bureau for Animal Resources
Independent African States
Joint FAO/WHO/OAU Regional Food and Nutrition Commission for Africa
Organization of African and Malagasy States
Organization of African Unity
Pan-African News Agency
Pan-African Postal Union
Pan-African Telecommunications Union
Shelter Afrique
Trans-East African Highway Authority
UAR-Libyan-Sudanese Economic Integration
Union of African Parliaments
Union of African Railways
Union of Independent African States
Union of National Radio and Television Broadcasters
Union of Nile States
United Arab Republic

APPENDIX 5

EQUATORIAL GUINEA

    African Accounting Council
    African Caribbean Pacific Group
    African Centre for Applied Research and Training in Social Development
    African Centre for Monetary Studies
    African Development Bank
    African Regional Centre for Technology
    African Timber Organization
    Central African Customs and Economic Union
    Conference of East and Central African States
    Customs and Economic Union of Central Africa
    Economic Commission for Africa
    Economic Community of Central African States
    Franc Zone
    Inter-African Bureau for Animal Resources
    Inter-African Coffee Organization
    Joint FAO/WHO/OAU Regional Food and Nutrition Commission for Africa
    Lomé II
    Ministerial Conference of West and Central African States on Maritime Transport
    Organization for the Coordination in Control of Endemic Diseases in Central Africa
    Organization of African Unity
    Organization of Wood Producing and Exporting African Countries
    Pan-African Postal Union
    Pan-African Telecommunications Union

ETHIOPIA

    African Bureau of Educational Sciences
    African Caribbean Pacific Group
    African Center for Monetary Studies
    African Centre for Applied Research and Training in Social Development
    African Centre for Monetary Studies
    African Civil Aviation Commission
    African Commission on Agricultural Statistics
    African Development Bank
    African Forestry Commission
    African Regional Centre for Technology
    African Regional Organization for Standardisation
    African Reinsurance Corporation
    African Union of National Radio and Television Broadcasting
    Afro-Asian Rural Reconstruction Organization
    Association of African Central Banks
    Association of African Development Finance Institutions
    Association of African Trade Promotion Organizations
    Commercial and Development Bank for Eastern and Southern Africa

Commission on African Animal Trypanosomiasis
Conference of East and Central African States
Conference of Independent African States
Coordination Commission for Liberation Movements of Africa
Desert Locust Control Organization for Eastern Africa
Eastern African Centre for Research on Oral Traditions and African National Languages
Eastern and Southern African Trade and Development Bank
Economic Commission for Africa
Independent African States
Inter-African Bureau for Animal Resources
Inter-African Coffee Organization
Inter-Governmental Authority on Drought and Development
Intergovernmental Authority on Development and Desertification
Joint FAO/WHO/OAU Regional Food and Nutrition Commission for Africa
Lomé II
Monrovia Group
Organization of African Unity
Organization of African and Malagasy States
Pan-African Freedom Movements for East, Central and Southern Africa
Pan-African Movement for Eastern and Central Africa
Pan-African News Agency
Pan-African Postal Union
Pan-African Telecommunications Union
Preferential Exchange Zone
Science Education Programme for Africa
Trans-East African Highway Authority
Union of African Railways
Union of Independent African States
Union of National Radio and Television Broadcasters

GABON

African Accounting Council
African and Malagasy Common Organization
African and Malagasy Council on High Education
African Bureau of Educational Sciences
African Caribbean Pacific Group
African Centre for Monetary Studies
African Civil Aviation Commission
African Commission on Agricultural Statistics
African Cultural Institute
African Data Processing Institute
African Development Bank
African Forestry Commission
African Intellectual Property Organization

APPENDIX 5

African Malagasy Union
African Patent Document and Information Centre
African Reinsurance Corporation
African Solidarity Fund
African Timber Organization
African Union of National Radio and Television Broadcasting
African and Malagasy Bureau of Legislative Studies
African and Malagasy Coffee Organisation
African and Malagasy Common Organization
African and Malagasy Industrial Property Office
African and Malagasy Institite of Bilingualism
African and Malagasy Institute of Applied Economics and Statistics
African and Malagasy Office of Industrial Property
African and Malagasy Organization of Economic Cooperation
African and Malagasy Sugar Agreement
African and Malagasy Union
African and Malagasy Union of Economic Cooperation
African and Malagasy Union of Posts and Telecommunications
African and Mauritian Advanced Training Centre for Administrative Personnel
African and Mauritian School of Architecture and Urbanism
African and Mauritian Union of Development Banks
Afro-Malagasy Economic Cooperation Organization
Agency for the Safety of Air Navigation in Africa and Madagascar
Air Afrique
Architectural Institute
Association of African Central Banks
Association of African Trade Promotion Organizations
Bank of Central African States
Central African Clearing House
Central African Customs and Economic Union
Central African Federation for Higher Education
Central African Monetary Union
Central African States Development Bank
Central Bank of the States of Equatorial Africa and Cameroun
Centre for Training of Cadres
Cocoa Producers Alliance
Commission for Technical Cooperation in Africa South of the Sahara
Commission on African Animal Trypanosomiasis
Communauté
Conference of African Ministers of Culture
Conference of East and Central African States
Conference of Heads of State of Equatorial Africa
Council on Administration of Information
Customs and Economic Union of Central Africa
Economic Commission for Africa
Equatorial Conference of Heads of State
Equatorial Customs Union
Equatorial Monetary Union

219

Franc Zone
French Equatorial Africa
Higher Education Foundation in Central Africa
Institute for Training and Demographic Research
Institute of Sciences and Veterinary Medicine
Inter-African Bureau for Animal Resources
Inter-African Coffee Organization
Inter-African Committee on Hydraulic Studies
Inter-African Travel Company
Inter-State School of Rural Equipment Engineers
Lomé II
Ministerial Conference of West and Central African States on Maritime Transport
Monetary Union of Equatorial Africa and Cameroun
Monrovia Group
Organization for Meat Marketing
Organization for the Coordination in Control of Endemic Diseases in Central Africa
Organization for the Development of African Tourism
Organization for the Development of Tourism in Africa
Organization of African Unity
Organization of Wood Producing and Exporting African Countries
Pan-African News Agency
Pan-African Postal Union
Pan-African Telecommunications Union
Shelter Afrique
Transequatorial Communications Agency
Union of African Parliaments
Union of African Railways
Union of National Radio and Television Broadcasters
Yaoundé I (Association)
Yaoundé II (Association)

GAMBIA

African Accounting Council
African Caribbean Pacific Group
African Center for Monetary Studies
African Centre for Applied Research and Training in Social Development
African Civil Aviation Commission
African Commission on Agricultural Statistics
African Development Bank
African Forestry Commission
African Groundnut Council
African Reinsurance Corporation
Association of African Central Banks
Association of African Development Finance Institutions
British West Africa

APPENDIX 5

Centre for Linguistic and Historical Studies through Oral Traditions
Club des Amis du Sahel
Common Organization for the Control of Dessert Locust and Bird Pests
Commonwealth
ECOWAS Fund
Economic Commission for Africa
Economic Community of West African States
Gambia River Development Organization
Industrial Property Organization for English-Speaking Africa
Inter-African Bureau for Animal Resources
International African Migratory Locust Organization
Joint Anti-Locust and Anti-Aviarian Organization
Joint FAO/WHO/OAU Regional Food and Nutrition Commission for Africa
Lomé II
Ministerial Conference of West and Central African States on Maritime Transport
Organization of African Unity
Pan-African News Agency
Pan-African Postal Union
Pan-African Telecommunications Union
Permanent Interstate Drought Control Committee for the Sahel
Science Education Programme for Africa
Senegambia, Union of
Shelter Afrique
Union of National Radio and Television Broadcasters
West Africa Rice Development Association
West African Clearing House
West African Examinations Council
West African Health Community
West African Insurance Consultative Association
West African Insurance Institute
West African Regional Group

GHANA

African Bureau of Educational Sciences
African Caribbean Pacific Group
African Center for Administrative Training and Research for Development
African Center for Monetary Studies
African Centre for Applied Research and Training in Social Development
African Centre for Monetary Studies
African Civil Aviation Commission
African Commission on Agricultural Statistics
African Cultural Institute
African Development Bank
African Forestry Commission
African Postal Union

African Regional Centre for Technology
African Regional Organization for Standardisation
African Reinsurance Corporation
African Timber Organization
African Union of National Radio and Television Broadcasting
Afro-Asian Rural Reconstruction Organization
Association of African Central Banks
Association of African Development Finance Institutions
Association of African Trade Promotion Organizations
Brazzaville Group
British West Africa
Casablanca Group
Centre for Linguistic and Historical Studies through Oral Traditions
Cocoa Producers Alliance
Commission on African Animal Trypanosomiasis
Commonwealth
Community of Independent African States
Conference of African Ministers of Culture
Conference of Independent African States
Coordination Commission for Liberation Movements of Africa
ECOWAS Fund
Economic Commission for Africa
Economic Community of West African States
Ghana-Guinea Union
Ghana-Guinea-Mali Union
Ghana-Upper Volta Customs Union
Independent African States
Industrial Property Organization for English-Speaking Africa
Inter-African Bureau for Animal Resources
Inter-African Coffee Organization
International African Migratory Locust Organization
Joint FAO/WHO/OAU Regional Food and Nutrition Commission for Africa
Lomé II
Ministerial Conference of West and Central African States on Maritime Transport
Organization of African and Malagasy States
Organization of African Unity
Organization of Wood Producing and Exporting African Countries
Pan-African Postal Union
Pan-African Telecommunications Union
Regional Centre for Training in Aerial Surveys
Union of African Railways
Union of African States
Union of Independent African States
Union of Independent African States
Union of National Radio and Television Broadcasters
West African Common Market
West Africa Rice Development Association
West African Clearing House

APPENDIX 5

West African Examinations Council
West African Health Community
West African Insurance Consultative Association
West African Insurance Institute
West African Regional Group

GUINEA

African Accounting Council
African and Malagasy Common Organization
African and Malagasy Council on High Education
African Caribbean Pacific Group
African Centre for Applied Research and Training in Social Development
African Civil Aviation Commission
African Commission on Agricultural Statistics
African Development Bank
African Forestry Commission
African Postal Union
African Regional Centre for Technology
African Regional Organization for Standardisation
African Reinsurance Corporation
African and Malagasy Bureau of Legislative Studies
African and Malagasy Common Organization
African and Malagasy Institite of Bilingualism
African and Malagasy Institute of Applied Economics and Statistics
African and Malagasy Office of Industrial Property
African and Malagasy Union of Posts and Telecommunications
Architectural Institute
Brazzaville Group
Casablanca Group
Centre for Linguistic and Historical Studies through Oral Traditions
Centre for Training of Cadres
Commission for Technical Cooperation in Africa South of the Sahara
Commission on African Animal Trypanosomiasis
Communauté
Communauté Financiere Africaine
Community of Independent African States
Conference of Independent African States
Coordination Commission for Liberation Movements of Africa
Council on Administration of Information
ECOWAS Fund
Economic Commission for Africa
Economic Community of West African States
Free Trade Area
French West Africa
Gambia River Development Organization

Ghana-Guinea Union
Ghana-Guinea-Mali Union
Independent African States
Institute for Training and Demographic Research
Institute of Sciences and Veterinary Medicine
Inter-African Bureau for Animal Resources
Inter-African Coffee Organization
Joint FAO/WHO/OAU Regional Food and Nutrition Commission for Africa
Lomé II
Mano River Union
Ministerial Conference of West and Central African States on Maritime Transport
Niger Basin Authority
Niger River Commission
Non-aligned Countries Working Group on Southern Africa
Oganization of Senegal River States
Organization for Coordination and Cooperation in the Control of Major Endemic Diseases
Organization for Meat Marketing
Organization for the Development of Tourism in Africa
Organization of African and Malagasy States
Organization of African Unity
Organization of Senegal River States
Pan-African News Agency
Pan-African Postal Union
Pan-African Telecommunications Union
Union of African Railways
Union of African States
Union of Independent African States
Union of Independent African States
Union of National Radio and Television Broadcasters
West Africa Rice Development Association
West African Clearing House
West African Regional Group

GUINEA-BISSAU

African Accounting Council
African Bureau of Educational Sciences
African Caribbean Pacific Group
African Development Bank
African Postal Union
African Regional Organization for Standardisation
African Reinsurance Corporation
Centre for Linguistic and Historical Studies through Oral Traditions
Conference of African Ministers of Culture
ECOWAS Fund

APPENDIX 5

Economic Commission for Africa
Economic Community of West African States
Gambia River Development Organization
Inter-African Bureau for Animal Resources
Joint FAO/WHO/OAU Regional Food and Nutrition Commission for Africa
Lomé II
Ministerial Conference of West and Central African States on Maritime Transport
Organization of African Unity
Pan-African News Agency
Pan-African Telecommunications Union
Permanent Interstate Drought Control Committee for the Sahel
Union of National Radio and Television Broadcasters
West Africa Rice Development Association
West African Clearing House

IVORY COAST

Abidjan-Niger Railway Regime
African Accounting Council
African Agricultural Credit Commission
African Bureau of Educational Sciences
African Caribbean Pacific Group
African Center for Administrative Training and Research for Development
African Centre for Monetary Studies
African Civil Aviation Commission
African Commission on Agricultural Statistics
African Cultural Institute
African Data Processing Institute
African Development Bank
African Forestry Commission
African Intellectual Property Organization
African Malagasy Union
African Patent Document and Information Centre
African Posts and Telecommunications Union
African Regional Organization for Standardisation
African Reinsurance Corporation
African Solidarity Fund
African Timber Organization
African Union of National Radio and Television Broadcasting
African and Malagasy Coffee Organisation
African and Malagasy Industrial Property Office
African and Malagasy Organization of Economic Cooperation
African and Malagasy Sugar Agreement
African and Malagasy Union
African and Malagasy Union of Posts and Telecommunications
African and Mauritian Advanced Training Centre for Administrative Personnel

African and Mauritian School of Architecture and Urbanism
African and Mauritian Union of Development Banks
Afro-Malagasy Economic Cooperation Organization
Agency for the Safety of Air Navigation in Africa and Madagascar
Air Afrique
Association of African Development Finance Institutions
Association of Market Production, European Community/African-Caribbean-Pacific States
Cattle and Meat Economic Community of the Council of the Entente States Organization
Central Bank of West African States
Centre for Linguistic and Historical Studies through Oral Traditions
Cocoa Producers Alliance
Commission for Technical Cooperation in Africa South of the Sahara
Common Organization for the Control of Dessert Locust and Bird Pests
Communauté Financiere Africaine
Community Development Fund
Conference of Administrators of Posts and Telecommunications of West Africa
Conference of African Ministers of Culture
Conseil de l'Entente
Customs Union of West African States
ECOWAS Fund
Economic Commission for Africa
Economic Community of West African States
Franc Zone
Free Trade Area
French West Africa
Institute for Training and Demographic Research
Institute of Sciences and Veterinary Medicine
Inter-African Bureau for Animal Resources
Inter-African Coffee Organization
Inter-African Committee on Hydraulic Studies
Inter-African Travel Company
Inter-State School of Rural Equipment Engineers
International African Migratory Locust Organization
Joint Anti-Locust and Anti-Aviarian Organization
Lomé II
Ministerial Conference of West and Central African States on Maritime Transport
Monetary Union of the States of West Africa
Monrovia Group
Mutual Aid and Loan Guarantee Fund of the Council of the Entente States
Niger Basin Authority
Niger River Commission
Office for Research on African Food and Nutrition
Organization for Coordination and Cooperation in the Control of Major Endemic Diseases
Organization for the Development of African Tourism
Organization of African Unity

APPENDIX 5

Organization of Wood Producing and Exporting African Countries
Pan-African Movement for Eastern and Central Africa
Pan-African Postal Union
Pan-African Telecommunications Union
Regional Centre for Solar Energy Research and Development
Road Transport Committee of the Entente Council
Union of African Parliaments
Union of African Railways
Union of National Radio and Television Broadcasters
West African Common Market
West Africa Rice Development Association
West African Development Bank
West African Economic Community
West African Monetary Union
Yaoundé I (Association)
Yaoundé II (Association)

KENYA

African Bureau of Educational Sciences
African Caribbean Pacific Group
African Center for Monetary Studies
African Centre for Applied Research and Training in Social Development
African Civil Aviation Commission
African Commission on Agricultural Statistics
African Development Bank
African Forestry Commission
African Regional Centre for Technology
African Regional Organization for Standardisation
African Reinsurance Corporation
Afro-Asian Rural Reconstruction Organization
Arusha Convention
Association of African Central Banks
Association of African Development Finance Institutions
Association of African Trade Promotion Organizations
British East Africa
Commercial and Development Bank for Eastern and Southern Africa
Commission on African Animal Trypanosomiasis
Commonwealth
Commonwealth Regional Health Secretariat for East, Central and Southern Africa
Conference of East and Central African States
Desert Locust Control Organization for Eastern Africa
East Africa Airways
East African Agriculture and Forestry Research Organization
East African Common Market
East African Common Services Organization

East African Community
East African Court of Appeal
East African Customs Union
East African Development Bank
East African Examinations Council
East African External Telecommunications Company
East African Federation
East African Freshwater Fisheries Research Organization
East African Harbours Corporation
East African High Commission
East African Industrial Licensing Council
East African Industrial Research Organization
East African Institue of Malaria and Vector-Borne Diseases
East African Institute for Medical Research
East African Marine Fisheries Research Organization
East African Post and Telecommunications Corporation
East African Railways Corporation
East African Railways and Harbours Administration
East African Tourist Travel Association
East African Trypanosomiasis Research Organization
East African Veterinary Research Organization
Eastern and Southern African Mineral Resources Development Centre
Eastern and Southern African Trade and Development Bank
Economic Commission for Africa
Industrial Property Organization for English-Speaking Africa
Inter-African Bureau for Animal Resources
Inter-African Coffee Organization
Inter-Governmental Authority on Drought and Development
Inter-University Committee for East Africa
Intergovernmental Authority on Development and Desertification
Joint FAO/WHO/OAU Regional Food and Nutrition Commission for Africa
Lake Victoria Fisheries Commission
Lomé II
Organization of African Unity
Pan-African Freedom Movements for East, Central and Southern Africa
Pan-African Movement for Eastern and Central Africa
Pan-African Postal Union
Pan-African Telecommunications Union
Preferential Exchange Zone
Regional Centre for Services in Surveying, Mapping and Remote Sensing
Science Education Programme for Africa
Shelter Afrique
Trans-African Highway Coordinating Commission [B]
Trans-East African Highway Authority
Union of African Railways
Union of National Radio and Television Broadcasters
University of East Africa

APPENDIX 5

LESOTHO

    African Accounting Council
    African Caribbean Pacific Group
    African Civil Aviation Commission
    African Commission on Agricultural Statistics
    African Development Bank
    African Forestry Commission
    African Postal and Telecommunications Union
    Association of African Development Finance Institutions
    Commercial and Development Bank for Eastern and Southern Africa
    Commonwealth
    Commonwealth Regional Health Secretariat for East, Central and Southern Africa
    Constellation of South African States
    Customs Union Agreement
    Eastern and Southern African Mineral Resources Development Centre
    Economic Commission for Africa
    High Commission Territories
    Inter-African Bureau for Animal Resources
    Joint FAO/WHO/OAU Regional Food and Nutrition Commission for Africa
    Lomé II
    Organization of African Unity
    Pan-African Telecommunications Union
    Preferential Exchange Zone
    Rand Monetary Area
    Regional Centre for Services in Surveying, Mapping and Remote Sensing
    Science Education Programme for Africa
    South African Customs Union
    Southern African Customs Union
    Southern African Development Coordination Conference
    Southern African Regional Commission for the Consevation and Utilisation of the Soil
    Southern African Transport and Communications Commission
    Trans-African Highway Coordinating Commission [B]
    Union of African Parliaments

LIBERIA

    African Accounting Council
    African Bureau of Educational Sciences
    African Caribbean Pacific Group
    African Centre for Applied Research and Training in Social Development
    African Centre for Monetary Studies
    African Civil Aviation Commission
    African Commission on Agricultural Statistics
    African Development Bank

African Forestry Commission
African Postal Union
African Regional Centre for Technology
African Regional Organization for Standardisation
African Reinsurance Corporation
African Timber Organization
African Union of National Radio and Television Broadcasting
Afro-Asian Rural Reconstruction Organization
Association of African Development Finance Institutions
Association of African Trade Promotion Organizations
Commission for Technical Cooperation in Africa South of the Sahara
Commission on African Animal Trypanosomiasis
Community of Independent African States
Conference of Independent African States
ECOWAS Fund
Economic Commission for Africa
Economic Community of West African States
Independent African States
Inter-African Bureau for Animal Resources
Inter-African Coffee Organization
Lomé II
Mano River Union
Ministerial Conference of West and Central African States on Maritime Transport
Monrovia Group
Non-aligned Countries Working Group on Southern Africa
Organization of African Unity
Organization of African and Malagasy States
Organization of Wood Producing and Exporting African Countries
Pan-African Postal Union
Pan-African Telecommunications Union
Science Education Programme for Africa
Shelter Afrique
Union of African Parliaments
Union of African Railways
Union of Independent African States
Union of National Radio and Television Broadcasters
West African Common Market
West Africa Rice Development Association
West African Clearing House
West African Examinations Council
West African Health Community
West African Insurance Consultative Association
West African Insurance Institute
West African Regional Group

APPENDIX 5

LIBYA

African Accounting Council
African Agricultural Credit Commission
African Center for Administrative Training and Research for Development
African Center for Monetary Studies
African Centre for Applied Research and Training in Social Development
African Civil Aviation Commission
African Development Bank
African Postal Union
African Regional Organization for Standardisation
African Reinsurance Corporation
African Union of National Radio and Television Broadcasting
Afro-Asian Rural Reconstruction Organization
Association of African Central Banks
Association of African Development Finance Institutions
Association of African Trade Promotion Organizations
Brazzaville Group
Casablanca Group
Commission for Controlling the Desert Locust in Northwest Africa
Conference of Administrators of Posts and Telecommunications of West Africa
Conference of Independent African States
Coordination Commission for Liberation Movements of Africa
Economic Commission for Africa
FAO Committee for Controlling the Deasrt Locust in Northwest Africa
Federation of Arab Republics
Free Trade Area
Independent African States
Inter-African Bureau for Animal Resources
Libyan-Moroccan Union
Lomé II
Maghreb Regional Economic Organization
Organization of African and Malagasy States
Organization of African Unity
Organization of African and Malagasy States
Pan-African Postal Union
Pan-African Telecommunications Union
UAR-Libyan-Sudanese Economic Integration
Union of African Railways
Union of Independent African States
Union of National Radio and Television Broadcasters
United Arab Republic

MADAGASCAR

African Accounting Council
African Bureau of Educational Sciences
African Caribbean Pacific Group
African Center for Monetary Studies
African Civil Aviation Commission
African Commission on Agricultural Statistics
African Development Bank
African Forestry Commission
African Intellectual Property Organization
African Malagasy Union
African Timber Organization
African Union of National Radio and Television Broadcasting
African and Malagasy Coffee Organisation
African and Malagasy Industrial Property Office
African and Malagasy Organization of Economic Cooperation
African and Malagasy Sugar Agreement
African and Malagasy Union
African and Malagasy Union of Economic Cooperation
African and Mauritian Union of Development Banks
Afro-Malagasy Economic Cooperation Organization
Agency for the Safety of Air Navigation in Africa and Madagascar
Association of African Central Banks
Association of African Development Finance Institutions
Commission for Technical Cooperation in Africa South of the Sahara
Communauté
Conference of Independent African States
Eastern African Centre for Research on Oral Traditions and African National Languages
Eastern and Southern African Mineral Resources Development Centre
Economic Commission for Africa
Indian Ocean Commission
Institute for Training and Demographic Research
Inter-African Bureau for Animal Resources
Inter-African Coffee Organization
Joint FAO/WHO/OAU Regional Food and Nutrition Commission for Africa
Lomé II
Monrovia Group
Organization of African Unity
Organization of Wood Producing and Exporting African Countries
Pan-African News Agency
Pan-African Postal Union
Pan-African Telecommunications Union

APPENDIX 5

MALAWI

    African Accounting Council
    African Bureau of Educational Sciences
    African Caribbean Pacific Group
    African Centre for Monetary Studies
    African Civil Aviation Commission
    African Commission on Agricultural Statistics
    African Development Bank
    African Forestry Commission
    African Postal and Telecommunications Union
    African Regional Organization for Standardisation
    Association of African Central Banks
    Commercial and Development Bank for Eastern and Southern Africa
    Commission on African Animal Trypanosomiasis
    Commonwealth Regional Health Secretariat for East, Central and Southern Africa
    Conference of East and Central African States
    Eastern and Southern African Mineral Resources Development Centre
    Eastern and Southern African Trade and Development Bank
    Economic Commission for Africa
    Federation of Rhodesia and Nyasaland
    Industrial Property Organization for English-Speaking Africa
    Inter-African Bureau for Animal Resources
    Inter-African Coffee Organization
    Joint FAO/WHO/OAU Regional Food and Nutrition Commission for Africa
    Lomé II
    Organization of African Unity
    Pan-African Telecommunications Union
    Regional Centre for Services in Surveying, Mapping and Remote Sensing
    Shelter Afrique
    Southern Africa Regional Tourism Council
    Southern African Development Coordination Conference
    Southern African Regional Commission for the Consevation and Utilisation of the Soil
    Southern African Transport and Communications Commission
    Trans-East African Highway Authority
    Union of African Railways
    Union of National Radio and Television Broadcasters
    Yaoundé I (Association)
    Yaoundé II (Association)

MALI

    African Accounting Council
    African Bureau of Educational Sciences
    African Caribbean Pacific Group

African Centre for Applied Research and Training in Social Development
African Centre for Monetary Studies
African Civil Aviation Commission
African Commission on Agricultural Statistics
African Development Bank
African Forestry Commission
African Groundnut Council
African Postal Union
African Posts and Telecommunications Union
African Reinsurance Corporation
African Society for the Development of the Millet-and-Sorghum-based Food Industry
African Solidarity Fund
African and Malagasy Union of Posts and Telecommunications
Agency for the Safety of Air Navigation in Africa and Madagascar
Association of African Central Banks
Association of African Development Finance Institutions
Association of African Trade Promotion Organizations
Brazzaville Group
Casablanca Group
Centre for Linguistic and Historical Studies through Oral Traditions
Club des Amis du Sahel
Commission for Technical Cooperation in Africa South of the Sahara
Commission on African Animal Trypanosomiasis
Common Organization for the Control of Dessert Locust and Bird Pests
Commonwealth
Communauté
Communauté Financiere Africaine
Community Development Fund
Conference of Administrators of Posts and Telecommunications of West Africa
Conference of Independent African States
Coordinating Committee of the Dakar-Ndjamena Highway
Customs Union of West African States
ECOWAS Fund
Economic Commission for Africa
Economic Community of West African States
Franc Zone
French West Africa
Ghana-Guinea-Mali Union
Institute for Training and Demographic Research
Integrated Development Authority of the Liptako-Gourma Region
Inter-African Bureau for Animal Resources
Inter-African Committee on Hydraulic Studies
Inter-African Travel Company
Inter-State School of Rural Equipment Engineers
International African Migratory Locust Organization
Joint Anti-Locust and Anti-Aviarian Organization
Joint FAO/WHO/OAU Regional Food and Nutrition Commission for Africa

APPENDIX 5

Liptako-Gourma Integrated Development Authority
Lomé II
Mali Federation
Mali Federation
Ministerial Conference of West and Central African States on Maritime Transport
Monetary Union of the States of West Africa
Niger Basin Authority
Niger River Commission
Office for Research on African Food and Nutrition
Organization for Coordination and Cooperation in the Control of Major Endemic Diseases
Organization for the Development of African Tourism
Organization for the Development of the Senegal River
Organization of African and Malagasy States
Organization of African Unity
Organization of Senegal River States
Pan-African News Agency
Pan-African Postal Union
Pan-African Telecommunications Union
Permanent Interstate Drought Control Committee for the Sahel
Preferential Exchange Zone
Regional Centre for Solar Energy Research and Development
Regional Centre for Training in Aerial Surveys
Trans-African Highway Coordinating Commission [A]
Union of African Railways
Union of African States
Union of National Radio and Television Broadcasters
West African Common Market
West Africa Rice Development Association
West African Clearing House
West African Customs Union
West African Economic Community
West African Monetary Union
West African Regional Group
Yaoundé I (Association)
Yaoundé II (Association)

MAURITANIA

African Bureau of Educational Sciences
African Caribbean Pacific Group
African Center for Administrative Training and Research for Development
African Centre for Monetary Studies
African Civil Aviation Commission
African Commission on Agricultural Statistics
African Cultural Institute

A GUIDE TO AFRICAN INTERNATIONAL ORGANIZATIONS

African Development Bank
African Forestry Commission
African Intellectual Property Organization
African Malagasy Union
African Patent Document and Information Centre
African Postal Union
African Regional Centre for Technology
African Reinsurance Corporation
African Society for the Development of the Millet-and-Sorghum-based Food Industry
African and Malagasy Industrial Property Office
African and Malagasy Organization of Economic Cooperation
African and Malagasy Union
African and Malagasy Union of Economic Cooperation
African and Malagasy Union of Posts and Telecommunications
Afro-Malagasy Economic Cooperation Organization
Agency for the Safety of Air Navigation in Africa and Madagascar
Air Afrique
Association of African Development Finance Institutions
Center for Industrial Studies of the Maghreb
Centre for Linguistic and Historical Studies through Oral Traditions
Club des Amis du Sahel
Commission for Technical Cooperation in Africa South of the Sahara
Common Organization for the Control of Dessert Locust and Bird Pests
Communauté
Communauté Financiere Africaine
Community Development Fund
Conference of African Ministers of Culture
Coordination Commission for Liberation Movements of Africa
Customs Union of West African States
ECOWAS Fund
Economic Commission for Africa
Economic Community of West African States
French West Africa
Institute for Training and Demographic Research
Inter-African Bureau for Animal Resources
Inter-African Committee on Hydraulic Studies
Inter-African Travel Company
Inter-State School of Rural Equipment Engineers
International African Migratory Locust Organization
Joint Anti-Locust and Anti-Aviarian Organization
Lomé II
Ministerial Conference of West and Central African States on Maritime Transport
Monetary Union of the States of West Africa
Monrovia Group
Office for Research on African Food and Nutrition
Organization for Coordination and Cooperation in the Control of Major Endemic Diseases

APPENDIX 5

Organization for the Development of African Tourism
Organization for the Development of the Senegal River
Organization of African Unity
Organization of Senegal River States
Pan-African News Agency
Pan-African Telecommunications Union
Permanent Consultative Committee of the Maghreb
Permanent Interstate Drought Control Committee for the Sahel
Regional Centre for Solar Energy Research and Development
Union of African Parliaments
Union of National Radio and Television Broadcasters
West African Common Market
West Africa Rice Development Association
West African Clearing House
West African Customs Union
West African Economic Community
West African Monetary Union
West African Regional Group
Yaoundé I (Association)
Yaoundé II (Association)

MAURITIUS

African Accounting Council
African and Malagasy Common Organization
African and Malagasy Council on High Education
African Bureau of Educational Sciences
African Caribbean Pacific Group
African Centre for Monetary Studies
African Commission on Agricultural Statistics
African Development Bank
African Forestry Commission
African Posts and Telecommunications Union
African Regional Centre for Technology
African Regional Organization for Standardisation
African Reinsurance Corporation
African Solidarity Fund
African and Malagasy Bureau of Legislative Studies
African and Malagasy Common Organization
African and Malagasy Institite of Bilingualism
African and Malagasy Institute of Applied Economics and Statistics
African and Malagasy Office of Industrial Property
African and Mauritian Advanced Training Centre for Administrative Personnel
African and Mauritian School of Architecture and Urbanism
Afro-Asian Rural Reconstruction Organization
Architectural Institute

237

Association of African Central Banks
Association of African Development Finance Institutions
Centre for Training of Cadres
Commercial and Development Bank for Eastern and Southern Africa
Commonwealth
Commonwealth Regional Health Secretariat for East, Central and Southern Africa
Conference of African Ministers of Culture
Council on Administration of Information
Eastern and Southern African Mineral Resources Development Centre
Eastern and Southern African Trade and Development Bank
Economic Commission for Africa
Indian Ocean Commission
Institute for Training and Demographic Research
Institute of Sciences and Veterinary Medicine
Inter-African Bureau for Animal Resources
Joint FAO/WHO/OAU Regional Food and Nutrition Commission for Africa
Lomé II
Organization for Meat Marketing
Organization for the Development of Tourism in Africa
Organization of African Unity
Pan-African Telecommunications Union
Preferential Exchange Zone
Shelter Afrique
Union of African Parliaments
Union of National Radio and Television Broadcasters

MOROCCO

African Accounting Council
African Agricultural Credit Commission
African Bureau of Educational Sciences
African Center for Administrative Training and Research for Development
African Centre for Applied Research and Training in Social Development
African Centre for Monetary Studies
African Civil Aviation Commission
African Commission on Agricultural Statistics
African Development Bank
African Forestry Commission
African Regional Centre for Technology
African Reinsurance Corporation
Afro-Asian Rural Reconstruction Organization
Association of African Central Banks
Association of African Development Finance Institutions
Association of African Trade Promotion Organizations
Brazzaville Group
Casablanca Group

APPENDIX 5

    Center for Industrial Studies of the Maghreb
    Commission for Controlling the Desert Locust in Northwest Africa
    Conference of Independent African States
    Coordination Commission for Liberation Movements of Africa
    Economic Commission for Africa
    FAO Committee for Controlling the Deasrt Locust in Northwest Africa
    Independent African States
    Institute for Training and Demographic Research
    Inter-African Bureau for Animal Resources
    Joint FAO/WHO/OAU Regional Food and Nutrition Commission for Africa
    Libyan-Moroccan Union
    Maghreb Regional Economic Organization
    Maghrebin Charter
    Organization of African and Malagasy States
    Organization of African Unity
    Pan-African Postal Union
    Pan-African Telecommunications Union
    Permanent Consultative Committee of the Maghreb
    Shelter Afrique
    Union of African Parliaments
    Union of African Railways
    Union of Independent African States
    Union of National Radio and Television Broadcasters

MOZAMBIQUE

    African Bureau of Educational Sciences
    African Commission on Agricultural Statistics
    African Development Bank
    African Regional Centre for Technology
    Commission on African Animal Trypanosomiasis
    Front Line African States
    Inter-African Bureau for Animal Resources
    Joint FAO/WHO/OAU Regional Food and Nutrition Commission for Africa
    Organization of African Unity
    Pan-African News Agency
    Pan-African Postal Union
    Pan-African Telecommunications Union
    Southern African Development Coordination Conference
    Southern African Transport and Communications Commission
    Union of African Railways

A GUIDE TO AFRICAN INTERNATIONAL ORGANIZATIONS

NAMBIA

    African Postal and Telecommunications Union
    Southern African Regional Commission for the Consevation and Utilisation of the Soil

---

NIGER

    African Accounting Council
    African and Malagasy Common Organization
    African and Malagasy Council on High Education
    African Bureau of Educational Sciences
    African Caribbean Pacific Group
    African Centre for Monetary Studies
    African Civil Aviation Commission
    African Commercial Union
    African Commission on Agricultural Statistics
    African Cultural Institute
    African Data Processing Institute
    African Development Bank
    African Forestry Commission
    African Groundnut Council
    African Intellectual Property Organization
    African Malagasy Union
    African Patent Document and Information Centre
    African Posts and Telecommunications Union
    African Regional Centre for Technology
    African Regional Organization for Standardisation
    African Reinsurance Corporation
    African Society for the Development of the Millet-and-Sorghum-based Food Industry
    African Solidarity Fund
    African Union of National Radio and Television Broadcasting
    African and Malagasy Bureau of Legislative Studies
    African and Malagasy Common Organization
    African and Malagasy Industrial Property Office
    African and Malagasy Institite of Bilingualism
    African and Malagasy Institute of Applied Economics and Statistics
    African and Malagasy Office of Industrial Property
    African and Malagasy Organization of Economic Cooperation
    African and Malagasy Sugar Agreement
    African and Malagasy Union
    African and Malagasy Union of Posts and Telecommunications
    African and Mauritian Advanced Training Centre for Administrative Personnel
    African and Mauritian School of Architecture and Urbanism
    African and Mauritian Union of Development Banks

APPENDIX 5

Afro-Malagasy Economic Cooperation Organization
Agency for the Safety of Air Navigation in Africa and Madagascar
Air Afrique
Architectural Institute
Association of African Development Finance Institutions
Association of African Trade Promotion Organizations
Benin-Niger Common Organization
Cattle and Meat Economic Community of the Council of the Entente States Organization
Central Bank of West African States
Centre for Linguistic and Historical Studies through Oral Traditions
Centre for Training of Cadres
Club des Amis du Sahel
Commission for Technical Cooperation in Africa South of the Sahara
Commission on African Animal Trypanosomiasis
Common Organization for the Control of Dessert Locust and Bird Pests
Communauté
Communauté Financiere Africaine
Community Development Fund
Conference of Administrators of Posts and Telecommunications of West Africa
Conference of African Ministers of Culture
Conseil de l'Entente
Coordinating Committee of the Dakar-Ndjamena Highway
Council on Administration of Information
Customs Union of West African States
ECOWAS Fund
Economic Commission for Africa
Economic Community of West African States
Franc Zone
French West Africa
Institute for Training and Demographic Research
Institute of Sciences and Veterinary Medicine
Integrated Development Authority of the Liptako-Gourma Region
Inter-African Bureau for Animal Resources
Inter-African Committee on Hydraulic Studies
Inter-African Travel Company
Inter-State School of Rural Equipment Engineers
International African Migratory Locust Organization
Joint Anti-Locust and Anti-Aviarian Organization
Joint FAO/WHO/OAU Regional Food and Nutrition Commission for Africa
Lake Chad Basin Commission
Liptako-Gourma Integrated Development Authority
Lomé II
Ministerial Conference of West and Central African States on Maritime Transport
Monetary Union of the States of West Africa
Monrovia Group
Mutual Aid and Loan Guarantee Fund of the Council of the Entente States
Niger Basin Authority

Niger River Commission
Niger-Nigeria Joint Commission for Cooperation
Office for Research on African Food and Nutrition
Organization for Coordination and Cooperation in the Control of Major Endemic Diseases
Organization for Meat Marketing
Organization for the Development of African Tourism
Organization for the Development of Tourism in Africa
Organization of African Unity
Pan-African News Agency
Pan-African Postal Union
Pan-African Telecommunications Union
Permanent Interstate Drought Control Committee for the Sahel
Regional Centre for Solar Energy Research and Development
Road Transport Committee of the Entente Council
Trans-African Highway Coordinating Commission [A]
Union of African Railways
Union of National Radio and Television Broadcasters
West African Common Market
West Africa Rice Development Association
West African Customs Union
West African Development Bank
West African Economic Community
West African Monetary Union
Yaoundé I (Association)
Yaoundé II (Association)

NIGERIA

African Accounting Council
African Bureau of Educational Sciences
African Caribbean Pacific Group
African Centre for Monetary Studies
African Civil Aviation Commission
African Commission on Agricultural Statistics
African Development Bank
African Forestry Commission
African Groundnut Council
African Regional Centre for Technology
African Regional Organization for Standardisation
African Reinsurance Corporation
African Timber Organization
African Union of National Radio and Television Broadcasting
Association of African Central Banks
Association of African Development Finance Institutions
Association of African Trade Promotion Organizations

APPENDIX 5

British West Africa
Centre for Linguistic and Historical Studies through Oral Traditions
Cocoa Producers Alliance
Commission for Technical Cooperation in Africa South of the Sahara
Commonwealth
Conference of Independent African States
Coordinating Committee of the Dakar-Ndjamena Highway
Coordination Commission for Liberation Movements of Africa
ECOWAS Fund
Economic Commission for Africa
Economic Community of West African States
Independent African States
Inter-African Bureau for Animal Resources
Inter-African Coffee Organization
International African Migratory Locust Organization
Joint FAO/WHO/OAU Regional Food and Nutrition Commission for Africa
Lake Chad Basin Commission
Lomé II
Ministerial Conference of West and Central African States on Maritime Transport
Monrovia Group
Niger Basin Authority
Niger River Commission
Niger-Nigeria Joint Commission for Cooperation
Non-aligned Countries Working Group on Southern Africa
Organization of African Unity
Organization of African and Malagasy States
Organization of Wood Producing and Exporting African Countries
Pan-African News Agency
Pan-African Postal Union
Pan-African Telecommunications Union
Regional Centre for Training in Aerial Surveys
Trans-African Highway Coordinating Commission [A]
Trans-African Highway Coordinating Commission [B]
Union of African Railways
Union of National Radio and Television Broadcasters
West African Common Market
West Africa Rice Development Association
West African Clearing House
West African Examinations Council
West African Health Community
West African Insurance Consultative Association
West African Insurance Institute
West African Regional Group

RWANDA

African and Malagasy Common Organization
African and Malagasy Council on High Education
African Bureau of Educational Sciences
African Caribbean Pacific Group
African Centre for Monetary Studies
African Civil Aviation Commission
African Commission on Agricultural Statistics
African Development Bank
African Forestry Commission
African Posts and Telecommunications Union
African Regional Centre for Technology
African Solidarity Fund
African Union of National Radio and Television Broadcasting
African and Malagasy Bureau of Legislative Studies
African and Malagasy Common Organization
African and Malagasy Institite of Bilingualism
African and Malagasy Institute of Applied Economics and Statistics
African and Malagasy Office of Industrial Property
African and Malagasy Sugar Agreement
African and Malagasy Union
African and Malagasy Union of Economic Cooperation
African and Malagasy Union of Posts and Telecommunications
African and Mauritian Advanced Training Centre for Administrative Personnel
African and Mauritian School of Architecture and Urbanism
Architectural Institute
Association of African Central Banks
Association of African Development Finance Institutions
Association of African Trade Promotion Organizations
Centre for Training of Cadres
Commercial and Development Bank for Eastern and Southern Africa
Commission on African Animal Trypanosomiasis
Common Organization for Economic Cooperation in Central Africa
Conference of African Ministers of Culture
Conference of East and Central African States
Council on Administration of Information
Development Bank of the Great Lakes States
Economic Commission for Africa
Economic Community of Central African States
Economic Community of the Great Lakes Countries
Energy Organization of the Great Lakes Countries
Institute for Training and Demographic Research
Institute of Sciences and Veterinary Medicine
Inter-African Bureau for Animal Resources
Inter-African Coffee Organization
Inter-African Travel Company
Inter-State Body for Lakes Tanganyika/Kivu Basin

APPENDIX 5

    Joint FAO/WHO/OAU Regional Food and Nutrition Commission for Africa
    Lakes Tanganyika and Kivu Basin Commission
    Lomé II
    Monrovia Group
    Organization for Meat Marketing
    Organization for the Development of African Tourism
    Organization for the Development of Tourism in Africa
    Organization for the Management and Development of the Kagera River Basin
    Organization of African Unity
    Pan-African Movement for Eastern and Central Africa
    Pan-African News Agency
    Pan-African Telecommunications Union
    Preferential Exchange Zone
    Trans-East African Highway Authority
    Yaoundé I (Association)
    Yaoundé II (Association)

SAO TOME PRINCIPE

    African Accounting Council
    African Caribbean Pacific Group
    African Development Bank
    Cocoa Producers Alliance
    Economic Commission for Africa
    Economic Community of Central African States
    Inter-African Bureau for Animal Resources
    Joint FAO/WHO/OAU Regional Food and Nutrition Commission for Africa
    Lomé II
    Ministerial Conference of West and Central African States on Maritime Transport
    Organization of African Unity
    Pan-African News Agency
    Pan-African Telecommunications Union
    Shelter Afrique

SENEGAL

    African Accounting Council
    African Agricultural Credit Commission
    African and Malagasy Common Organization
    African and Malagasy Council on High Education
    African Bureau of Educational Sciences
    African Caribbean Pacific Group
    African Center for Administrative Training and Research for Development
    African Centre for Applied Research and Training in Social Development

African Centre for Monetary Studies
African Civil Aviation Commission
African Commission on Agricultural Statistics
African Cultural Institute
African Data Processing Institute
African Development Bank
African Forestry Commission
African Groundnut Council
African Intellectual Property Organization
African Malagasy Union
African Patent Document and Information Centre
African Posts and Telecommunications Union
African Regional Centre for Technology
African Regional Organization for Standardisation
African Reinsurance Corporation
African Solidarity Fund
African Union of National Radio and Television Broadcasting
African and Malagasy Bureau of Legislative Studies
African and Malagasy Common Organization
African and Malagasy Industrial Property Office
African and Malagasy Institite of Bilingualism
African and Malagasy Institute of Applied Economics and Statistics
African and Malagasy Office of Industrial Property
African and Malagasy Organization of Economic Cooperation
African and Malagasy Sugar Agreement
African and Malagasy Union
African and Malagasy Union of Economic Cooperation
African and Malagasy Union of Posts and Telecommunications
African and Mauritian Advanced Training Centre for Administrative Personnel
African and Mauritian School of Architecture and Urbanism
African and Mauritian Union of Development Banks
Afro-Malagasy Economic Cooperation Organization
Agency for the Safety of Air Navigation in Africa and Madagascar
Air Afrique
Architectural Institute
Association of African Development Finance Institutions
Association of African Trade Promotion Organizations
Association of Market Production, European Community/African-Caribbean-Pacific States
Central Bank of West African States
Centre for Linguistic and Historical Studies through Oral Traditions
Centre for Training of Cadres
Club des Amis du Sahel
Commission for Technical Cooperation in Africa South of the Sahara
Commission on African Animal Trypanosomiasis
Common Organization for the Control of Dessert Locust and Bird Pests
Communauté
Communauté Financiere Africaine

APPENDIX 5

Community Development Fund
Conference of Administrators of Posts and Telecommunications of West Africa
Conference of African Ministers of Culture
Coordinating Committee of the Dakar-Ndjamena Highway
Coordination Commission for Liberation Movements of Africa
Council on Administration of Information
Customs Union of West African States
ECOWAS Fund
Economic Commission for Africa
Economic Community of West African States
Franc Zone
French West Africa
Gambia River Development Organization
Institute for Training and Demographic Research
Institute of Sciences and Veterinary Medicine
Inter-African Bureau for Animal Resources
Inter-African Committee on Hydraulic Studies
Inter-African Travel Company
Inter-State School of Rural Equipment Engineers
International African Migratory Locust Organization
Joint Anti-Locust and Anti-Aviarian Organization
Joint FAO/WHO/OAU Regional Food and Nutrition Commission for Africa
Lomé II
Mali Federation
Mali Federation
Ministerial Conference of West and Central African States on Maritime Transport
Monetary Union of the States of West Africa
Monrovia Group
Mutual Aid and Loan Guarantee Fund of the Council of the Entente States
Office for Research on African Food and Nutrition
Oganization of Senegal River States
Organization for Coordination and Cooperation in the Control of Major Endemic Diseases
Organization for Meat Marketing
Organization for the Development of African Tourism
Organization for the Development of Tourism in Africa
Organization for the Development of the Senegal River
Organization of African Unity
Organization of Senegal River States
Pan-African News Agency
Pan-African Postal Union
Pan-African Telecommunications Union
Permanent Interstate Drought Control Committee for the Sahel
Regional Centre for Solar Energy Research and Development
Regional Centre for Training in Aerial Surveys
Senegambia, Union of
Union of African Parliaments
Union of African Railways

Union of National Radio and Television Broadcasters
West African Common Market
West Africa Rice Development Association
West African Development Bank
West African Economic Community
West African Monetary Union
West African Regional Group
Yaoundé I (Association)
Yaoundé II (Association)

SEYCHELLES

African Caribbean Pacific Group
African Centre for Monetary Studies
African Commission on Agricultural Statistics
African Cultural Institute
African Development Bank
Commonwealth Regional Health Secretariat for East, Central and Southern Africa
Conference of African Ministers of Culture
Eastern and Southern African Mineral Resources Development Centre
Economic Commission for Africa
Indian Ocean Commission
Institute for Training and Demographic Research
Inter-African Bureau for Animal Resources
Lomé II
Organization of African Unity
Pan-African Telecommunications Union
Union of National Radio and Television Broadcasters

SIERRA LEONE

African Bureau of Educational Sciences
African Caribbean Pacific Group
African Centre for Applied Research and Training in Social Development
African Centre for Monetary Studies
African Civil Aviation Commission
African Cultural Institute
African Development Bank
African Forestry Commission
African Regional Centre for Technology
African Reinsurance Corporation
African Union of National Radio and Television Broadcasting
Afro-Asian Rural Reconstruction Organization
Association of African Central Banks

APPENDIX 5

Association of African Development Finance Institutions
Association of Market Production, European Community/African-Caribbean-Pacific States
British West Africa
Centre for Linguistic and Historical Studies through Oral Traditions
Commission for Technical Cooperation in Africa South of the Sahara
Commission on African Animal Trypanosomiasis
Commonwealth
Conference of African Ministers of Culture
Conference of Independent African States
ECOWAS Fund
Economic Commission for Africa
Economic Community of West African States
Free Trade Area
Industrial Property Organization for English-Speaking Africa
Inter-African Bureau for Animal Resources
Inter-African Coffee Organization
International African Migratory Locust Organization
Joint FAO/WHO/OAU Regional Food and Nutrition Commission for Africa
Lomé II
Mano River Union
Ministerial Conference of West and Central African States on Maritime Transport
Monrovia Group
Organization of African Unity
Organization of African and Malagasy States
Pan-African News Agency
Pan-African Postal Union
Pan-African Telecommunications Union
Science Education Programme for Africa
Shelter Afrique
Union of African Parliaments
Union of National Radio and Television Broadcasters
West African Common Market
West Africa Rice Development Association
West African Clearing House
West African Examinations Council
West African Health Community
West African Insurance Consultative Association
West African Insurance Institute

SOMALIA

African and Malagasy Common Organization
African and Malagasy Council on High Education
African Caribbean Pacific Group
African Center for Administrative Training and Research for Development

African Center for Monetary Studies
African Civil Aviation Commission
African Development Bank
African Postal Union
African Regional Centre for Technology
African Reinsurance Corporation
African and Malagasy Bureau of Legislative Studies
African and Malagasy Common Organization
African and Malagasy Institite of Bilingualism
African and Malagasy Institute of Applied Economics and Statistics
African and Malagasy Office of Industrial Property
Architectural Institute
Association of African Central Banks
Association of African Development Finance Institutions
Association of African Trade Promotion Organizations
Centre for Training of Cadres
Commercial and Development Bank for Eastern and Southern Africa
Commission for Technical Cooperation in Africa South of the Sahara
Commission on African Animal Trypanosomiasis
Conference of East and Central African States
Conference of Independent African States
Coordination Commission for Liberation Movements of Africa
Council on Administration of Information
Desert Locust Control Organization for Eastern Africa
Eastern African Centre for Research on Oral Traditions and African National Languages
Eastern and Southern African Mineral Resources Development Centre
Eastern and Southern African Trade and Development Bank
Economic Commission for Africa
Industrial Property Organization for English-Speaking Africa
Institute of Sciences and Veterinary Medicine
Inter-African Bureau for Animal Resources
Inter-Governmental Authority on Drought and Development
Intergovernmental Authority on Development and Desertification
Joint FAO/WHO/OAU Regional Food and Nutrition Commission for Africa
Lomé II
Monrovia Group
Organization for Meat Marketing
Organization for the Development of Tourism in Africa
Organization of African Unity
Organization of African and Malagasy States
Pan-African Freedom Movements for East, Central and Southern Africa
Pan-African Movement for Eastern and Central Africa
Pan-African Postal Union
Pan-African Telecommunications Union
Preferential Exchange Zone
Regional Centre for Services in Surveying, Mapping and Remote Sensing
Shelter Afrique

APPENDIX 5

Union of National Radio and Television Broadcasters
Yaoundé I (Association)
Yaoundé II (Association)

SOUTH AFRICA

African Postal and Telecommunications Union
Commission for Technical Cooperation in Africa South of the Sahara
Constellation of South African States
Customs Union Agreement
Rand Monetary Area
South African Customs Union
Southern Africa Regional Tourism Council
Southern African Customs Union
Southern African Development Bank
Southern African Regional Commission for the Consevation and Utilisation of the Soil

SUDAN

African Accounting Council
African Bureau of Educational Sciences
African Caribbean Pacific Group
African Center for Administrative Training and Research for Development
African Center for Monetary Studies
African Centre for Applied Research and Training in Social Development
African Civil Aviation Commission
African Development Bank
African Forestry Commission
African Groundnut Council
African Postal Union
African Regional Centre for Technology
African Regional Organization for Standardisation
African Reinsurance Corporation
African Society for the Development of the Millet-and-Sorghum-based Food Industry
Afro-Asian Rural Reconstruction Organization
Association of African Central Banks
Association of African Development Finance Institutions
Association of African Trade Promotion Organizations
Commission on African Animal Trypanosomiasis
Conference of East and Central African States
Conference of Independent African States
Desert Locust Control Organization for Eastern Africa

Eastern African Centre for Research on Oral Traditions and African National Languages
Economic Commission for Africa
Independent African States
Industrial Property Organization for English-Speaking Africa
Inter-African Bureau for Animal Resources
Inter-Governmental Authority on Drought and Development
Intergovernmental Authority on Development and Desertification
Joint FAO/WHO/OAU Regional Food and Nutrition Commission for Africa
Lomé II
Non-aligned Countries Working Group on Southern Africa
Organization of African Unity
Pan-African News Agency
Pan-African Postal Union
Pan-African Telecommunications Union
Trans-East African Highway Authority
UAR-Libyan-Sudanese Economic Integration
Union of African Parliaments
Union of African Railways
Union of Independent African States
Union of National Radio and Television Broadcasters
Union of Nile States

SWAZILAND

African Bureau of Educational Sciences
African Caribbean Pacific Group
African Centre for Monetary Studies
African Civil Aviation Commission
African Development Bank
African Postal and Telecommunications Union
African Reinsurance Corporation
Association of African Development Finance Institutions
Association of African Trade Promotion Organizations
Commercial and Development Bank for Eastern and Southern Africa
Commonwealth
Commonwealth Regional Health Secretariat for East, Central and Southern Africa
Constellation of South African States
Customs Union Agreement
Eastern and Southern African Mineral Resources Development Centre
Economic Commission for Africa
High Commission Territories
Inter-African Bureau for Animal Resources
Joint FAO/WHO/OAU Regional Food and Nutrition Commission for Africa
Lomé II
Organization of African Unity

APPENDIX 5

Pan-African Postal Union
Pan-African Telecommunications Union
Preferential Exchange Zone
Rand Monetary Area
Regional Centre for Services in Surveying, Mapping and Remote Sensing
Science Education Programme for Africa
South African Customs Union
Southern Africa Regional Tourism Council
Southern African Customs Union
Southern African Development Coordination Conference
Southern African Regional Commission for the Consevation and Utilisation of the Soil
Southern African Transport and Communications Commission
Trans-East African Highway Authority
Union of African Railways

TANZANIA

African Accounting Council
African Bureau of Educational Sciences
African Caribbean Pacific Group
African Centre for Monetary Studies
African Civil Aviation Commission
African Commission on Agricultural Statistics
African Development Bank
African Forestry Commission
African Regional Centre for Technology
African Regional Organization for Standardisation
African Reinsurance Corporation
African Timber Organization
African Union of National Radio and Television Broadcasting
Arusha Convention
Association of African Central Banks
Association of African Development Finance Institutions
British East Africa
Commission on African Animal Trypanosomiasis
Commonwealth
Commonwealth Regional Health Secretariat for East, Central and Southern Africa
Conference of East and Central African States
Coordination Commission for Liberation Movements of Africa
Desert Locust Control Organization for Eastern Africa
East Africa Airways
East African Agriculture and Forestry Research Organization
East African Common Market
East African Common Services Organization
East African Community

East African Court of Appeal
East African Customs Union
East African Development Bank
East African Examinations Council
East African External Telecommunications Company
East African Federation
East African Freshwater Fisheries Research Organization
East African Harbours Corporation
East African High Commission
East African Industrial Licensing Council
East African Industrial Research Organization
East African Institue of Malaria and Vector-Borne Diseases
East African Institute for Medical Research
East African Marine Fisheries Research Organization
East African Post and Telecommunications Corporation
East African Railways Corporation
East African Railways and Harbours Administration
East African Tourist Travel Association
East African Trypanosomiasis Research Organization
East African Veterinary Research Organization
Eastern African Centre for Research on Oral Traditions and African National Languages
Economic Commission for Africa
Front Line African States
Industrial Property Organization for English-Speaking Africa
Inter-African Bureau for Animal Resources
Inter-African Coffee Organization
Inter-State Body for Lakes Tanganyika/Kivu Basin
Inter-University Committee for East Africa
Intergovernmental Authority on Development and Desertification
Joint FAO/WHO/OAU Regional Food and Nutrition Commission for Africa
Lake Victoria Fisheries Commission
Lakes Tanganyika and Kivu Basin Commission
Lomé II
Organization for the Management and Development of the Kagera River Basin
Organization of African Unity
Organization of Wood Producing and Exporting African Countries
Pan-African Freedom Movements for East, Central and Southern Africa
Pan-African Movement for Eastern and Central Africa
Pan-African News Agency
Pan-African Postal Union
Pan-African Telecommunications Union
Preferential Exchange Zone
Science Education Programme for Africa
Southern African Development Coordination Conference
Southern African Transport and Communications Commission
Tanzania-Zambia Railway Authority
Union of African Railways

APPENDIX 5

Union of National Radio and Television Broadcasters
University of East Africa

TOGO

    African Accounting Council
    African and Malagasy Common Organization
    African and Malagasy Council on High Education
    African Bureau of Educational Sciences
    African Caribbean Pacific Group
    African Center for Administrative Training and Research for Development
    African Centre for Applied Research and Training in Social Development
    African Centre for Monetary Studies
    African Civil Aviation Commission
    African Commercial Union
    African Commission on Agricultural Statistics
    African Cultural Institute
    African Data Processing Institute
    African Development Bank
    African Forestry Commission
    African Intellectual Property Organization
    African Patent Document and Information Centre
    African Posts and Telecommunications Union
    African Regional Centre for Technology
    African Regional Organization for Standardisation
    African Reinsurance Corporation
    African Solidarity Fund
    African Union of National Radio and Television Broadcasting
    African and Malagasy Bureau of Legislative Studies
    African and Malagasy Coffee Organisation
    African and Malagasy Common Organization
    African and Malagasy Institite of Bilingualism
    African and Malagasy Institute of Applied Economics and Statistics
    African and Malagasy Office of Industrial Property
    African and Malagasy Sugar Agreement
    African and Malagasy Union
    African and Malagasy Union of Economic Cooperation
    African and Malagasy Union of Posts and Telecommunications
    African and Mauritian Advanced Training Centre for Administrative Personnel
    African and Mauritian School of Architecture and Urbanism
    African and Mauritian Union of Development Banks
    Agency for the Safety of Air Navigation in Africa and Madagascar
    Air Afrique
    Architectural Institute
    Association of African Development Finance Institutions
    Association of African Trade Promotion Organizations

Cattle and Meat Economic Community of the Council of the Entente States
    Organization
Central Bank of West African States
Centre for Linguistic and Historical Studies through Oral Traditions
Centre for Training of Cadres
Cocoa Producers Alliance
Commission on African Animal Trypanosomiasis
Communauté
Communauté Financiere Africaine
Conference of African Ministers of Culture
Council on Administration of Information
ECOWAS Fund
Economic Commission for Africa
Economic Community of West African States
Franc Zone
Institute for Training and Demographic Research
Institute of Sciences and Veterinary Medicine
Inter-African Bureau for Animal Resources
Inter-African Coffee Organization
Inter-African Committee on Hydraulic Studies
Inter-African Travel Company
Inter-State School of Rural Equipment Engineers
International African Migratory Locust Organization
Lomé II
Ministerial Conference of West and Central African States on Maritime Transport
Monetary Union of the States of West Africa
Monrovia Group
Mutual Aid and Loan Guarantee Fund of the Council of the Entente States
Office for Research on African Food and Nutrition
Organization for Coordination and Cooperation in the Control of Major Endemic
    Diseases
Organization for Meat Marketing
Organization for the Development of African Tourism
Organization for the Development of Tourism in Africa
Organization of African Unity
Organization of African and Malagasy States
Pan-African News Agency
Pan-African Postal Union
Pan-African Telecommunications Union
Road Transport Committee of the Entente Council
Union of African Railways
Union of National Radio and Television Broadcasters
West African Common Market
West Africa Rice Development Association
West African Customs Union
West African Development Bank
West African Monetary Union
Yaoundé I (Association)

APPENDIX 5

Yaoundé II (Association)

TUNISIA

    African Accounting Council
    African Agricultural Credit Commission
    African Bureau of Educational Sciences
    African Caribbean Pacific Group
    African Center for Administrative Training and Research for Development
    African Centre for Monetary Studies
    African Commercial Union
    African Commission on Agricultural Statistics
    African Development Bank
    African Forestry Commission
    African Regional Organization for Standardisation
    African Reinsurance Corporation
    African Union of National Radio and Television Broadcasting
    Afro-Asian Rural Reconstruction Organization
    Association of African Central Banks
    Association of African Development Finance Institutions
    Association of African Trade Promotion Organizations
    Center for Industrial Studies of the Maghreb
    Commission for Controlling the Desert Locust in Northwest Africa
    Conference of Independent African States
    Coordination Commission for Liberation Movements of Africa
    Economic Commission for Africa
    FAO Committee for Controlling the Deasrt Locust in Northwest Africa
    Independent African States
    Institute for Training and Demographic Research
    Inter-African Bureau for Animal Resources
    Joint FAO/WHO/OAU Regional Food and Nutrition Commission for Africa
    Maghreb Regional Economic Organization
    Maghrebin Charter
    Organization of African Unity
    Organization of African and Malagasy States
    Pan-African News Agency
    Pan-African Postal Union
    Pan-African Telecommunications Union
    Permanent Consultative Committee of the Maghreb
    Trans-African Highway Coordinating Commission [A]
    Union of African Parliaments
    Union of African Railways
    Union of Independent African States
    Union of National Radio and Television Broadcasters

UGANDA

African Bureau of Educational Sciences
African Caribbean Pacific Group
African Center for Monetary Studies
African Centre for Applied Research and Training in Social Development
African Commission on Agricultural Statistics
African Development Bank
African Forestry Commission
African Regional Centre for Technology
African Regional Organization for Standardisation
African Reinsurance Corporation
Arusha Convention
Association of African Central Banks
Association of African Development Finance Institutions
Association of African Trade Promotion Organizations
British East Africa
Commercial and Development Bank for Eastern and Southern Africa
Commonwealth
Commonwealth Regional Health Secretariat for East, Central and Southern Africa
Conference of East and Central African States
Coordination Commission for Liberation Movements of Africa
Desert Locust Control Organization for Eastern Africa
East Africa Airways
East African Agriculture and Forestry Research Organization
East African Common Market
East African Common Services Organization
East African Community
East African Court of Appeal
East African Customs Union
East African Development Bank
East African Examinations Council
East African External Telecommunications Company
East African Federation
East African Freshwater Fisheries Research Organization
East African Harbours Corporation
East African High Commission
East African Industrial Licensing Council
East African Industrial Research Organization
East African Institue of Malaria and Vector-Borne Diseases
East African Institute for Medical Research
East African Marine Fisheries Research Organization
East African Post and Telecommunications Corporation
East African Railways Corporation
East African Railways and Harbours Administration
East African Tourist Travel Association
East African Trypanosomiasis Research Organization
East African Veterinary Research Organization

APPENDIX 5

Eastern and Southern African Trade and Development Bank
Economic Commission for Africa
Industrial Property Organization for English-Speaking Africa
Inter-African Bureau for Animal Resources
Inter-African Coffee Organization
Inter-Governmental Authority on Drought and Development
Inter-University Committee for East Africa
Intergovernmental Authority on Development and Desertification
International African Migratory Locust Organization
Joint FAO/WHO/OAU Regional Food and Nutrition Commission for Africa
Lake Victoria Fisheries Commission
Lomé II
Organization for the Management and Development of the Kagera River Basin
Organization of African Unity
Pan-African Movement for Eastern and Central Africa
Pan-African News Agency
Pan-African Postal Union
Pan-African Telecommunications Union
Preferential Exchange Zone
Regional Centre for Services in Surveying, Mapping and Remote Sensing
Science Education Programme for Africa
Shelter Afrique
Trans-African Highway Coordinating Commission [B]
Trans-East African Highway Authority
Union of National Radio and Television Broadcasters
University of East Africa

UPPER VOLTA   (Burkina Fasso)

Abidjan-Niger Railway Regime
African Accounting Council
African Agricultural Credit Commission
African and Malagasy Common Organization
African and Malagasy Council on High Education
African Bureau of Educational Sciences
African Caribbean Pacific Group
African Centre for Applied Research and Training in Social Development
African Centre for Monetary Studies
African Commercial Union
African Commission on Agricultural Statistics
African Cultural Institute
African Data Processing Institute
African Development Bank
African Forestry Commission
African Intellectual Property Organization
African Malagasy Union

African Patent Document and Information Centre
African Posts and Telecommunications Union
African Reinsurance Corporation
African Society for the Development of the Millet-and-Sorghum-based Food Industry
African Solidarity Fund
African Union of National Radio and Television Broadcasting
African and Malagasy Bureau of Legislative Studies
African and Malagasy Common Organization
African and Malagasy Industrial Property Office
African and Malagasy Institite of Bilingualism
African and Malagasy Institute of Applied Economics and Statistics
African and Malagasy Office of Industrial Property
African and Malagasy Organization of Economic Cooperation
African and Malagasy Sugar Agreement
African and Malagasy Union
African and Malagasy Union of Posts and Telecommunications
African and Mauritian Advanced Training Centre for Administrative Personnel
African and Mauritian School of Architecture and Urbanism
African and Mauritian Union of Development Banks
Afro-Malagasy Economic Cooperation Organization
Agency for the Safety of Air Navigation in Africa and Madagascar
Air Afrique
Architectural Institute
Association of African Development Finance Institutions
Association of African Trade Promotion Organizations
Cattle and Meat Economic Community of the Council of the Entente States Organization
Central Bank of West African States
Centre for Linguistic and Historical Studies through Oral Traditions
Centre for Training of Cadres
Club des Amis du Sahel
Commission for Technical Cooperation in Africa South of the Sahara
Commission on African Animal Trypanosomiasis
Common Organization for the Control of Dessert Locust and Bird Pests
Communauté
Communauté Financiere Africaine
Community Development Fund
Conference of African Ministers of Culture
Conseil de l'Entente
Coordinating Committee of the Dakar-Ndjamena Highway
Council on Administration of Information
Customs Union of West African States
ECOWAS Fund
Economic Commission for Africa
Economic Community of West African States
Franc Zone
French West Africa

APPENDIX 5

Ghana-Upper Volta Customs Union
Institute for Training and Demographic Research
Institute of Sciences and Veterinary Medicine
Integrated Development Authority of the Liptako-Gourma Region
Inter-African Bureau for Animal Resources
Inter-African Committee on Hydraulic Studies
Inter-African Travel Company
Inter-State School of Rural Equipment Engineers
International African Migratory Locust Organization
Joint Anti-Locust and Anti-Aviarian Organization
Joint FAO/WHO/OAU Regional Food and Nutrition Commission for Africa
Liptako-Gourma Integrated Development Authority
Lomé II
Mali Federation
Ministerial Conference of West and Central African States on Maritime Transport
Monetary Union of the States of West Africa
Monrovia Group
Mutual Aid and Loan Guarantee Fund of the Council of the Entente States
Niger Basin Authority
Niger River Commission
Office for Research on African Food and Nutrition
Organization for Coordination and Cooperation in the Control of Major Endemic Diseases
Organization for Meat Marketing
Organization for the Development of African Tourism
Organization for the Development of Tourism in Africa
Pan-African News Agency
Pan-African Postal Union
Pan-African Telecommunications Union
Permanent Interstate Drought Control Committee for the Sahel
Regional Centre for Solar Energy Research and Development
Regional Centre for Training in Aerial Surveys
Road Transport Committee of the Entente Council
Union of National Radio and Television Broadcasters
West African Common Market
West Africa Rice Development Association
West African Customs Union
West African Development Bank
West African Economic Community
West African Monetary Union
West African Regional Group
Yaoundé I (Association)
Yaoundé II (Association)

ZAIRE

    African Accounting Council
    African and Malagasy Common Organization
    African and Malagasy Council on High Education
    African Bureau of Educational Sciences
    African Caribbean Pacific Group
    African Centre for Applied Research and Training in Social Development
    African Centre for Monetary Studies
    African Commission on Agricultural Statistics
    African Development Bank
    African Forestry Commission
    African Groundnut Council
    African Postal Union
    African Postal and Telecommunications Union
    African Regional Centre for Technology
    African Regional Organization for Standardisation
    African Reinsurance Corporation
    African Solidarity Fund
    African Timber Organization
    African Union of National Radio and Television Broadcasting
    African and Malagasy Bureau of Legislative Studies
    African and Malagasy Common Organization
    African and Malagasy Institite of Bilingualism
    African and Malagasy Institute of Applied Economics and Statistics
    African and Malagasy Office of Industrial Property
    African and Malagasy Sugar Agreement
    African and Malagasy Union of Posts and Telecommunications
    Architectural Institute
    Association of African Central Banks
    Association of African Development Finance Institutions
    Association of African Trade Promotion Organizations
    Central African Clearing House
    Central African Economic Union
    Centre for Training of Cadres
    Commission for Technical Cooperation in Africa South of the Sahara
    Commission on African Animal Trypanosomiasis
    Common Organization for Economic Cooperation in Central Africa
    Conference of East and Central African States
    Coordination Commission for Liberation Movements of Africa
    Council on Administration of Information
    Development Bank of the Great Lakes States
    Economic Commission for Africa
    Economic Community of Central African States
    Economic Community of the Great Lakes Countries
    Energy Organization of the Great Lakes Countries
    Institute for Training and Demographic Research
    Institute of Sciences and Veterinary Medicine

APPENDIX 5

Inter-African Bureau for Animal Resources
Inter-African Coffee Organization
Inter-African Travel Company
Inter-State Body for Lakes Tanganyika/Kivu Basin
International African Migratory Locust Organization
Joint FAO/WHO/OAU Regional Food and Nutrition Commission for Africa
Lakes Tanganyika and Kivu Basin Commission
Lomé II
Ministerial Conference of West and Central African States on Maritime Transport
Monrovia Group
Organization for Meat Marketing
Organization for the Development of African Tourism
Organization for the Development of Tourism in Africa
Organization of Wood Producing and Exporting African Countries
Pan-African News Agency
Pan-African Telecommunications Union
Trans-African Highway Coordinating Commission [B]
Union of African Parliaments
Union of African Railways
Union of Central African States
Union of National Radio and Television Broadcasters
United States of Central Africa
Yaoundé I (Association)
Yaoundé II (Association)

ZAMBIA

African Bureau of Educational Sciences
African Caribbean Pacific Group
African Center for Administrative Training and Research for Development
African Centre for Monetary Studies
African Commission on Agricultural Statistics
African Cultural Institute
African Development Bank
African Forestry Commission
African Regional Centre for Technology
African Regional Organization for Standardisation
African Reinsurance Corporation
Association of African Central Banks
Association of African Development Finance Institutions
Association of African Trade Promotion Organizations
Commercial and Development Bank for Eastern and Southern Africa
Commission on African Animal Trypanosomiasis
Commonwealth
Commonwealth Regional Health Secretariat for East, Central and Southern Africa
Conference of African Ministers of Culture

A GUIDE TO AFRICAN INTERNATIONAL ORGANIZATIONS

    Conference of East and Central African States
    Coordination Commission for Liberation Movements of Africa
    Eastern and Southern African Mineral Resources Development Centre
    Eastern and Southern African Trade and Development Bank
    Economic Commission for Africa
    Federation of Rhodesia and Nyasaland
    Front Line African States
    Industrial Property Organization for English-Speaking Africa
    Inter-African Bureau for Animal Resources
    Inter-State Body for Lakes Tanganyika/Kivu Basin
    Joint FAO/WHO/OAU Regional Food and Nutrition Commission for Africa
    Lakes Tanganyika and Kivu Basin Commission
    Lomé II
    Pan-African Movement for Eastern and Central Africa
    Pan-African News Agency
    Pan-African Telecommunications Union
    Preferential Exchange Zone
    Preferential Trade Area for East and Southern Africa
    Regional Centre for Services in Surveying, Mapping and Remote Sensing
    Science Education Programme for Africa
    Shelter Afrique
    Southern African Development Coordination Conference
    Southern African Transport and Communications Commission
    Tanzania-Zambia Railway Authority
    Trans-East African Highway Authority
    Union of African Railways
    Union of National Radio and Television Broadcasters

ZIMBABWE

    African Bureau of Educational Sciences
    African Caribbean Pacific Group
    African Development Bank
    African Forestry Commission
    African Postal and Telecommunications Union
    Commercial and Development Bank for Eastern and Southern Africa
    Commonwealth
    Commonwealth Regional Health Secretariat for East, Central and Southern Africa
    Eastern and Southern African Mineral Resources Development Centre
    Economic Commission for Africa
    Federation of Rhodesia and Nyasaland
    Front Line African States
    Industrial Property Organization for English-Speaking Africa
    Inter-African Bureau for Animal Resources
    Inter-African Coffee Organization
    Joint FAO/WHO/OAU Regional Food and Nutrition Commission for Africa

APPENDIX 5

Lomé II
Pan-African News Agency
Pan-African Postal Union
Pan-African Telecommunications Union
Preferential Exchange Zone
Southern African Development Coordination Conference
Southern African Transport and Communications Commission
Trans-East African Highway Authority
Union of National Radio and Television Broadcasters

APPENDIX 6

NUMBER OF MEMBERSHIPS BY GROUPS

	N	AVERAGE NUMBER OF MEMBERSHIPS	RANGE
All Africa	52	53.4	2 - 111
All Africa (Without Namibia and S. Africa)	50	55.3	14 - 111
"New" States (Independent 1968 or later)	11	22.8	16 - 48
"Old" States (Independent prior to 1968)	41	60.8	10 - 111
East Africa (Kenya, Tanzania, Uganda)	3	74.3	72 - 77
Former British Colonies (Botswana, The Gambia, Ghana, Kenya, Lesotho, Malawi, Mauritius, Nigeria, Seychelles, Sierra Leone, Swaziland, Uganda, Zambia, Zimbabwe)	14	45.4	16 - 74
Former French Colonies (Algeria, Benin, Central African Republic, Chad, Comoros, Congo, Djibouti, Gabon, Guinea, Ivory Coast, Madagascar, Mali, Mauritania, Morocco, Niger, Senegal, Togo, Tunisia, Upper Volta)	19	73.0	18 - 111
Former Portuguese Colonies (Angola, Cape Verde, Guinea-Bissau, Mozambique, Sao Tome Principe)	5	18.2	14 - 22
Maghreb (Algeria, Egypt, Libya, Morocco, Tunisia)	5	40.5	40 - 41
Microstates (Cape Verde, Comoros, Djibouti, Equatorial Guinea, Guinea-Bissau, Sao Tome Principe, Seychelles)	7	18.7	14 - 24

MAPS

1A.	Customs Union of West African States	271
1B.	Southern African Customs Union	273
2A.	Central African Economic and Customs Union	275
2B.	Entente Council	277
3A.	African Postal Union	279
3B.	Southern African Development Co-ordination Conference	281
4A.	African Posts and Telecommunications Union	283
4B.	African Postal and Telecommunications Union	285
5A.	African and Malagasy Common Organization	287
5B.	East African Community	289

AFRICA
Political Boundaries

AFRICA
Political Boundaries

AFRICA
Political Boundaries

275

AFRICA
Political Boundaries

AFRICA
Political Boundaries

AFRICA
Political Boundaries

AFRICA
Political Boundaries

AFRICAN POSTS AND
TELECOMMUNICATIONS
UNION

AFRICA
Political Boundaries

AFRICAN AND MALAGASY COMMON ORGANIZATION

AFRICA
Political Boundaries

BIBLIOGRAPHY

N.B. Citations included are generally scholarly monographs and journal articles. If there is a paucity of information about an organization, other sources may be used. This is not intended to be exhaustive, but a broad sampling of the material available. Most sources are in English with a few in French; there is a rich continental literature in this field that is largely unmentioned.

GENERAL

Aboussier. Gabriel D'. 1961. *L'afrique vers l'unité*. Issy: Edition St. Paul.
African International Organization Directory 1984/85. 1984. Munich: K.G. Saur.
Ajala, A. 1973. *Pan-Africanism: Evolution, Progress and Prospects*. London: André Deutsch.
Ajomo, M. A. 1976. "Regional Economic Organizations, the African Experience," *International Comparative Law Quarterly*, XXV.
Ake, Claude. 1967. *A Theory of Political Integration*. New York: Odyssey Press.
Andmicheal. Berdahun. 1979. *Regionalism and the United Nations*. Dobbs Ferry, N.Y.: Oceana Publications.
Andic, F., et.al. 1971. *Theory of Economic Integration for Developing Countries*. Toronto: University of York Studies in Economics.
Ansari, Javed. 1986. *The Political Economy of International Economic Organization*. Boulder, Colorado: Lynne Rienner Publishers, Inc.
Anglin, Douglas G. 1983 " Economic Liberation and Regional Co-operation in Southern Africa: SADCC and PTA." *International Organization*, vol. 37.
Armah, Kwesi. 1965. *Africa's Golden Road: An Outline History of the Various Movements Towards African Unification*. Exeter, N.H.: Heinemann.
Azevedo, Mario. 1988. "Obstacles to Pan-Africanism: Real or Imaginary?" *Africa and the World*, 1:4.
Axline, Andrew. 1977. "Underdevelopment, Dependence and Intergration: the Politics of Regionalism in the Third World." *International Organization*.
Balassa, Bela. 1961. *A Theory of Economic Integration*. Homewood: Irwin Press.
Barbour, K.M. 1972. "Industrialization in West Africa: the Need for Subregional Groupings within an Integrated Economy." *Journal of Modern African Studies,* 10:3.
Boateng, E.A. 1978."*African Unity: the Dream and the Reality."* Accra: Ghana Academy of Arts and Science.
_____. 1966. *Outlook for African Unity*. Legon: University of Ghana.
Boutros-Ghali, Boutros. 1971. "Les difficultés institutionelles du panafricanism." Geneva: Institute de Hautes Études Internationale.
British Information Services. 1965. *Pan-africanism*. London.
Butete, C. M. 1985. "PTA: Toward an African Common Market," *Africa Report*, 30:1.
Cantori, L. and S.L. Spiegal. 1970. *The International Politics of Region: A Comparative Approach*. Englewood Cliffs, N.J.: Prentice-Hall.
Chidzero, B.T.G. 1965 "The Meaning of Economic Intergration in Africa," *East Africa Journal*,11:8.
Chime, Sam. 1977. *Integration and Politics among African States: Limitations and Horizons of Midterm Theorizing*. Uppsala: Scandinavian Institute of African Studies.
Chrisman, Robert, ed. 1974. *Pan-Africanism*. New York: Bobbs-Merrill.

Clark, John F. 1974. "Patterns of Support for International Organizations in Africa, 1964-1970." Paper prepared for Canadian African Studies Association.

_____. 1974 "Patterns of Support for International Organizations in Africa." Paper presented to Canadian Studies Association.

_____. n.d. "Relations among International Organizations in Africa." Dissertation presented to Syracuse University (dissertation abstracts vol. 35, 11a, p.7378A).

Cohen, John M. 1971. "Leadership Identity Problems and Regional Integration and Political Development." Paper presented at Social Science Council Conference, Makerere University, Kampala.

Constantin, F. 1972. "L'integration regionale en afrique noire," *Revue française de science politique,* 22.

Cooper, C.A. and B.F. Massell. 1965. "Towards a General Theory of Customs Unions for Developing Countries." *Journal of Political Economy,* vol. 73.

Cox, Richard 1965. *Pan-Africanism in Practice.* London: Oxford University Press

Currie, David P. (ed.) 1964. *Federalism and the New Nations of Africa.* Chicago: University of Chicago Press.

Dahlberg, Kenneth A. 1970. Regional Integration: The Neo-functional versus a Configurative Approach." *Integrational Organization,* XXIV.

DaSilvia Cunha, J.M. 1964. *Regionalism: The Solution for Africa.* Lisbon:----

Davidson, Basil, and Adenekan Ademola, eds. 1953. *The New West Africa.* London:----

Davis, Lenwood G. 1972. *Pan-Africanism: A Selected Bibliography.* Portland, Oregon.

_____. 1972. "Pan-africanism: An Intensive Bibliography." *Genéve afrique,* 11:2.

Decraene, P. 1970. *Le Panafricanisme.* Paris: Presses Universitaire de France.

Dimitrov, Th. D. 1973. *Documents of International Organization: A Bibliographic Handbook.* London: International University Publishers.

Diop, Cheikh Anta. 1978. *Black Africa: The Economic and Cultural Basis for a Federated State.* Westport, Connecticut: L. Hill.

_____. 1976. *Technical Co-operation among African Countries.* New York: United Nations.

Dolan, Micheal B. "Neofunctionalism: Problem Shift in a Theory of Regional Integration." Papers of the Peace Science Society International, No. 25.

Duchein, R.N. 1957. "The Pan-African Manifesto." Accra:----

DeLancey, Mark W. 1980. *Aspects of International Relations in Africa.* Indiana University, African Studies Program.

El-Agraa, A.M., and A.J. Jones. *Theory of Customs Unions.* New York: St.Martin's Press.

El-Ayouty, Yassin, and H.C. Brooks. 1973. *Africa and International Organization.* The Hague: Martinus Nijhoff.

Elkan, Peter G. 1975. "Measuring the Impact of Economic Integration Among Developing Countries," *Journal of Common Market Studies,* XIV(1).

Esedbe, Olisanwuche. 1982. *Pan-Africanism: The Idea and the Movement.* Washington: Howard University Press.

Falk, Peter, and Sual Menlovitz, eds. 1973. *Regional Politics and World Order,* San Francisco: W.H. Freeman.

Fanon, Frantz. 1966. *On the Problem of Unity in Africa.* Lagos: African Statement.

Geiss, Immanuel. 1974. *The Pan-African Movement.* London: Methuen.

_____. 1969. "Pan-Africanism," *Journal of Contemporary History,* 4:1.

Green, Reginald H.J., and K.G.V. Krishna. 1967. *Economic Cooperation in Africa: Retrospect and Prospect.* Nairobi: Oxford University Press.

_____ and Ann Seidman. 1968. *Unity or Poverty? The Economics of Pan-Africanism*. Harmondsworth: Penguin.
Gregg, Robert W. 1966. "The U.N.Regional Economic Commissions and Integration in the Underdeveloped Regions," *International Organization*, XX(2).
Gruhn, Isebill V. 1967. "Functionalism in Africa: Scientific and Technical Integration." Unpublished dissertation. University of California, Berkeley.
_____. 1972. "The External Factor in African Regional Integration." Paper presented at African Studies Association, Philadelphia.
Haas, Ernst B. 1975. "Is There a Hole in the Whole? Knowledge, Technology, Interdependence and the Construction of International Regimes," *International Organization*, 29 (3).
_____. 1975. "The Obsolescence of Regional Integration Theory." Berkeley: Institute of International Studies, Research Series, No. 25.
_____. 1976. "Turbulent Fields and the Theory of Regional Integration," *International Organization*, 30 (2).
Hama, Boubou. 1966. *Enquéte sur les foundationss et la genése de l'unité africaine*. Paris: Presence Africaine.
Hazelwood, Arthur (ed). 1967. *African Integration and Disintegration: Case Studies in Economic and Political Union*. London: Oxford University Press.
Hensen, Roger D. 1967. "Regional Integration: Reflections on a Decade of Theoretical Efforts," *World Politics* XX:2.
Integration Legal Materials. Washington: America Society of International Law (bi-monthly).
Jacob, Jean Francois. 1977. *La panafricaisme*. Paris: R. Laffont.
Jacob, Philip E., and James V. Toscano, eds. 1964. *The Integration of Political Communities*. Philadelphia: J.B. Lippincott.
Johns, David H. 1971. "Diplomatic Activity, National Development, and Regional Integration." Paper presented at Makerere University Social Science Conference.
Kahnert, F. 1969. *Economic Integration among Developing Countries*. Paris: OECD.
Kapteyn, P.J.G., et. al. 1981. *International Organization and Integration.*(2 vols.) The Hague: Martinius Nijhoff.
Keohane, Robert O., and Joseph S. Nye. 1975. "International Interdependence and Integration," in Fred I. Greenstein and Nelson W. Polsby, eds., *Handbook of Political Science*, Vol. 8. Reading, Massachusetts: Addison-Wesley Publishing Co.
_____. 1974. "Transgovernmental Relations and International Organization," *World Politics*, XXVII:9.
Kiang, Chien-Kuen. 1956. "Conditions for Federation." Unpublished dissertation, University of Nebraska.
Kitamura, H. 1966. "Economic Theory and the Economic Integration of Underdeveloped Regions," in M.S. Wionczek, ed., *Latin American Economic Integration*. New York: Frederick A. Praeger.
Kohn, Hans, and Wallace Sokolsky. 1965. *African Nationalism in the Twentieth Century*. Princeton: D. Van Nostrand Co.
Krasner, Stephen D. 1981. "Power Structures and Regional Development Banks," *International Organization*, 35.
Krauss, M.B. 1973. *Economics of Integration: A Book of Readings*. London: George Allen and Unwin.
Langley, J. Ayodele. 1963. *Pan-africanism and Nationalism in West Africa 1900-1945; A Study in Ideology and Social Classes*. Oxford: Clarendon Press.

Legum, Colin. 1965. *Pan-Africanism; A Short Political Guide*. New York: Praeger Publishers.
Leys, Colin. 1982. "African Economic Development in Theory and Practice," *Daedalus*, III:2.
Lindberg, Leon N., and Stuart A. Scheingold, eds. 1971. *Regional Integration: Theory and Research*. Cambridge: Harvard University Press.
Machlup, F. 1977. *A History of Thought on Economic Integration*. New York: Columbia University Press.
Manchyo, B. Chango. 1968. *Pan-africanism*. Kampala: Makerere University Press.
Makonnen, Ras. 1973. *Pan-africanism from Within*. New York: Oxford University Press.
Marasinghe, M. L. 1984. "An Review of Regional Economic Integration in Africa with Particular Reference to Equatorial Africa," *International and Comparative Law Quarterly*, 33.
Martin, Jane. (ed.) 1969. *Bibliography on African Regionalism*. Boston: Boston University African Studies Center.
Martin, Tony. 1983. *Pan-African Connection: From Slavery to Garvey and Beyond*. Cambridge: Schenkman Publishing Co.
Mazrui, Ali. 1967. *Towards A Pax Africana*. Chicago: University of Chicago Press.
Mazzeo, Domenico. 1984. *African Regional Organizations*. Cambridge: Cambridge University Press.
Morrison, Donald G. and H.M. Stevenson. 1972. "Integration and Instability: Patterns of African Political Development," *The American Political Science Review*, LXVI:3.
M'Buyinza, E., ed. 1982. *Pan-Africanism or Neocolonialism? The Bankruptcy of OAE*. London: Zed Press.
Merle, Marcel, ed. 1968. *L'afrique Noire Contemporarie*, 2nd. ed. Paris: Librarie Armand Colin.
Mezu, Sebastian O., ed. 1965. *The Philosophy of Pan-Africanism: A Collection of Papers*. Washington: Georgetown University Press.
Mutharika, B.W.T. 1972. *Towards Multinational Economic Cooperation in Africa*. New York: Praeger Publishers.
Mytelka, Lynn K. 1973. "The Salience of Gains in Third World Integrative Systems," *World Politics*, XXV:2.
Ngoudi, N. 1971. La Réussite de l'intégration Economique en Afrique," *Presence Africaine*.
Nkrumah, Kwame. 1963. *Africa Must Unite!* New York: Praeger Publishers.
Nye, Joseph S., Jr. 1968. *International Regionalism*. Boston: Little Brown & Co.
_____. 1971. *Peace in Parts: Integration and Conflict in Regional Organization*. Boston: Little Brown & Co.
O'leary, J.O. 1978. *Systems Theory and Regional Integration: the Market Model of International Politics*. Washington: University Press of America.
Okadigbo, Chuba. 1987. "The Odyssey and Future of Pan-Africanism," *Africa and the World*, 1:1.
Onwuka, Ralph, and Amadu Sesay. 1985. *The Future of Regionalism in Africa*. New York: St. Martin's Press.
Oshisanya, Samuel A. 1980. *The Ultimate End of Pan-africanism*.
Osei-Kwame, Peter. 1980. *A New Conceptual Model for the Study of Political Integration in Africa*. Lanham, Maryland: University Press of America.
Padmore, George. 1963. *History of the Pan-African Congress; Colonial and Coloured Unity, A Program of Action*. London: Hammersmith.
Pan-African Journal. Published by Greenwood Periodicals for Pan-African Institute.

Philip, Kjeld. 1972. *Intra-African Economic Co-operation and Africa's Relations with the EEC*. New York: United Nations Economic Commission for Africa.

Povolny', Mojmú. 1963. *Africa in Search of Unity*. Chicago: Czechoslovakian Foreign Institute in Exile.

Ramphul, Radha Krishna. 1983. "The Role of International and Regional Organizations in the Peaceful Settlement of Internal Disputes (with Special Emphasis in the Organization of African Unity)," *Georgia Journal of International and Comparative Law*, 13.

Ranjeva, Raymond. 1978. *La succession d'organisations internationales en Afrique*. Paris: Editions A. Pedone.

Robson, Peter. 1968. *Economic Integration in Africa*. London: George Allen and Unwin.

Roemer, Michael. 1982. "Economic Development in Africa," *Daedelus* III:2.

Rothchild, Donald. 1960. *Toward Unity in Africa*. Washington: Public Affairs Press.

_____, ed. 1968. *Politics of Integration*. Nairobi: East African Publishing House.

Sackey, Joseph A. 1978. "Political Economy of Regional Integration in West Africa." Paper presented to Canadian Studies Association.

Sanger, Clyde. 1964. "Toward Unity in Africa," *Foreign Affairs*, 42:2.

Santos, Eduardo Dos. 1968. *Pan-africanismo de ontem e de hoje*. Lisbon:-.

Schiavone, Guiseppe. 1983. *International Organization*. Chicago, St. James Press.

Shaw, Timothy. 1972. "International Organization and the Politics of Southern Africa: Regional Integration or Liberation ?" Paper presented at Canadian Studies Association.

_____ and Sola Ojo. 1982. *Africa and the International Political System*. Washington, D.C.: University Press of America for the Department of International Relations, University of Ife (Nigeria).

Simai, M., and P. Garam. 1977. *Economic Integration: Concepts, Theories and Problems*. ---: International Publications.

Sixth Pan-Africanist Congress: Resolutions and Speeches. 1974. Dar Es Salaam: Tanzania Publishing House.

Smith, John Graham. 1973. *Regional Economic Co-operation and Integration in Africa*. Bibliographic Series, 2. Toronto: McGill University.

Sohn, Louis B. (ed.) 1971. *Basic Documents of African Regional Organizations*. Dobbs Ferry, NY: Oceana Publications.

Statesman's Yearbook. Annual. London: Macmillan and Co.

Tefera, Asfaw. 1963. *Africa's March to Unity*. Lagos: Ribway.

Teitgen, P.H. 1971. *Les organizations régionales internationales*. Monchreatien.

Teshome, Adera. 1963. *Nationalist Leaders and Africa [sic] Unity*. Addis Ababa: Ethiopian National Patriotic Association.

Tharp, Paul A., Jr., ed. 1971. *Regional International Organizations: Structures and Functions*. New York: St. Martins Press.

Thomas, Charles M. 1965. *Pan-africanism; Its Significance for the United States*. Maxwell Air Force Base: Document Research Division.

Thompson, Vincent Bakpetu. 1984. *Africa and Unity: The Evolution of Pan-Africanism*. Harlow: Longmans.

Tinbergen, J. 1965. *International Economic Integration*. 2nd. ed. New York: Elsevier.

Udechuku, G.C. 1974. *African Unity and International Law*. Ithaca: Cornell University Press.

Union of International Associations. 1984. *African International Organization Directory*. London: K.G. Saur.

Wallerstein, Immanuel. 1967. *Africa, the Politics of Unity*. New York: Random House.
Waters, A.R. 1970. "A Behavioral Model of Pan-African Disintegration," *African Studies Review*, XIII:3.
Welch, Claude E. 1962. *Awakening Africa; Conferences of Independent African States*. Accra.
———. 1966. *Dream of Unity, Pan-africanism and Unification*. Ithaca: Cornell University Press.
Williams, Gwyneth. 1987. *Third World Political Organizations*. 2nd ed. London: The MacMillan Press, Ltd.
Wionczek, Miguel S. 1966, 1967. "Economic Integration and Regional Distribution of Industrial Activities: A Comparative Study," *East African Economic Review*, 1:1.
Woodie, Francis. 1970. *Les Institutions internationales régionales en Afrique Occidentale et Centrale*. Paris: R. Durand-Auzias.

EAST AFRICA

Asare, F.B.1977 "Le communauté de l'afrique de l'est." Paris: Administration Internationale, 3e cycle.
Beck, A. 1972. "The East African Community and Regional Research in Science and Medicine." Paper presented at African Studies Association, Philadelphia.
Bigirwenkya, K. 1972. "Regional Co-operation: The East African Experience." Daker, Senegal: Institute Africaine de Développement Economique et de Plantation.
Chime, Chimelu. 1977. *Integration and Politics Among East African States; Limitations and Horizons of Mid-term Theorizing*. Uppsala: The Scandinavian Institute of African Studies.
Colloton, Carol. 1972. "Political Integration in East Africa," *Journal of International and Comparative Studies*, 5:3.
Donohey, Roxanne. 1972. "East African Unity: Political Differences vs. Economic Interests," *Journal of International and Comparative Studies*, 5:3.
Dreyer, Elwood G. 1951. "The Federation Movement in British Central Africa." Unpublished dissertation, Georgetown University.
Dunne, James R. "East African Federation: Background and Economic-Political Events of 1946-1964." Unpublished dissertation, State University of New York at Albany.
Ghai, Yashpal P. 1974. "State Trading and Regional Economic Integration: The East African Experience," *Journal of Common Market Studies*, XII:3.
———. 1976. "Reflections on Law and Economic Integration: in East African." Uppsala: Scandinavian Institute of African Studies.
Gitelson, Susan A. 1973. "Can the UN be an Effective Catalyst for Regional Integration? The Case of the EAC," *Journal of Developing Areas*, 8:1.
Hazelwood, Arthur. 1975. *Economic Integration: The East African Experience*. London: Heinemann.
———. 1979. "The End of the East African Community: What Are the Lessons for Regional Integration Schemes?" *Journal of Common Market Studies*, 18:1.
International Conciliation. 1970. No. 580 devoted to East African Community.
Kappeler, D. 1978. "Causes et conséquences de l'intégration de la Communaunté Est-africaine en politique étrangère, XLIII:3.
Kennedy, T.A. 1959. "The East African Customs Union," *Makerere Journal*, 3.
Masell, B.F. 1963. *East African Economic Union: An Evaluation and Some Implications for Policy*. Santa Monica: Rand Corp.

Mazzeo, Domenico. 1975. *Foreign Assistance and the East African Services, 1960-70*. Munich: Weltforum Verlag.
Mbogoro, D.A.K. 1978. "Les groupements régionaux et le développement économique: quelques leçons tirées du plan d'intégration de l'afrique de l'est," *Cahiers éconmiques et sociaux*, XVI:2.
Ndegwa, P. 1965. *The Common Market and Development in East Africa*. Nairobi: East African Publishing House.
Nixson, F.I. 1973. *Economic Integration and Industrial Location: an East African Case Study*. London: Longmans.
Nye, Joseph S. 1965. *Pan-Africanism and East African Integration*. Cambridge: Harvard University Press.
Potholm, Christian, and Richard A. Fredland. 1980. *Integration and Disintegration in East Africa*. Lanham, Maryland: University Press of America.
Ravenhill, John. 1979. "Regional Integration and Development in Africa: Lessons from the East African Community," *Journal of Commonwealth and Comparative Politics*, 17:3.
Robson, Peter, and Colin Leys, eds. 1965. *Federation in East Africa: Opportunities and Problems*. Nairobi: Oxford University Press.
_____. 1968. "L'udeac et la communauté de l'Afrique de l'est." *BCEAEC Etudes et Statistiques*, 131.
Rosberg, Carl G., and Aaron Segal. 1963. "An East African Federation," *International Conciliation*, 543.
Segal, Aaron. 1967. "The Integration of Developing Countries: Some Thoughts on East Africa and Central America," *Journal of Common Market Studies*, V:3.
Seidman, Ann. "Problems and Possibilities for East African Economic Integration." Paper presented at African Studies Association.
Sircar, P.K. "Toward a Greater East African Community," *Africa Quarterly*, XVI:3
United Nations. 1971. *Co-operation for Economic Development in Eastern Africa*, 9 parts. New York.
Wionczek, M.S. 1967. "Economic Integration and Regional Distribution of Industrial Activities: A Comparative Study," *East African Economic Review*.

ORGANIZATION OF AFRICAN UNITY (OAU)

Abdallah, R. 1974, "L'unité africaine de premiers congrés panafricaines la fin de la premiére décennie de l'oua." *Revue juridique* (Tunis), i.
Akindele, R. A. 1971. "The Organization of African Unity and the UN: A Study of the Problems of Universal-Region Relationships in the Organization and Maintenance of International Peace and Security," *Canadian Yearbook of International Law, IX*.
Akinyemi, A. Bdanji. 1981. "The Organization of African Unity and African Identity," *African Quarterly*, 20:3-4.
Akuchu, Gemuh E. 1975. " The Problem of OAU's Ineffectiveness in Peaceful Settlement: A Case Study of Casual Factors in the Nigerian-British Conflict." Paper presented at Conference on Role of International Organization in African International Politics, University of South Carolina.
Aluko, O. 1973. "The OAU Liberation Committee after a Decade: An Appraisal," *Quarterly Journal of Administration*, VIII:1.
Aluko, S. A. 1963. "Problems of Financial and Monetary Integration." *Nigerian Journal of Economic and Social Studies*.

Amate, C.O.C. 1986. *Inside the OAU; Pan-Africanism in Practice*. New York: St. Martin's Press.
Amonoo, H. R. 1964. "The Organization of African Unity: Its Defects and Solutions." *Panafricanist Review*, 1:1.
Andemicael, Berhanykun. 1976. *The OAU and the UN: Relations between the Organization of African Unity and the United Nations*. New York: UNITAR.
Azare, F.B. 1965. "The Background to OAU," *Africa and the World*, II.
Cervenka, Zdenek. 1969. *The Organization of African Unity and its Charter*. London: C. Hurst & Co.
Chukwurah, A.O. 1973. "The Organization of African Unity and African Territorial and Boundary Problems: 1963-1973," *Indian Journal of International Law*, XIII:2.
Dieshit, R. D. 1966. "O.A.U. Promises and Performances," *African Quarterly*.
Dugard, C.J.R. 1967. "The Organization of African Unity and Colonialism," *International and Comparative Law Quarterly*, XVI:1.
El-Ayouty, Yassin. (ed.) 1975. *The OAU after Ten Years: Comparative Perspectives*. New York: Praeger Publishers.
_____. 1975. " O.A.U. Meditation in the Arab-Isreali Conflict," *Genéve Afrique*, XIV:1.
Elias, T.O. 1965. "The Charter of the Organization of African Unity," *American Journal of International Law*, LXI:2.
Fredland, Richard A. 1973. "The Organization of African Unity at 10: Can It Survive?" *African Affairs*.
Hanning, H. 1981. "Lifebelt for Africa: The OAU in the 1980's," *The World Today*.
Hoskyns, Catherine. 1967. "Trends and Development in the Organization of African Unity," *Yearbook of World Affairs*, XXI.
_____. 1969. *Case Studies in African Diplomacy: I. The Organization of African Unity and the Congo Crisis 1964-65*. Dar Es Salaam: Oxford University Press.
Kafoma, Kweci, ed. 1988. *OAU; 25 Years On*. London: From Publishers.
Kamal, Humayun A. 1973. "Organization of African Unity," *Pakistan Horizon*, 26:1.
Kamanu, Onyeonoro S. 1974. "Secession and the Right of Self-Determination: an O.A.U. Dilemma," *The Journal of Modern African Studies*, 12:3.
Legum, Colin. 1964. "The Specialized Commissions of the OAU," *Journal of Modern African Studies*, 2:4.
_____. 1975. "The Organization of African Unity: A Success or Failure?" *International Affairs*, LI.
_____. 1964. "The Specialized Commissions of the OAU," *Journal of Modern African Studies*, II:2.
Markakis, J. 1966. "The Organization of African Unity; A Progress Report," *Journal of Modern African Studies*, IV:2.
Mayall, J. 1973. "African Unity and the O.A.U.: the Place of a Political Myth in African Diplomacy," *Yearbook of World Affairs*.
Mazrui, Ali. 1977. "Rights of States or of People--Where Should the OAU Focus?" *New African* (London).
Mini, M. 1973. "Class Struggle and African Unity, Ten Years of O.A.U.," *Mainstream*, XI.
Meyers, B.David. 1974. "Interregional Conflict Management by the Organization of African Unity," *International Organization*, XXVIII:3.
_____. "The Organization of African Unity: An Annotated Bibliography." Mimeograph.

_____. 1976. "O.A.U.'s Administrative-Secretary General," Paper presented at Conference on International Organization in African Politics, University of South Carolina, and in *International Organization*, XX.
Nambiar, K.R. 1963. "The Charter of the Organization of African Unity," *Indian Journal of International Law*, III.
Noviki, Margaret. 1983. "The Addis Summit: A Test for African Unity," *Africa Report*, 28:5.
Padelford, Norman J. 1964. "The Organization of African Unity: Background and Events in its Establishment," *International Organization*, XVIII:3.
Pazzanita, Anthony G. 1985. "Legal Aspects of Membership in the Organization of African Unity," *Case Western Reserve Journal of International Law*, 17:1.
Polhemus, James H. 1974 "The Provisional Secretariat of the O.A.U., 1963-1964," *The Journal of African Studies*, 12:2.
Saenz, P. 1970. "The Organization of African Unity in the Subordinate African Regional System," *African Studies Review*, III:2.
Sesay, Amadu, et.al. 1984. *The OAU After Twenty Years*. Boulder, Colorado: Westview Press.
Tandon, Yashpal. 1972. "Organization of African Unity: A Forum for African International Relations," *Round Table*, 246.
Telli, Diallo. 1965. "The Organization of African Unity," *African Forum*, 1:2.
Thompson, V.B. 1966. "A Catalogue of Betrayal: UN and OAU in the African Crisis." *Africa and the World*.
Thompson, W., and R.R. Bissell. 1973. "Development of the African Subsystem: Legitimacy and Authority in the OAU," *Policy*, V:3.
Topouzis, Daphne. 1989. "The OAU: A Charter for Human Rights," *Africa Report*, 34:4.
Tiewul, A. 1975. "Relations between the United Nations and the OAU in the Settlement of Secessionist Conflicts," *Harvard International Law Journal*, XVI.
Touval, S. 1967. "The Organization of African Unity and African Borders," *International Organization*, XXI:1.
Wild, P. 1966. "The OAU and the Algerian-Morocco Border Conflict: A Study of New Machinery for Peace-keeping and for the Peaceful Settlement of Disputes among African States," *International Organization*, XX:1.
Wolfers, Arnold. 1976. *Politics in the Organization of African Unity*. London: Methuen & Co., Ltd.
Woronoff, Jon. 1970. *Organizing African Unity*. Metuchen, N.J.: Scarecrow Press.
Young, William B. and Richard Pyle. 1974. "The OAU: Ten Years Old and Getting Stronger." Paper presented at International Studies Association.

SOUTHERN AFRICA

Amin, Samir. 1987. *SADCC: Prospects for Disengagement and Development in Southern Africa*. United Nations University.
Anglin, Douglas C. 1985. "SADCC After Nkomati," *African Affairs*, XXVI:1.
_____. 1983. "Economic Liberation and Regional Cooperation in Southern African: SADCC and PTA," *International Organization*, 37.
Boyd, J. Barron, Jr. 1984. "The Southern African Development Coordination Conference: A Subsystemic Analysis." Paper presented at International Studies Association.
Cobbe, J.H. 1980. "Integration among Unequals: The Southern African Customs Union and Development," *World Development*, VIII:4.

Cownie, David S. n.d. "Regional Cooperation for Development: A Review and Critique of the Southern African Development Coordination Conference." Paper prepared at National Institute of Development, Research and Documentation, University of Botswana.

———. 1984. "Botswana and the SADCC: Expanding External Options through Regional Cooperation." Paper presented at African Studies Association.

Hill, Christopher R. 1983. "Regional Cooperation in Southern Africa," *African Affairs*, 82:327.

Lee, Margaret C. 1989. *The Political Economy of Development in Southern Africa*. Nashville, Tennessee: Winston-Derek Publishers.

Liebenow, J. Gus. 1982. "SADDC: Challeging the 'South African Connection,'" Universities Fieldstaff Reports, 13.

Makoni, Simba. 1987. "SADCC's New Strategy," *Africa Report*.

Maasdrop, G. G. 1984. *SADCC: A post -Nkomati Evaluation*. Braamfontien: South African Institute of International Affairs.

Marquard, Leopold. 1971. *A Federation of South Africa*. New York: Oxford University Press.

Matthews, Jacquelin. 1984. "Economic Integration in Southern Africa: Progress or Decline?" *South African Journal of Economics*, 52.

Morna, Colleen Lowe. 1987. "SADCC and the Private Sector," *Africa Report*, 32:3.

Mwase, Ngla. 1985. "The African Preferential Trade Area: Towards a Sub-regional Economic Community in Eastern and Southern Africa, " *Journal of World Trade Law*, 19.

Thompson, Carol B. 1987. "SADCC's Struggle for Economic Liberation," *Africa Report*, 32:3.

Turner, Biff. 1971. "A Fresh Start for the Southern African Customs Union," *African Affairs*, 70:280.

Vale, Peter. 1982. "Prospects for Transplanting European Models of Regional Integration to South Africa," *Politikon*, 9:2.

FRANCOPHONE (WEST) AFRICA

Abangwu, George C. 1975. "Systems Approach to Regional Integration in West Africa," *Journal of Common Market Studies*, XIII:1-2.

Adedeji, A. 1970. "Prospects of Regional Economic Cooperation in West Africa," *Journal of Modern African Studies*, VIII:2.

Adamo, Lebum L. 1978. Coperation or Neocolonialism: Francophone Africa," *Africa Quarterly* (New Dehi), XVIII:1.

Aderigbe, A.B. 1963. "West African Integration: An Historical Perspective," *Nigerian Journal of Economic and Social Studies*.

Agyeman-Dickson, John de'g. 1953. "Federation in the West Africa: A Study in Political Geography." Unpublished dissertation, University of Michigan.

Amacbree, Igolima. 1973. "Problems of Integration in West Africa," (review), *The American Journal of Economics and Sociology*, 32:2.

Bakary, B. 1978. "Les changes d'une intégration monétaire et économique au sein de la sous-région ouest africaine," *Banaguel*, 374.

Balassa, B. 1978. "Advantages comparés et perspectives de l'intégration économique en Afrique de l'Ouest," *Cahiers économiques et sociaux*, XVI.

Baloro, J. 1977. "Economic Integration in West Africa: An Examination of the Mechanism for Dispute Settlement," S.I.:s.n.
Barbour, K.M. 1972. "Industrialisation in West Africa," *Journal of Modern African Studies*, 10:3.
Bornstein, R. 1972. "The Organization of Senegal River States," *Journal of Modern African Studies*, X:2.
Crone, D. 1982. *Industrialization and Regionalism in ECOWAS and ASEAN: Nigeria and Indonesia in Regional and World Systems*, East Lansing: Michigan State University.
David, J. 1973. La communauté économique de l'Afrique de l'ouest." *Marchés tropicaux et méditerranéens*.
Delaborde, Michael. 1968. "New Developments in French-Speaking Africa," *Civilisations*, XVIII:1.
Diagne, P. 1972. *Pour l'Unité Ouest-Africaine: micro-états et intégration économique*. Paris: Anthropos.
Diakha, Dieng. 1965. "From UAM to OCAM," *African Forum*, 1:2.
Diejomoah, V.P. and M.A.Iyoda, eds. 1980. *Industrialization in the Economic Community of West African States (ECOWAS)*. Ibadan: Heinemann.
DuBois, Victor D. 1965. "The Search for Unity in French-Speaking Africa," University Fieldstaff Reports, VII.
_____. "Crisis in OCAM." American Universities Fieldstaff Reports, XIV:2.
Ekue, A.K. 1976. "L'organisation Commune Africaine et Mauricienne," *Revue française d'études politiques africaines,* 130.
Elias, T.O. 1978. "The Economic Community of West Africa," *Yearbook of World Affairs*, XXXII.
Ernst, Andrew H. 1976. "Formation of the Economic Organization of West African States: A Customs Union and Free Trade Area for Regional Development," *Georgia Journal of International and Comparative Law,* 6.
Espallargeas, M. 1983. "L'Autorité du Bassin de Niger: la Coopération inter-Africaine pour l'utilization et l'amé du bassin du Niger," *Le mois en Afrique,* Nos. 205-206.
Fessard, deFoucault, B. 1972. "Vers un réménageement des relations entre les états riverains du fleuve sénégal?" *Revue de défense nationale.*
Foltz, W.J. 1965. *From French West Africa to the Mali Federation*. New Haven: Yale University Press.
Gautron, Jean -Claude. 1976. "The Loménagement du bassin su fleuve sénégal." *Annuaire français de droit international,* XIII.
_____. 1976. "La communauté économique de l'Africique de l'Ouest: antécédents et perspectives,"*Annauire Francais de Droit Internationale.* Paris: Centre National de la Recherche Scientifique.
_____. 1970. "Les métamorphoses d'un groupment sous-régional: l'Organisation des états riverains du sénégal." *Année Africaine.*
Gerardin, Hubert. 1982. "L'intégration monetaire et économique régionale: une alternative pour le développement des PMA? L' Afrique de L'Ouest," *Mondes en développement,* vol.10, no.39.
Gray-Johnson, C. 1973. *Senegambia: the Need for Integration.* Dakar: IDEP.
Harrell-Bond, Barbara. 1979. "ECOWAS: The Economic Community of West African States," American Universites Fieldstaff Reports, 6.
Hedrich, M., and K. von Der Ropp. 1978. "Perspectives d'intégration régionale en Afrique de l'Ouest," *Afrique Contemporaine*, XVI.

Hippolyte, M. 1968. "De Nouakchott à Niamey, l'itinéraire de l'OCAM," *Revue française d'études politiques africaines*, XXXIV.
Ilori, C.D. 1973. "Trade Contraints: A Barrier to Economic Co-operation in West Africa," *Journal of Economic and Social Studies*, 15:3.
Jalloh, A.A. 1973. *Political Integration in French-Speaking Africa*. Berkeley: Institute of International Studies, University of California.
Jouve, E. 1975. "L'OUA et la libération de l'Afrique," *Annuaire du Tiers Monde*, I.
Kurtz, D.M.1970. "Political Integration in Africa: The Mali Federation," *Journal of Modern African Studies*, VIII:3.
Mytelka, Lynn K. 1970. "Common Market with some Uncommon Problems: UDEAC Chooses Cooperation despite Unequally Shared Poverty and Some Severe Clashes of Interest," *Africa Report*, XV.
Ndongko, W. A. 1976. "The Economic Implications of Multimembership in Regional Groupings: the Case of Cameroon and Nigeria," *Africa Spectrum* (Hamburg), 11:3.
Nguyen, Q. L.1982. "Development of the Senegal River Basin: An Example in International Co-operation," *Natural Resources Forum*, 6.
_____. 1974. "A Geneaology of Francophone West and Equatorial African Regional Organizations," *Journal of Modern African Studies*, XII:2.
_____. 1968. "New Departures in Equatorial African Integration," *Africa Today*, XV:5.
_____. 1970. "UDEAC: Problems of a Common Market," *Africa Report*, 15:7.
_____. 1968. "OCAM: de Tananarive Niamey." *Jeune Afrique*, supplement 367.
Ojo, O. 1975. "Economic Integration: the Nigerian Experience since Independence," The Hugue: Institute of Social Studies (Occasional Papers, 54).
Ojo, O.J.B. 1980. "Nigeria and the Formation of ECOWAS," *International Organization*, XXXIV:4.
Okolo, Julius Emeka. 1987. "Intra-ECOWAS Trade Liberalization." Paper prepared for International Studies Association.
_____. 1984. "West African Regional Integration: ECOWAS," paper prepared for International Studies Association.
_____. 1987. "Intra-ECOWAS Trade Liberalization: An Assessment." Paper prepared for International Studies Association.
_____. 1987. *West African: Regional Cooperation and Development*. Boulder, Colorado: Westview Press.
Onitiri, H.M.A. "Towards a West African Economic Community," in Eicher and Carl Leidholm, eds. *Growth and Development of the Nigerian Economy*. East Lansing: Michigan State University Press.
Onwuka, R.I. 1982. *Development and Integration in West Africa: the Case of the Economic Community of West African States*. Ife: University of Ife Press.
_____. 1977. "Independence within the Economic Community of West African States," *West Africa* (London), Nos.3144/3145.
Oudes, Bruce J. 1968. "OCAM Comes of Age," *Africa Report*.
Panter-Brick, Kurt. 1965. "The Union Africaine et Malgache" in Austin and Weiler, *Inter-State Relations in Africa*. Freiburg: i. Br.
Peureux, G. 1961. "La création de l'union africaine et malgache et les conférences des chefs d'était d'expression française," *Revue juridique et politique d'outremer*.
Prevost, P. 1968. "L'Union douanière et économique de l'Afrique central, "*Revue française d'ètudes politiques africaines*, XXXIV.

Plessz, N.G. 1968. *Problems and Prospects of Economic Integration in West Africa*. Montreal: McGill University Press.
Ramamurthi, T.G. 1970. "The Dynamics of Regional Integration in West Africa," *India Quarterly*, XXVI:3.
"Report on ECOWAS." 1982. *West Africa*.
Robson, Peter. 1983. *Integration, Development and Equity: Economic Integration in West Africa*. London: Allen and Unwin.
_____. 1965. "The Problem of Senegambia," *Journal of Modern African Studies*, III:3.
_____. 1968. "L'UDEAC et la Communauté de l'Afrique de l'est," *BCEAEC Etudes et Statistiques*, 131.
Ross, C.G. 1982. "Development of the Gambia River Basin; A Planning Methodology," *Economic Planning*, 18:2.
Sircar, P.K. "Regional Development through Cooperation: Two Examples from West Africa," *Africa Quarterly*, XVII:1.
Sackey, J.A. 1979. "West African Integration; Some Further Reflections," University of West Indies, Department of Economics.
_____. 1978. "Regional Development through Cooperation: Two Examples from West Africa." *Africa Quarterly*, XVII:1.
Symposium on West African Integration. 1963. *Nigerian Journal of Economic and Social Studies*.
Tevoedjre, Albert. 1965. *Pan-Africanism in Action: An Account of the UAM*. Cambridge, Massachusetts: Center for International Affairs, Harvard University. 2nd ed., 1984. College Park: University of Maryland Press.
Thompson, V. 1972. *West Africa's Council of the Entente*. Ithaca: Cornell University Press.
_____ and Richard Adloff. 1958. *French West Africa*. Stanford: Stanford University Press.
Vinay, B. 1971. "Coopération intra-africaine et intégration-l'expérience de l'UDEAC," *Penant*, LXXXI.
Yadi, Melchiade. 1975. "Promotion du développement industriel équilibré des pays-membres de l'UDEAC et de la CAE," *Études Internationales*, VI:1.
Zagaris, Bruce. 1978. "Economic Community of West African States (ECOWAS): An Analysis and Prospects," *Case Western Reserve Journal of International Law*.

OTHERS

Alting von Geusau, F.A.M., ed. 1977. *The Lomé Convention and a New International Economic Order*. Leyden: Sijthoff.
Asante, S.K.B. 1981. "Lomé II: Another Machinery for Updating Dependency," *Development and Cooperation*, III.
_____. 1981. "The Lomé Convention: towards Perpetuation of Dependence or Promotion of Interdependence," *Third World Quarterly, III:4*
Baza, G. 1970. "Tentatives de coordination industrielle au sein de l'Union douaniére et économique de l'Afrique du centre," *Cahiers congolais de la recherche et du développement* (Kinshasa).
Bouazizi, M.M. 1977. "Essai sur l'integration économique, cas de la libye, la tunisie, l'algerie et le maroc." Paris: *Science économique*.
Bruyas, J. 1975. "La convention ACP-CEE de Lomé (28 février 1975)," *Annuaire du Tiers Monde*, I.

Coffee, P. 1975. "The Lomé Agreement and the EEC: Implications and Problems," *Three Banks Review*, 108.
Cole, B. 1983. "The Mano River Union: Ten Years, Not Out," *West Africa*, 3451.
Cox, Richard. 1964. *Pan-Africanism in Practice (PAFMECSA 1958-1964)*. London: Oxford University Press.
Dolan, Michael B. 1977. "The Lomé Convention and Europe; A Relationship with the Third World: A Critical Analysis." Paper prepared for International Studies Association.
_____. "Part 2: New Bonds Between Ex-French and Ex-Belgian Colonies; The Acceptance of Congo-Leopoldville by O.C.A.M.," American Universities Field Staff Reports, VII:4
Dvorin, Eugene P. 1955. "The Central African Federation; A Political Analysis." Unpublished dissertation, University of California at Los Angeles.
Efrat, Edgar Shlomo. 1962. "The Application of Federalism to Emergent States in Central Africa." Unpublished dissertation, University of Texas.
Ekue, A.K. 1967." L'Organization Commune Africaine et Mauricienne," *Revue française d'études politiques africaine*, 130.
Fordwor, Kwame Donkoh. 1980. *The African Development Bank*. New York: Pergamon.
French, Howard. 1984. "African Development Bank," *African Business*, 73.
Galtung, P. 1976. "The Lomé Convention and Neo-capitalism," *Africa Review*, VI:1.
Gautron, Jean-Claude. 1980. "De Lomé I à Lomé II: la Convention ACP-EEC du 31 Octobre 1979," *Cahiers de droit européen*, XVI:4.
Ghai, Dahram. 1973. "The Association Agreement between the European Economic Community and the Partner States of the East African Community," *Journal of Common Market Studies*, XII:1.
Gillet, J. F. 1965. *Les organismes communs aux états de l'Afrique centrale: secretariat général de la conférence des chefs d'état de l'Afrique équatoriale*. Brazzaville.
Gitelson, Susan Aurelia. 1973. "Can the U.N. Be an Effective Catalyst for Regional Integration? The Case of the East African Community," *Journal of Developing Areas*, 8:1.
Green, R.H. 1976."The Lomé Convention: Updated Dependence or Departure toward Collective Self-reliance? *African Review*, VI:1.
Gruhn, Isebill V. 1971. "The Commission for Technical Cooperation in Africa, 1960-65." *Journal of Modern African Studies*, IX:3.
_____. 1976. "The Lomé Convention: Inching towards Independence," *International Organization*, XXX:2.
Hazelwood, Arthur, ed. 1967. *African Integration and Disintegration: Case Studies in Economic and Political Union*. London: Oxford University Press.
_____. 1970. *Les états du Groupe de Brazzaville aux Nations Unies*. Paris: Colin.
Jalloh, A. A. 1969. "The Politics and Economies of Regional Political Integration in Central Africa." Unpublished dissertation, University of California.
Kiano, Gikonyo. 1956. "The Federation Issue in Multi-Racial East and Central Africa. "Unpublished dissertation, University of California at Berkeley.
Mytelka, Lynn K. 1977. "The Lomé Convention and a New International Division of Labour," *Journal of European Integration*, I:1.
Maumon, M. 1968. "La cooperation industriélle dans les pays de l'UDEAC." Paris: Secretariat d'état aux affairs étrangéres changé de la coopération.

_____. 1970. "A Common Market with some Uncommon Problems: UDEAC Choses Cooperation despite Unequally Shared Provety and Some Severe Clashes of Interest," *Africa Report*, XV.

_____. 1972. "Decision Making and the Single Tax System in the Custom and Economic Union of Central Africa (UDEAC)." Paper prepared for African Studies Association.

_____. 1973. "Foreign Aid and Regional Integration: the UDEAC Case," *Journal of Common Market Studies*, 12:2.

_____. 1973. "A Geneology of Francophone West and Equatorial Africa Studies," *Journal of Modern African Studies*, 12:2.

_____. 1977. "The Lomé Convention and a New International: Division of Labour," *Journal of European Integration*, I:1.

_____. 1978. "Dependence and Regional Integration: UDEAC," in Larry Gould and Harry Targ, *Global Dominance and Dependence*. Columbus: Kings Court Communications.

Olofin, Sam. 1977. "ECOWAS and the Lomé Convention: An Experiment in Complementary [sic] of Conflicting Customs Union Arrangements," *Journal of Common Market Studies*, 16.

Peureux, G. 1961. "La création de l'union africaine et malgache et les conference des chefs d'états d'expression française," *Revue juridique et politique d'outremer*.

Prevost, R. 1968. "L'Union douaniére et économique de l'Afrique central," *Revue française d'études politique africanes*.

Proctor, J.H. 1967. "The Gambia's Relations with Senegal: The Search for Partnership," *Journal of Community Political Studies*, V:2.

Rama, R.S. 1968. "OCAM: An experiment in Regional Cooperation," *African Quarterly*, 8.

Segal, A. 1967. "The Integration of Development Countries: Some Thoughts on East African and Central American," *Journal of Common Market Studies*, V:3.

Shingiro, Victor. 1972. "La cooperation régionale en matiére industrielle: l'example de l'UDEAC et ses leçons," Genéve: Memoire présenté pour le diplôme, l'Institute Universitaire des Hautes Etudes Internationale.

Tevoedjre, Albert. 1984. *Pan-Africanism in Action: An Account of the UAM*. Lanham, Maryland: University Press of America.

Thompson, V., and R. Adloff. 1958. *French West Africa*. London: Oxford University Press.

Touré, A. 1975. *Integration régionale et structures économique: le cas de la CEAD*. Nancy: Université de Nancy.

Twitchett, Carol C. 1978. "Towards a New ACP-EC Convention," *World Today*, 34:12.

United States General Accounting Office. 1986. "African Development Bank; a More Independent Evaluation System is Needed."

Vinay, B. 1971. "Coopération intra-africaine et intégration: l'experiénce de l'UDEAC," *Penant*, LXXXI.

Wall, D. 1976. "The European Community's Lomé Convention: STABEX and the Third World Aspiration." London: Trade Policy Research Centre.

_____. 1971. "The Case for an African Defense Organization," *Africa Report*.

Wanthier, Claude. 1987. "PANA: The Voice of Africa," *Africa Report*, 32:2.

INDEX

Abbas, Ferhat 159
Abselwahab 159
Acronyms, alphabetical listing of 185
ADB 13, 15
Adedeji, Adebayo 159
Adjei, Ako 159
Africa divisions 24
Africa Reinsurance Corporation 48
African and Malagasy Common Organization 194, 269
African and Malagasy Organization of Economic Cooperation 192
African and Malagasy Union 192
African and Malagasy Union of Development Banks 192
African and Malagasy Union of Economic Cooperation 193
African and Malagasy Union of Posts and Telecommunications 193
African and Mauritian Union of Development Banks 193
African bloc 22
African Caribbean Pacific Group 196
African Development Bank 12, 47, 178, 193
    funding 47
    institutions associated 48
    management 47
African Development Bank Group 193
African Development Fund 47, 195
African disputes considered by the OAU (table) 28
African International Association 191
African Malagasy Union 191
African Postal and Telecommunications Union 191, 269
African Postal Union 192, 269
African Posts and Telecommunications Union 193, 269
African Telecommunications Union 192
Air Afrique 192
Allaf, Ely Ould 159
All-African People's Conference(s) 191
    Congress 177
Alomenu, H. S. 159
Alphabetical listing of acronyms 185
Amin, Idi 12, 25
Amin, Samir 160
Appendices 181
Appiah, Joe 160
Arab-African Union of States 198
Arusha Convention 195
Associated States of Africa 192
Association of African Central Banks 195
Association of African Development Finance Institutions 48

Atante, Philip 160
Ayari, Chedly 160

Background of international organizations 3
Bank of Central African States 191
Beheiry, Mamoun Ahmed 160
Benin-Niger Common Organization 192
Berlin Conference 177
Bibliography 291
Blumeris, Frederick Arthur 161
Blyden, Dr. Edward Wilmot 160
Bonaventura, Kidwingira 161
Brazzaville Group 192
British East Africa 177, 191
British West Africa 161, 162, 177, 191
Brumby, P.J. 161

Cabou, Daniel 161
Caiore, Augustus 161
Carpenter, Muhamadu A. 161
Carrington, Edwin 161
Casablanca Group 178, 193
Casely-Hayford, Joseph 161
CEAO 178, 179
Central African Customs and Economic Union 178, 194
Central African Economic and Customs Union 13, 269
Central African Economic Union 194
Central African Federation 191
Central African Monetary Union 195
Central Bank of the States of Equatorial Africa and Cameroun 192
Central Bank of West African States 191
Chronology 177
Club des Amis du Sahel 196
Commission for Technical Cooperation in Africa South of the Sahara 191
Commission of Fifteen on Refugees 22
Commission of Mediation, Conciliation, and Arbitration 23, 27, 194
Common market 18
Common Organization for Economic Cooperation in Central Africa 195
Commonwealth 45, 191
Communauté 45, 175, 192
Community of Independent African States 192
Conference of East and Central African States 194
Conference of Heads of African and Malagache States and Governments 191
Conference of Heads of State of Equatorial Africa 192
Conference of Independent African States 172, 177, 178, 192
Conflict resolution 21, 27, 34
Conseil de l'Entente 192
Contact Group of 5 179

Coordinating Commission on Assistance to Refugees 22
Corruption 20
Council of the Entente 162, 168
Countries and number of memberships 199
Cudjoe, Seth Dzifanu 162
Customs and Economic Union of Central Africa 194
Customs union 8, 9, 14, 15, 20, 37, 43
Customs Union of Central African States 43
   development bank 43
   single tax 43
Customs Union of West African States 192, 269

Dehinde, A.E. 162
Delaney, MArtin R. 162
Desert Locust Control Organization for Eastern Africa 17
Diaby-Ouattara, Aboubacar 162
Diallo, Aliou Samba 162
Diallo-Telli, Boubacar 162
Diori, Hamani 162
Distributable pool 29, 31, 39
DuBois, William E.B. 163
Dzakpasu, Cornelius K. 163

EAC 9, 18, 169
EACSO 178
East African Common Market 194
East African Common Services Organization 29, 193
East African Community 7, 11, 12, 29, 173, 178, 179, 194, 269
   conflict in 11
   problems 29
East African Community Institutions (table) 33
East African Court of Appeal 29, 191
East African Customs Union 31, 191
East African Development Bank 194
East African Examinations Council 17
East African Federation 193
East African Harbours Corporation 193
East African High Commission 191
East African Railways Corporation 193
East African Tourist Travel Association 191
Eastman, T. Ernest 163
Eboucha-Babackas, M. 163
Economic collaboration, impediments 8
Economic Commission for Africa 13, 21, 192
Economic Community of Central African States 197
Economic Community of Eastern Africa 194
Economic Community of West Africa 178
Economic Community of West African States 13, 37, 196

favorable characteristics 38
   regional disputes 37
   treaty 37
Economic development 19
Economy of scale 3, 15
ECOWAS 18, 179
ECOWAS Fund 196
Ekangaki, Nzo 163
El-Fouly, M. 163
Entente Council 269
Equatorial Conference of Heads of State 191
Equatorial Customs Union 192
Equatorial Office of Posts and Telecommunications 16
Eteki, William-Aurélian 163
Eton, Vincent 164
European Community 5
   success 6
European Free Trade Area 5
European Fund for Overseas Development 45

Fall, Cheikh Ibrahima 164
Fanon, Franz 164
Federation of Arab Republics 195
Federation of East African States 192
Federation of Rhodesia and Nyasaland 191
Felleke, Zawdu 164
Foalem, Ambroise 164
Fordwor, Kwame D. 164
Founding dates of African international organizations 191
Franc Zone 18, 191
Francophone states 13
Free Trade Area 194
French acronyms with English equivalents 191
French Community 18, 177
French Equatorial Africa 18, 177, 191
French West Africa 18, 162, 75, 177, 191
Front Line States 41, 191
Functionalism 4, 14, 15, 32
Fund for Cooperation, Compensation and Development (ECOWAS) 38

Ganou, Silimane 164
Gardiner, Robert Kweku Atta 165
Garvey, Marcus 165
Ghana-Guinea Union 192
Ghana-Guinea-Mali Union 192
Ghana-Upper Volta Customs Union 192
Gillet, Jean-François 165
Gold Coast 177

INDEX

Gueye, Dieumb Ojibail 165

Haile Selassie 165, 177
Hassan, Hassan M. 165
Hazlewood, Arthur 7, 30
Historical attempts at union 6
Horton, James Africanus Beale 166
Houphouët-Boigny, Félix 166

Independent African States 192
Individuals in the leadership of African international organizations 159
Infrastructure development 7
Integration 8, 14, 15, 23, 31, 37, 43
    start-up costs 6
Integrators 11, 12
Inter-African Bureau for Soils 191
Inter-African Bureau of African Health 16
International civil servants 22
International organization
    measure for the success 35
Intraregional cooperation 24

Jagne, Alieu B. 166
John, Malick 166
Johnson, James 166
Joudiou, Christian 166

Kane, Falilou 166
Kanza, Thomas R. 166
Karefa-Smart, Dr. John Musselman 167
Kaunda, Kenneth 167
Kaya, Paul 167
Keita, Drissa 167
Keita, Founéké 167
Keita, Modibo 167
Kenya budget for international organizations 183
Kenyatta, Jomo 167
Kodjo, Edem 168
Konaté, Tiéoulé 168
Kotso, Nathaniels E.K. 168
Kouyaté, Garan 168

Lagos Plan of Action 28
Lake Chad Basin Commission 194
Landeroin, Ms 168
Landlocked states 9
League of Nations 4, 166
Liberation Committee of the OAU 27

Libyan-Moroccan Union 198
Limitations on international co-operation 26
Limited competence 15
Liptako-Gourma Integrated Development Authority 17
Loi Cadre 33
Lomé I 45, 46, 179, 196
Lomé II 179, 197
Lomé III 179, 198
Lomé IV 46, 179
Lusaka Declaration 41
Lusaka Manifesto 178, 195

Maghrebin Charter 191
Mahamane, Brah 168
Main African international organizations 15
Makoni, Simbarashe 168
Makonnen, Ras 168
Mali Federation 33, 178, 192
Mamadou Samb, Mour 168
Maps 269 *ff.*
Materu, M.E.A. 169
Mazrui, Ali 169
Mbita, Hashim Iddi 169
Mboumoua, William Etexi 169
Microstates 3
Minhas, B.S. 169
Mobutu Sese Sekou 12
Models 14, 15, 16
    use of 18
    of African international organization 15
Mondjanagni, A.C. 169
Monetary Union of Equatorial Africa and Cameroun 193
Monetary Union of the States of West Africa 193
Monrovia Group 178, 193
Moutia, Sidney 169
Multinational business 7, 38
Mung'omba, Wila d'Israeli 169
Munu, Momodou 170

N'Diaye, Babacar 170
Nduwayo, Alieu M.B. 170
Neo-imperialism 26, 172
New industry 10
Ngom, Moussa 170
Niger Basin Authority 179, 194
Niger River Commission 193
Nigeria Trust Fund 47
N'Jie, Pierre Saar 170

Nkrumah, Kwame 4, 11, 21, 160, 170, 295
Nomvete, Bax 170
Non-African acronyms 191
Number of memberships by groups 267
Nyerere, Julius 11, 12, 23, 171

Obote, Milton 171
OCAM 12, 18, 178, 179
Oganization of Senegal River States 194
Okelo-Odongo, Thomas 171
Olatunde-Oshinibi, Ayotunde 171
Olufolabi, F. Olufemi 171
Onu, Peter 171
Organization Commune Africaine et Malgache 33
    conflict resolution 34
    demise 34, 36
    institutions associated with 34
    objectives 33
Organization for the African Community 193
Organization for the Development of the Senegal River 178
Organization for West African Economic Cooperation 191
Organization of African and Malagasy States 193
Organization of African Unity 12, 21, 178, 193
    accomplishments 26
    budget 25
    charter 16
    dispute settlement 22
    objectives 21
    organs 21, 27
    specialized agencies 25
Organizational leadership 20
Ould Soueid Ahmed, Abdullah 171
Oumarou, Ide 172

Pacific-African-Caribbean States 13, 45
    results 46
Padmore, George 172
PAFMECA 169, 177
PAFMECSA 169, 178
PAFMESA 169
Pan-African Congress 164, 176, 177, 179, 191
Pan-African Federation 191
Pan-African Freedom Movements for East, Central and Southern Africa 192
Pan-African Movement for Eastern and Central Africa 192
Pan-African News Agency 179, 197
Pan-African Postal Union 197
Pan-African Telecommunications Network 195
Pan-African Telecommunications Union 197

Pan-Africanism 4, 12, 21, 160, 162, 164, 166, 170, 172, 174, 176
Pan-Africanist Manifesto 178, 192
Philip, Prof. Kjeld 172
Political will 1, 10, 13, 14, 15, 16, 18, 19, 28, 31, 32, 36
Popular support 21
Preferential Trade Area 29
Preferential Trade Area for Eastern and Southern Africa 197

Quaison-Sackey, Alex 172

Rand Monetary Area 196
Reasons for integration 15
Regional co-operation 5, 9, 26, 42
    difficulty 8
    stability 11
Regional organization 16
Regionalism 4, 8, 14, 33

SADCC 17, 179
Scientific, Technical, and Research Committee 14, 178
Self-help organizations 17
Senegambia, Union of 197
Seydou, Amadou 172
Shelter Afrique 48
Significant dates relating to African international organizations 177
Simpore, Mamadou 172
Single-purpose organizations 15
Sired, Ismail Amri 172
Société Internationale Financière pour les Investissements et le Developpement en Afrique 48
Solidarity Fund (of Customs Union of Central African States) 43
Sory Balde, Ibrahim 172
South African Customs Union 177, 191
Southern African Customs Union 195, 269
Southern African Development Bank 197
Southern African Development Coordination Conference 13, 17, 41, 269
    donor conference 42
    impact 42
    problems 42
    program of action 41
Sovereignty 4
    surrender of 9, 11, 12
Spillover 5, 14
STABEX 45
SYSMIN 45

Tanganika, Gahuranyi 173
Tanzania-Zambia Railway Authority 194
Taylor, Alwyn B. 173

INDEX

Tazara 178
Tchanque, Pierre 173
Technical cooperation 16, 29
Tevoedjre, Albert 173
Touré, Bakary 173
Touré, Ahmed Sekou 21, 173
Transequatorial Communications Agency 192
Traoré, Diawa-Mory 174
Trickle-down 10
Tsiranana, Philip 174
Tubman, Robert C. 174
Typology of African international organizations 15

UAM 178
UAS 178
UDE 178
UDEAC 179
UEAC 178
UMOA 178
Union of African Railways 195
Union of African States 193
Union of Central African Republics 192
Union of Central African States 194
Union of Independent African States 192
Union of the Republics of Central Africa 192
United Arab Republic 195
United Nations 16, 21, 22, 24, 25, 36
　　charter 16
United States of Central Africa 194
Universal Negro Improvement Association 191
University of East Africa 14

Variables affecting international organization (table) 19

Wacha, D.S.O. 174
WACU 178, 192
WADB 178, 196
Wako, D.M. 174
WARDA 178
West African Common Market 194
West African Customs Union 178, 192
West African Development Bank 178, 196
West African Economic Community 195
　　Development Fund 195
West African Monetary Union 193
West African Regional Group 194
Williams, A.O. 174
Williams, Henry Sylvester 174

315

Windapo, Adesoye 175
Worku, Arega 175

Yaoundé I 45, 193
Yaoundé II 46, 195

LIBRARY USE ONLY
DOES NOT CIRCULATE